Knowledge Capitalism

'. . .offers the business practitioner an excellent balance between analysis and prescription'
    Hirotaka Takeuchi, co-author of *The Knowledge-Creating Company*

'No stone is left unturned in this sweeping and insightful analysis of the knowledge game in this new economy'
    John Seely Brown, Chief Scientist, Xerox Corporation; Director, Xerox PARC

'A winner . . . It is the best book that I have seen for a CEO on the strategy to use, if you want the best from the Knowledge that exists in your organization . . . I recommend it for all planning teams, everywhere'
    Bob Buckman, Buckman Laboratories, US

'At a time when the "Knowledge Economy" has become an everyday expression, it is important that the concept is better understood. This book on "Knowledge Capitalism" has the great merit of conveying an account of the subject which will be useful alike to a business and to an academic public.'
    Chris Freeman, SPRU, University of Sussex

'. . . a pathbreaking survey of the knowledge economy written with the maturity of a practical manager, the insights of a seasoned academic and the deftness of an informed chronicler. Burton-Jones pushes the boundaries of management thought and practice by providing challenging business scenarios and suggesting ways to benefit from them commercially. It will add significant value for managers and consultants in knowledge intensive businesses, and in the graduate seminar as well'
    Keith Bradley, Professor of Management, City University Business School; Co-author of *Managing Knowledge: Experts, Agencies, and Organizations*

'. . . a comprehensive look at the state of knowledge in the New Economy . . . It will be one of my reference books for the near future'
    Gordon Petrash, PricewaterhouseCoopers, Chicago, Intellectual Asset Management Practice; Dow, Global Director for Intellectual Asset and Caplital Management

'This book impresses with its breadth of coverage, its research detail and the synthesis of analysis . . . it touches upon something important for many people— work, its nature, its shortage for some, its changes and its future direction. Highly recommended, given its significance and thoughtful analysis'
    Dr John Burgess, University of Newcastle, Australia

Further comments on Knowledge Capitalism can be found on the author's website at http://www.burton-jones.com/capitalism.asp

Knowledge Capitalism
Business, Work, and Learning
in the New Economy

ALAN BURTON-JONES

OXFORD
UNIVERSITY PRESS

OXFORD

UNIVERSITY PRESS

Great Clarendon Street, Oxford OX2 6DP

Oxford University Press is a department of the University of Oxford.
It furthers the University's objective of excellence in research, scholarship,
and education by publishing worldwide in

Oxford New York

Athens Auckland Bangkok Bogotá Buenos Aires Calcutta
Cape Town Chennai Dar es Salaam Delhi Florence Hong Kong Istanbul
Karachi Kuala Lumpur Madrid Melbourne Mexico City Mumbai
Nairobi Paris São Paulo Singapore Taipei Tokyo Toronto Warsaw

and associated companies in Berlin Ibadan

Oxford is a registered trade mark of Oxford University Press
in the UK and in certain other countries

Published in the United States
by Oxford University Press Inc., New York

British Library Cataloguing in Publication Data

Data available

Library of Congress Cataloging in Publication Data

Burton-Jones, Alan.
    Knowledge capitalism: business, work, and learning in the new economy/
Alan Burton-Jones.
    p. cm.
Includes index.
    1. Knowledge management.   2. Information resources management.
3. Intellectual capital.   I. Title.
HD30.2.B87 1999   658.4′038—dc21   99–31583

ISBN 0–19–829622–3

10 9 8 7 6 5 4 3 2 1

Typeset by Hope Services (Abingdon) Ltd.
Printed in Great Britain
on acid-free paper by
Bookcraft Ltd
Midsomer Norton, Somerset

PREFACE

As we approach the dawn of the twenty-first century, inflation is down, productivity is up, the US locomotive is powering away, the former communist bloc is rapidly embracing western-style capitalism—but everywhere there is a sense of unease.

Many of the symptoms of the malaise are obvious, if not their causes. In the USA, despite an economic 'dream run' 10 per cent of the current workforce are worse off than they were a quarter of a century ago. Japan, Asia's industrial superpower and still the world's second largest economy, continues to flounder in recession. Throughout the West, despite falling inflation and rising corporate profits, economic growth is largely restricted to retailing and services. The public sector is disintegrating. Commodity prices are falling. Small business sentiment is apprehensive and consumer confidence low.

Large labour-intensive manufacturing firms, which are able to relocate their production, are rapidly establishing themselves in the third world where labour is cheap and government regulations few. Meantime small firms, less able to relocate, less able to borrow from the bank, and forced by governments to provide an ever-increasing array of employee benefits, have, in the majority, simply ceased to grow.

Since the industrial era, most people, whether workers, owners, or investors, have perceived their careers and fortunes to be inextricably linked to one or other industry and 'the firm'. Now they see whole industries declining, massive changes occurring to the structure of firms, and jobless growth. As yet they have little understanding of what is causing these changes, what it means to their future, or what they can do to help themselves.

The malaise is spreading throughout society. For the family breadwinners and others in mid-corporate career, downsizings, delayerings, retrenchments, and job losses are occurring all around. The ever-present question is 'Who will be next?' Charting a course for their children which might offer better, long-term prospects of job security is equally problematic. For many young people, particularly early school-leavers, growing disillusionment and lack of a sense of purpose and self-worth have become critical. From their perspective the news they hear is largely bad, and if those they respect in society have no sense of security or direction, they have little cause for optimism.

Many of those at or approaching retirement age are facing more years of life than they have money in the bank to afford. Meantime pensions and all other publicly funded benefits for the aged are being reduced. The spreading sense of economic insecurity is also affecting society in other ways. Extremist factions are appearing across the West, touting simplistic economic messages and attributing real or imagined grievances to other minority groups as convenient scapegoats.

Buffeted by the forces of change, individuals, businesses, and social communities perceive themselves to be at risk. Despite all these obvious symptoms of economic insecurity and related social unease, politicians and the media have provided little coherent explanation as to what is happening in the economy.

The purpose of this book is essentially to shed light on these issues and to suggest ways in which some of them at least might be tackled. The fundamental proposition of the book is that among the various factors currently causing change in the economy, none is more important than the changing role of *knowledge*. Over recent years much attention has been given to the growing economic importance of technology, information, business processes, quality control, human capital, and corporate capabilities and competencies—all knowledge-related factors. Viewed individually, such factors can provide valuable insights, but their links to the fundamental role played by knowledge within the firm and in the economy are not always obvious.

As the title of this book suggests, knowledge is fast becoming the most important form of global capital—hence 'knowledge capitalism'. Paradoxically, knowledge is probably the least understood and most undervalued of all economic resources. The central theme of this book is, therefore, the nature and value of knowledge and how it is fundamentally altering the basis of economic activity, thus business, employment, and all of our futures. The central message is that we need to reappraise many of our industrial era notions of business organization, business ownership, work arrangements, business strategy, and the links between education, learning, and work.

The terrain covered in discussing these issues is necessarily broad, and involves a synthesis of ideas and concepts derived from many disciplines. This interdisciplinary perspective has been largely shaped from personal experience gained while consulting at the nexus between IT and business strategy. Much of the book's discussion, however, inevitably centres on changes to the role of the firm and to relationships between its stakeholders. The book's intended readership, therefore, includes firm owners and managers interested in the strategic implications of the knowledge economy; individuals concerned about their personal career prospects; plus students, educators, and others interested in the changing links between education, learning, and work. Naturally many readers will fall into more than one of these categories. The distinction between managers and workers these days is becoming increasingly blurred, as is the distinction between learning and working, and we are all owners, at least of our own intellectual capital—in that sense we are all knowledge capitalists! The book is divided into four parts.

Part I, 'The Knowledge Revolution', describes the fundamental shift that is occurring, particularly in the western world, from an economy based largely on physical resources to one based on knowledge. The role of knowledge is explained and shown to subsume more limited concepts of economic change based on information and services. The increasing importance of knowledge is discussed in relation to theories of the firm, firm–market boundaries, and firm ownership and control.

Conventional thinking regarding the organization and ownership of firms and the centrality of the employment relationship is challenged. New models based on knowledge-centred organization and knowledge supply as distinct from labour supply are proposed. The knowledge characteristics of work are shown to be critical in determining which functions and activities will be retained within the firm (internalized) and which will be provided by external resources (externalized).

Part II, 'Navigating Knowledge Markets', presents empirical evidence of the links between firms' decisions to use externalized resources and the knowledge characteristics of the work involved. Comparative statistics are provided from the USA, Europe, and other OECD countries. First, the decline in traditional forms of employment is analysed and contrasted with the growth of more flexible work arrangements. Next, the growth of independently mediated services is discussed in the context of both staffing services and outsourcing and predictions made regarding the potential convergence of different forms of mediated service involving supply of people and 'solutions'. Knowledge supply is then discussed in relation to dependent and independent forms of self-employment, micro firms, and networks. The implications of these various trends are discussed from the perspectives of firms, workers, service providers, governments, and other stakeholders.

Part III, 'The Knowledge-Based Firm', continues the theme of knowledge supply, but switches focus to discuss the knowledge characteristics of work likely to be retained within the firm. The increasing value of the firm's intellectual resource base is shown to be redefining its role and reshaping organizational structures and business strategies. The development of the firm into a knowledge-based enterprise is discussed and an evolutionary model based on stages of knowledge growth is then proposed. Strategies to succeed in the knowledge-based economy are also examined. This is followed by an analysis of how the emergence of the knowledge-based firm is likely to lead to changing patterns of firm ownership and how workers, owners, and investors will need to adjust to the new ownership structures.

Part IV, 'The Knowledge Escalator', discusses how economic demand for an increasingly skilled workforce will necessitate a move to lifelong learning. This leads to an analysis of the implications of the learning imperative, including the use of learning technologies, the development of a global learning industry, and changes to the relationships involving learners, educators, and firms. The book concludes with a look at the future of knowledge capitalism and what governments, firms, and individuals can do to ensure a profitable transition to the global knowledge economy of the next millennium.

ACKNOWLEDGEMENTS

Many of the ideas that appear in this book have been amassed whilst working in the UK and Australia, in the course of IT and management consulting assignments. My thanks therefore are due to all those who directly or indirectly, and sometimes unwittingly, contributed to this book's conception, in particular Peter Fancke and Bernie Dilger at Colonial, Collin Hiss at Lumley Technology, Brian Mitchell at Oracle Corporation, Geoff Slocombe at Digital, Maurice Castro at Australia Post, Peter Cheshire while at ICI, and Jack Melbourne while at Fluor Daniel.

Thanks to all those who provided comments and suggestions on early versions of the manuscript, including Lester Thurow, Martin Carnoy, Chris Freeman, Peter Sherer, Stuart Macdonald, Rob Grant, John Burgess, Mark Wooden, and a number of anonymous reviewers. For insightful suggestions and guidance along the way, my thanks to David Musson at Oxford University Press.

Julie Sibthorpe and the staff at BRISQ, Kate Purcell at IER, Marg Hearn at RCSA, Bruce Steinberg at NATSS, Todd Wheatland at Kelly Services, Carol D'Amico at the Hudson Institute, Howard Fullerton, Sharon Cohany and Charlie Muhl at the BLS, and Mark Kefford and the team at Information Dynamics all provided invaluable assistance with research material. My thanks also to Guy Standing and Arnulf Gruebler for allowing me to reproduce material.

For some invaluable personal insights on technology and industry trends I would like to thank John Bowmer at Adecco, Carl Camden at Kelly Services, Wendy Coles at GM, Steve Denning at the World Bank, Leif Edvinsson at Skandia, Bipin Junnarkar at Datafusion, Gordon Petrash at PriceWaterhouseCoopers, Melissie Rumizen at Buckman Laboratories, Hubert Saint-Onge at the Mutual Group, and Jeff Taylor at TMP Interactive.

Last but not least I have my family, both in Australia and the UK, to thank. Joan for her constructive criticism and keeping her sense of humour, Andrew for his analytical skills and for keeping me 'on track', Katherine and Ivor for staying in touch, and Dylys for her enthusiasm and unflagging support.

A.B.-J.

CONTENTS

LIST OF FIGURES

LIST OF TABLES

PART I

THE KNOWLEDGE REVOLUTION

There is a tide in the affairs of men
Which taken at the flood leads on to fortune.
   (William Shakespeare, *Julius Caesar*, IV. iii)

1

The Rise of Knowledge Capital

Since ancient times, wealth and power have been associated with the owner-ship of physical resources. The traditional factors of production, materials, labour, and money, have been largely physical in nature. Historically the need for knowledge has been limited, and access to it largely controlled by those owning the means of production. Steam power, physical labour, and money capital largely facilitated the Industrial Revolution of some two and a half cen-turies ago.

In contrast, future wealth and power will be derived mainly from intangible, intellectual resources: knowledge capital. This transformation from a world largely dominated by physical resources, to a world dominated by knowledge, implies a shift in the locus of economic power as profound as that which occurred at the time of the Industrial Revolution. We are in the early stages of a 'Knowledge Revolution', the initial impact of which is becoming apparent in the volatility of markets, uncertainty over future direction within governments and businesses, and the insecurity over future career and job prospects felt by individuals.

In order to gauge the implications of this new economic paradigm on work, jobs, employers, and employees, it is first necessary to appreciate how it is changing the traditional inputs to wealth creation: materials, labour, and money. This chapter therefore focuses on the nature of knowledge and its role as a factor of production. First, the growth of a knowledge-based economy is discussed in the context of a post-industrial society, in which goods are being replaced by services. We then take a closer look at knowledge itself and the key characteristics that determine its economic value. The role of information technology in facilitating the growth of the knowledge economy is then dis-cussed.

The chapter concludes with an overview of how the shift to a knowledge economy is beginning to change the economic landscape and, in particular, to impact work and jobs.

GOODS, SERVICES, AND KNOWLEDGE

The theory of a post-industrial society has been in existence now for over a quarter of a century.[1] According to this theory, the production of goods would decline in favour of services, knowledge would become the basis of economic growth and productivity, and occupational growth would occur mainly in white-collar managerial and professional jobs. Actual trends in economic growth and employment have been broadly consistent with these predictions. In the half-century up to 1970, agricultural employment, previously the staple employment source of most economies, declined across the West in favour of manufacturing and services. Between 1970 and 1990, manufacturing employment itself declined in all the G7 countries: USA, Japan, Germany, UK, France, Canada, and Italy.[2]

Delineating the boundaries between goods and services has always been problematic. A film, for example, may be sold as a video (a good) or delivered via your television (a service). The strong growth of services over recent years is clearly linked to the connection between services and goods-producing sectors. As manufacturers outsource non-core functions to specialist service organizations, employment in *services* increases and employment in *manufacturing* declines.

Service has been defined as an activity where output is characteristically consumed at the same time as it is produced, such as having a haircut or taking a taxi-ride. On the other hand, not all services are consumed as they are produced—particularly those that can be electronically time-shifted. From these few examples it can be seen that defining the services sector, and distinguishing its growth separately from the more traditional goods-producing sector, is not a straightforward matter. *The Economist*'s definition of services as 'anything sold in trade that could not be dropped on your foot' is perhaps as good as any.[3]

In fact, as both goods and services become more knowledge and information intensive, the distinction between them is becoming both less apparent and in many cases less relevant. Knowledge is becoming the defining characteristic of economic activities, rather than either goods or services. Unfortunately statistical reporting based on the knowledge characteristics of different types of economic activity is not yet an accepted practice. Meantime economic perspectives remain limited by the 'industrial lenses' through which the world is still defined and described.

KNOWLEDGE AS A FACTOR OF PRODUCTION

The central tenet of this book is that *knowledge* is transforming the nature of production and thus work, jobs, the firm, the market, and every aspect of economic activity. Yet knowledge is currently a poorly understood and thus undervalued economic resource. Even after the invention of the magnetic compass and the telescope, many sailors still hugged the coastline believing that the world ended at the horizon. In South America today there are tribal people who build their long-houses with the central pole protruding through the roof, because they still believe that the sun literally rests on it at midday. When it comes to valuing knowledge, the perspectives of many politicians, firms, and individuals in today's western world are often as far removed from economic reality as those of older or more primitive societies are from physical reality.

We need new sets of lenses through which to view the emerging knowledge economy and new models to predict and plan future strategies, whether national, corporate, or personal. The starting point for this process must be to understand the nature of knowledge and its role as an input to production.

Defining Knowledge

Since words such as data, information, and knowledge are often used loosely to describe the same phenomena, it is important to commence with a few definitions that will be adopted from here onwards. This is essentially to achieve consistency and avoid semantic confusion. For the purpose of this book, therefore, data are defined as any signals which can be sent by an originator to a recipient—human or otherwise. Information is defined as data which are intelligible to the recipient. Finally, knowledge is defined as the cumulative stock of information and skills derived from use of information by the recipient. Where the recipient is a human being, knowledge thus reflects the processing (thinking or cognition) by the brain of the 'raw material' supplied in the form of information (see Figure 1.1).

Other connotations of knowledge, which tend to differentiate it from data and information, are that it represents 'truth' and therefore offers a reliable basis for action.[4] To be knowledgeable thus implies having capabilities or competencies likely to be valuable in the future as well as the present.

The value of information is also dependent on the recipient's prior knowledge. If we have no previous knowledge of a particular subject, it is usually difficult if not impossible to make sense of data related to that subject. Conversely, the more we know about a subject, the better able we are to evaluate and use new data about it.

Whether there is any objective reality to know about, whether notions of truth or belief are a reflection of that reality, and how we know what we know, have long engaged epistemologists and more recently information theorists and researchers in artificial intelligence and cognitive science.[5] No doubt these enquiries will continue into the foreseeable future; meantime however the above 'working definitions' of data, information, and knowledge will probably suffice for the purpose of this discussion.

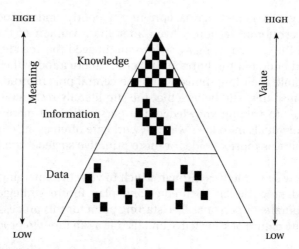

FIG. 1.1. Data, information, and knowledge

It can be seen from these working definitions that knowledge subsumes information, which represents both the input to knowledge development and the form in which knowledge is transferred—its 'circulatory system'. The traditional economic view of information and knowledge is that they are the same thing. In practice it can be seen that they are different, but strongly complementary.[6]

Knowledge acquisition (*learning*) and creation (*invention, innovation*) can only occur to any significant degree in the human brain. On the other hand knowledge is clearly 'reflected' in other ways. A firm's knowledge capital, often referred to as its intellectual capital or intellectual assets, can be identified in its workforce (human capital), its customers' demands and preferences (customer capital), and its systems, products, processes, and capabilities (structural capital). The value of the knowledge assets of a firm may thus significantly exceed the value of its tangible assets, as shown by the market valuations of firms such as Microsoft or Netscape.[7]

The world's stock of knowledge is today growing faster than ever before. At the same time as our stock of knowledge is increasing, our reliance on traditional physical forms of capital is reducing, further accentuating the importance of knowledge, in all its forms, as the principal form of capital in the new economy. US companies for example have been reported as needing 20 per cent less in tangible assets to produce one dollar's worth of sales than they did a quarter-century ago.[8]

Whatever supporting artefacts may be used, therefore, such as computers and communications, and however much data and information are produced, knowledge itself remains the paramount resource and thus the key to economic progress. This is why we need to move beyond the limited concept of an information-based economy to the broader and more powerful concept of a knowledge-based economy.

Knowledge Characteristics

A useful distinction can be made between knowledge about something and knowledge about how to do something ('know-how'): for example, I may know about computers but not know how to program a computer. Knowledge about something generally relates to concepts and theories, and know-how to the acquisition of skills through practical implementation of such concepts and theories. Learning on the job in a work situation is a classic example of acquiring knowledge or skills through practice. Another popular term to describe this aspect of knowledge acquisition is 'learning by doing'.

Knowledge can be further classified according to whether it can be made explicit, or whether it remains implicit or tacit. The critical difference between these two aspects of knowledge relates to how easy or difficult it is to codify or express the knowledge in terms which enable it to be *understood* by a broad audience. If knowledge can be *codified* in this way, it can be made explicit and thus readily transferable. Conversely, if it cannot be made explicit, it must remain tacit (literally 'silent'), thus difficult, if not impossible, to transfer. As Michael Polanyi put it in his seminal work 'The Tacit Dimension', 'we can know more than we can tell'.[9]

Two other important concepts associated with the transfer of knowledge are 'stickiness' and 'absorptive capacity'. Stickiness refers to the difficulty often associated with codifying knowledge, i.e. turning it into explicit transmittable information. Readers will doubtless have encountered the problem of stickiness on occasion, when trying to get 'a thought down on paper'. In the firm, internal stickiness often hinders effective transfer of knowledge between individuals or departments.[10]

Whereas stickiness slows down the export of knowledge, absorptive capacity affects how easily the recipient can understand it.[11] Prior knowledge of a particular 'knowledge domain' or subject, as noted earlier, tends to make it easier to understand new information that is related to that knowledge domain. The converse is also true, as many firms and individuals have found to their cost, when venturing into new knowledge domains.

By way of example, let's assume you or I could receive coaching from the men's singles champion at Wimbledon and let's also assume we are both highly receptive to this idea. He may be able to explain aspects of his game, how to serve, volley, etc. He is, however, unlikely to be able to transfer the knowledge that enables him to play well enough to win Wimbledon. If he could, you or I might be able to emulate him quite easily, assuming of course we were also reasonably athletic in the first place! In the real world, to have a hope of winning Wimbledon, apart from natural talent (tacit knowledge), we would probably need a lot of personal coaching, involving transfer of explicit and some tacit knowledge, plus a great deal of practice, i.e. learning by doing. The difficulty of becoming a Wimbledon champion, without natural talent, special coaching, and years of practice, is an example of how hard it can be to transfer knowledge—particularly where critical components of that knowledge are tacit.

Naturally other factors may also inhibit successful knowledge transfer (i.e. transmission and receipt), such as the complexity of the subject matter and the receptivity and retentive ability of the recipient. Finding that one's message falls on 'deaf ears' or 'goes in one ear and out the other' are problems we have all encountered.

THE ENABLING ROLE OF INFORMATION TECHNOLOGY

The change from a physical to an increasingly non-physical information and knowledge-based economy has been mainly achieved through the commercial application of information technology (IT). It is therefore useful to examine how the IT industry has evolved and how current IT trends are likely to affect the development of the knowledge economy.

The combination of constantly declining costs and constantly improving performance has enabled the IT industry to become one of the fastest and most highly productive growth sectors in the world economy, pervading most aspects of economic activity. Information systems (IS), a branch of IT, uses systems analysis and design tools to represent the 'real world' (as perceived by users), the main aim being to achieve as accurate and complete a representation of it as possible. In this way a complex process, which perhaps has been the idiosyncratic knowledge of a particular individual, can be transformed into more generalizable knowledge, or decomposed into items of information which can be accessed and, if required, reassembled at low cost. Other IT functions then provide the capabilities to program, process, store, and transfer these 'knowledge models'. The application of IT has dramatically improved our ability to access and use data and information. This has increased our stock of knowledge, which in turn has enabled us to evaluate and use yet more information. IT can thus be seen to play an enabling role, facilitating both the development and the transfer of knowledge.

The Growth and Commercial Application of Information Technology

Between the mid-1950s and the mid-1900s, the cost of computer power, as compared to the cost of manual information processing, fell by 8,000 per cent. Between 1950 and 1980, the time required for a single electronic operation fell by a factor of 80 million.[17]

In 1900, less than 18 per cent of the total workforce in the USA were engaged in data- and information-handling tasks. By 1980 it had risen to over 50 per cent. Of these information-handling tasks, approximately 19 per cent were associated with R&D, education and training, and design work, which may be classified as adding to the long-term 'knowledge stock' of businesses. The balance of 81 per cent was associated with transient data and information related to day-to-day operational management.[13]

On present trends, over 80 per cent of the workforce are likely to be involved in information-handling tasks by 2020, of whom a much higher proportion than at present are likely to be engaged in knowledge-building and decision-making activities. Routine management of transient information will by that time have been massively automated and the focus of workers retained in the firm will be knowledge management. Workforce reductions are therefore likely to be equally massive if the educational qualifications of workers do not keep pace with the speed of technological change (see Chapter 10).

Flowing from the growth in volume and complexity of information handling, five distinct stages in the commercial application of IT for commercial purposes can be identified from the early 1960s to today. The evolving commercial focus of IT and the parallel progression from data, through information management, and now towards knowledge management is depicted in Table 1.1. Dates shown are intended as indicative rather than definitive.

Table 1.1. *The changing focus of IT*

	Stage				
	1	2	3	4	5
Technical focus	Centralized file handling	Distributed computing	Personal computing	Local networking	Local and global networking
Timeline (approximate)	1960s	1970s	1980s	1990–5	1995–2000+
Business focus	Data management	Data management	Information management	Information management	Knowledge management
Workforce skills	Low	Low	Medium	Medium	High

During the 1960s and 1970s businesses opted to use IT to control and standardize their operations, rather than for innovation or experimentation as in the scientific sphere. The commercial application of IT has thus tended to have a 'levelling' effect, reducing the specific to the general, the idiosyncratic to the standard, tacit knowledge to explicit knowledge, scarce goods and services to commodities. As Table 1.1 shows, the 1990s have been marked by improvements in information management techniques and the spread of networking, first within the firm and latterly across its borders. These moves have enabled firms to improve both access to and sharing of information among workers, customers, and suppliers, which in turn has helped to create a platform for decision support, organizational learning, and knowledge sharing. Combined with these developments, routine functions and applications have continued to be automated and standardized.

One of the major reasons the commercial application of IT has had a neutral or levelling effect has been the tendency by firms to adopt standard software packages, as noted above. SAP R/3, for example, developed by the German firm SAP.AG, is one of the most comprehensive and sophisticated commercial applications packages on the market today, currently boasting 16,500 installations worldwide, mainly in government and large commercial organizations.[14]

From a knowledge perspective, one of the most striking features of SAP is the extent to which it provides extremely comprehensive standards for financial, logistical, and human resource systems in a variety of industrial settings. It provides, in detailed, explicit terms, a set of best practices for operating many of the routine functions of a business. A major benefit of such an approach to users, in addition to other benefits such as cost savings, is that they can elect to rely on externally provided knowledge of best practices, rather than have to develop and maintain that knowledge themselves. The risk is that in doing so they may lose the benefits of firm-specific or tacit knowledge embedded in internal processes and procedures which are replaced by the standard system. Firm-specific knowledge of course is not necessarily a good thing in itself—only if it contributes to the firm's success. The success of SAP, along with many other software packages, indicates that purchasers have believed the value of standardization to exceed the value of firm-specific knowledge.

Recognizing, to some extent, the danger implicit in standardizing their routine operations, firms have also been making increasing attempts to locate and abstract the idiosyncratic or job-specific knowledge of particular workers or groups of workers which they believe is likely to be of lasting value to them. Early efforts based on concepts of artificial intelligence and expert systems were generally not found to be effective. New approaches to the same issues, however, are now becoming more popular, particularly due to improvements in data collection and networking technologies. At GM, for example, field technicians are provided with voice-driven PCs that they wear on their belts. When they finish a particular repair, they describe the procedure aloud, their words being converted automatically into electronic text files. The company plans to collect this information centrally over an intranet, enabling technicians at GM's headquarters to review the reports and decide whether to use the information to alter service procedures or add to training materials.[15]

From Information Management to Knowledge Management

To manage information implies that it can first be defined and preferably measured. Saint-Onge highlights the fact that the great majority of knowledge within organizations is in practice tacit, or unarticulated.[16] The challenge for any organization therefore is to develop a culture that facilitates not only exchange of (manageable) explicit knowledge but also renewal of (less manageable) tacit knowledge.

In their book *The Knowledge-Creating Company*, Nonaka and Takeuchi describe how knowledge creation in the firm demands a series of repeated interactions between tacit and explicit knowledge, involving four possible permutations: tacit to explicit; explicit to explicit; explicit to tacit; and tacit to tacit.[17] To date, firms have tended to focus their use of IT on the first two of these permutations. On the *tacit to explicit* dimension, firms have concentrated on developing systems that would enable them to dispense with the idiosyncratic and often tacit knowledge of particular workers. Where such knowledge has been deemed potentially valuable, efforts have been made to convert it into explicit rules-based systems. Hence the massive growth of the standard application package industry and the focus on achieving company-wide best practices by adherence to standard rules and procedures. On the *explicit to explicit* dimension, firms have found the computational storage and communication capabilities of IT ideal for accurately recording and managing large volumes of data. This has led, among other things, to the growth of the database industry, as firms seek to slice, dice, and view (explicit) data in ever more sophisticated ways.

IT has, however, not been used to the same extent to date to help address the second two 'knowledge' permutations, *explicit to tacit* and *tacit to tacit*. This appears to be partly because the available technologies have been ill suited to the task and partly because of firms' preoccupation with controlling and providing access to information, rather than acquiring and building knowledge. As Bipin Junnarkar, former head of Monsanto's Knowledge Management initiative, and now CEO of Datafusion, says, 'nowadays it's not content that people lack, but context. Firms have emphasized completeness of information rather than clarity of understanding, the result being that many data warehousing and data mining projects have not met firms' expectations.'[18]

Firms are nowadays beginning to address the explicit to tacit dimension through case-based systems, which provide a richer array of contextual information. By studying the details of previous corporate experience in a situation analogous to one in which they find themselves, end users are often able to derive more value than by simply reading a set of prescribed rules or procedures. The net result (hopefully) is that they will better absorb the lessons that can be learned from the past and, in so doing, increase their own level of tacit knowledge. The *tacit to tacit* dimension may also be partially assisted by a more context-sensitive approach to providing information. The lessons of experience tend to be encapsulated in the story rather than spelt out explicitly. In this sense, some of the tacit knowledge of the originator may be effectively transferred to the recipient.

Most sharing of tacit knowledge has however traditionally occurred face to face, for example, master and apprentice, teacher and pupil. IT systems have some way to go before they can simulate the real world immediacy of physical face-to-face contact, although developments in virtual reality systems offer a hint of things to come.

In summary, it can be seen that firms' perceptions of the value of data, information, and knowledge need to change in order for them to derive maximum benefits from the use of IT. Much of the focus to date has been on rule making, standardizing and commoditizing knowledge, rather than creating or acquiring it. As firms look for new ways to gain a competitive edge, they may be expected to switch the focus of their IT initiatives towards the provision of case-based as well as rule-based information, improving informational clarity, and assisting the processes of creating and sharing tacit knowledge.

SIGNS OF THE EMERGING KNOWLEDGE ECONOMY

Assisted by IT and other advanced technologies, the balance of economic activity is shifting from manufacturing and production of physical goods to information handling, knowledge accumulation, and production of knowledge goods—or as Negroponte put it, 'from atoms to bits'.[19] The contrast between the old industrial economy and the emerging knowledge economy is indeed characterized by a shift from reliance on tangible, physical resources to intangible, mental resources. This trend to intangibility in turn presages the growth of a virtual economy, one which is not only less dependent on physical capital, but also, as a result, free of traditional organizational and geographical boundaries. Signs of the emerging knowledge economy are apparent in the increasing use of symbolic rather than physical goods, the lessening need for physically massed/collocated resources, and the declining importance of traditional boundaries defined by business functions, industries, and nations. Let us take a look at some of these features of the new economy.

Growth of Symbolic Goods

A single personal computer is capable of manipulating symbols representing data about practically any subject. This offers the potential for massive economies of scale, which cannot be matched by equipment designed solely to perform tasks involving physical objects. The machinery used in farming for example cannot be used to manufacture automobiles, or cook hamburgers. The symbolic representation of information means that its value is independent of the physical characteristics of those symbols. An electronic file may represent details of banking transactions, orders for equipment, or clearance instructions for cargo. If one compresses the symbols for transmission purposes, it does not change the nature or value of the data. In contrast, an automobile compressed to one hundredth of its size does not retain the value of a full-size model.[20]

Money was probably the first type of capital to be symbolically mediated. Money itself had previously replaced the barter system as people found it more convenient to exchange monetary tokens such as coins or paper for other goods. Various other media were also used for these functions. An often cited example is that of the American colonists at the turn of the eighteenth century who used seashells for their medium of exchange. The Indians ran the 'central bank' for this monetary system, converting the shells into animal pelts, which were used to store wealth, and for trade.[21]

Monetary systems based on exchange of physical tokens, whether animal pelts, seashells, or gold, have all progressively been replaced by exchange of electronic symbols. Most money in the world is thus stored, exchanged, and controlled electronically. Within a very few years, smart cards and electronic banking will virtually replace the need for other media. At that point, money will have effectively dematerialized and retail bank branches will have largely disappeared. Where you deposit or borrow funds will be progressively less affected by geography—which also raises interesting issues for national banks and national governments.

We are all accustomed to reading newspapers, studying books, and viewing computer screens. What all these media provide are representations in symbolic form of the real physical world. Most of our knowledge is thus gained vicariously, i.e. without having physically to visit or inspect the reality we are learning about. The better symbolic representations of the real world become, the less we need to visit it, unless of course we need to do something other than learn about it. Looking at a picture of food is no substitute for eating it! On the other hand, if all we wish to do is to select and order food, we can probably learn as much as we need to know about it on a computer screen and by sending an electronic message to convey our order request—an example of electronic commerce.

Business nowadays is increasingly about exchange of symbolic goods, electronic symbols representing information about the physical goods which we need to know to conduct the transactions. The faster and cheaper it becomes for business to acquire the knowledge it needs, the more efficient it can become. There is thus a continuing incentive to improve how knowledge about the real world is symbolically represented and communicated. This in turn removes physical barriers and borders to transacting business—as we will see.

Demassification

Historically, the means of production needed to be physically collocated, or 'massed', to achieve maximum productive efficiency. This principle of massed resources worked as well for the pharaohs of Egypt as it did later for Henry Ford's production line. The need for physical concentration or massing of labour, materials, and money has led to the development of cities, armies, schools, and factories. IT has already played a significant role in reducing our dependency upon these human and material concentrations. As more efficient systems for logistics management are developed, technology is likely further to reduce the need for physical resources to be concentrated. Just-in-time systems and computer-integrated manufacturing are already streamlining production, 'demassifying' factories, inventories, and workforces. Self-paced learning has started to replace mass teaching, offering new hope to a profession currently looking at the spectre of mass education (see Chapter 10). Even military forces have moved away from the massed approach to warfare, favouring smaller, more technologically intensive units.

In those industries that are more information or knowledge intensive, such as the IT industry itself, the concept of working on the move, or from a home office, is already well accepted. If all the employees of many modern organizations were to look for a desk at their office location simultaneously, many would be left standing. Telephone, facsimile, email, and video conferencing are progressively replacing the need for much routine face-to-face contact. On the other hand, as mentioned earlier, such technologies cannot as yet convey the full nuances and subtleties of physical face-to-face communication or, for example, the 'atmosphere' of a busy office. Newspaper offices are a case in point. Such places are typically large, open-plan spaces, buzzing with noise, full of computers, and littered with documents. Hardly the type of place to be quietly creative. Yet, on the whole, journalists prefer to work in such environments because they facilitate rapid knowledge transfer.[22] The same can be said today for many businesses that depend upon frequent informal social interaction.

It can be expected therefore that activities that depend on the transfer of explicit knowledge will be most easily demassed and distributed. Conversely activities which depend upon frequent and informal sharing of tacit knowledge between people will tend to remain physically collocated—at least for the short term.

Boundaryless Enterprise

The boundaries between economic activities are eroding within the firm, between industries, and between nations.[23] They are also eroding between the firm and the market—a subject that will be discussed in detail in Chapter 2.

The concept of the division of labour, first enunciated by Adam Smith in *The Wealth of Nations* (1776) and subsequently adopted as the model for production line manufacturing, was based on boundaries at the micro level, i.e. the assignment of a task to a worker. Smith's famous example of pin manufacture characterized the division of labour thus:

one man draws out the wire, another straightens it, a third cuts it, a fourth points it, a fifth grinds it at the top for receiving the head; to make the head requires two or three distinct operations; to put it on, is a peculiar business, to whiten the pins is another; it is even a trade by itself to put them into the paper; and the important business of making a pin is, in this manner, divided into about eighteen distinct operations, which, in some manufactories, are all performed by distinct hands, though in others the same man will sometimes perform two or three of them.[24]

This task-centred view of manufacturing, based on efficiency through specialization, is now giving way to process-centred production activities, emphasizing the importance of teamwork and interchangeability of tasks. Instead of deskilling (if not dehumanizing) labour, by endless repetition of simple tasks, modern production processes rely upon fewer, more skilled workers, carrying out more tasks. Fewer task and hierarchical boundaries— greater cross-functionalism—these are the hallmarks of modern production methods.

The progressive disintegration of boundaries can also be seen at the industry level. Old demarcation lines between industries involved in banking, insurance, and other financial services, which applied less than twenty years ago, have subsequently eroded. The convergence we are witnessing of publishing, entertainment, and the media with the information and telecommunications industries is another example of the removal of industry boundaries.

It is clear that the traditional limitations placed on economic activities because of dependency on particular national or regional locations are breaking down. We are in an era of increasing globalization. Financial globalization is virtually complete. The collapse of communism and the growth of Asia have opened up new opportunities to the entrepreneurs of the West. From American sports equipment to German automobiles and Australian steel, all types of commodities previously manufactured in the West are now produced in the East. Computer software is routinely developed around the world. Other goods and services are beginning to be traded globally as electronic commerce starts to develop. Improved communications and control systems are facilitating the relocation of physically intensive production to countries with the lowest-cost labour, fewest regulations, and largest domestic markets for western goods. In parallel, political moves to reduce national tariff barriers are clearing the non-technical barriers to global trade.

As productive activities become less reliant on physical inputs and more on knowledge inputs, countries reliant for their wealth on physical resources will be progressively disadvantaged. According to the World Bank, in the mid-1990s Australia still enjoyed the highest per capita productive wealth in the world ($US835,000 per person). Japan in contrast was fifth on the world league table ($US565,000 per person). Such statistics suggest Australia's 'lucky country' tag should still apply. Why is Australia not then still the economic superpower it was at the beginning of the twentieth century, on a par at that time with the USA? The answer lies in those same statistics from the World Bank. Eighty per cent ($US668,000 per capita) of Australia's productive wealth comes from its natural physical resources, land, minerals, primary produce— only 20 per cent ($US167,000 per capita) from knowledge and skills. In contrast, Japan's per capita wealth is only 20 per cent natural resources (a mere

$US113,000 per capita) but a staggering 80 per cent ($US452,000 per capita) is derived from knowledge and skills.[25]

Unlike any other resource, knowledge transcends firm, industry, and national boundaries. Many other factors will continue to drive globalization, from mobile speculative capital to the ambitions of large corporations and the need for poorer countries to look beyond their borders for food and aid. Knowledge however will continue to find its way to all corners of the planet. A few decades hence, there will be one economy—a global knowledge economy.

WORK AND CAREERS

A major question—for many people the most important question—posed by the changing nature of economic activity is whether the future knowledge economy will provide more or fewer opportunities for work than are at present available.

During the 1990s we have witnessed an unprecedented number of work-force reductions and disposals of under-performing physical assets. The ensuing effects on employment have received much public attention, although their underlying causes, permanent nature, and future direction have been less publicized and less well understood. Some writers have augured the demise of the firm as an institution, others the demise of work or possibly the demise of the capitalist system. More sanguine observers have interpreted the effects as part of an economic correction to conditions of imbalance between the developed and developing regions of the world. Politicians—forever optimists—have pointed to the incidence of reducing inflation and growth of small business activity as positive omens for job creation and employment. Little wonder that the average citizen is confused, apprehensive, and uncertain as to how best to secure or retain work and how to help his or her children in preparing for their future careers. Later chapters will discuss the characteristics of future work in some detail; however, the following perspectives may help to shed some light on these issues.

Innovation, Substitution, and Compensation

The Austrian economist Joseph Schumpeter, in the 1930s, was one of the first economists to recognize the profound implications of technological innovation. For Schumpeter, innovation lay at the centre of economic change, causing 'gales of creative destruction'. He proposed a taxonomy of technological change based on three stages: invention, innovation, and diffusion.[26]

Innovative products, processes, or services result from the inventiveness of individuals or groups. Following innovation, the process of diffusion commences, determined by the rate of adoption of the process, product, or service by the market. This gives rise to a familiar sigmoid-shaped curve, the 'S' curve of growth; where, after a slow start, successful innovations of all types have been shown to grow slowly for a while then enter a period of rapid growth, before flattening out (see Fig. 1.2).

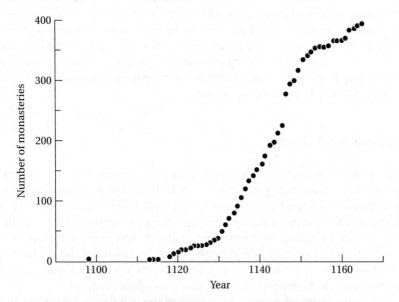

FIG. 1.2. The initial diffusion of Cistercian monasteries in Europe
Source: A. Gruebler (1995), *Time for a Change: Rates of Diffusion of Ideas, Technologies, and Social Behaviors*, WP-95-82, Laxenburg: International Institute for Applied Systems Analysis. Reproduced from P. L. Janauschek (1877), *Originum Cisterciensium*, i, Vienna: A. Hoeler.

Major innovations tend to produce clusters of related innovative products and services which may take many decades to reach maturity.[27] These long cycles or long waves of change, taking about half a century each, had been identified before the First World War by the Dutch economist van Gelderen and in the 1920s by the Russian Kondratieff.

Five long waves, each characterized by a distinctive style, can be identified as having occurred since the latter half of the eighteenth century: water power, steam transport, steel and electricity, Fordist production techniques, and most recently IT and biotechnology.[28]

Carlotta Perez has identified the tendency for each long wave to lead to what she terms a 'technological style'. According to Perez, rapid economic growth occurs where there is a strong positive match between the new techno-economic paradigm and the current socio-institutional framework. 'Mismatches' occur where society and its institutions are not yet prepared for the new paradigm or style. In the latter case, a downsizing in the economy will occur, leading to slow growth or depression. This will be followed by an upswing when the necessary reforms are implemented to allow the new paradigm.[29]

In summary, both Schumpeterian and long wave theories of the economic effects of technological innovation imply that their effects can be both positive and negative, dependent on timing and other circumstances. What matters is society's ability to understand and use technological innovations and more importantly the knowledge they represent, in a way that ensures that the positive effects *compensate* for the negative effects. As future chapters will show, understanding how technological change is increasing the economic importance of knowledge is the critical first step.

Compensation Theories

According to some theorists, the revolution in economic activities which is being caused by continuing improvements in IT and other technologies will result in unavoidable and massive net loss of work. Such pessimistic forecasts are not supported by classical compensation theories. According to such theories, for which considerable supporting evidence has been gathered in the past, savings in labour requirements caused by innovations should be compensated by other factors, which will ensure that the labour saved will be reabsorbed into the economy. Thus equilibrium will be restored.

Considerable debate continues to rage as to the validity and relative merits of various compensation theories. On one aspect, both proponents and critics of compensation theories are closer to agreement, i.e. that *process* innovation almost always implies direct substitution involving efficiency gains and thus loss of existing work. The effects of 'business process re-engineering' during the 1990s are recent evidence of this. New *product* innovations in contrast imply additional work opportunities. Price decreases resulting from innovations generally lead to increased demand, thus growth in supply and related work opportunities. However, new products are usually the result of new and better processes—a 'chicken and egg' situation. The growth of the IT industry itself is evidence of this phenomenon.

Empirical evidence of technological displacement on work and jobs to date has been largely ambivalent. Studies conducted during the 1980s in several OECD countries indicated that technologically induced change up to that time had had either a neutral or mildly positive effect on net employment.[30] Such studies also tend to show, however, that work opportunities are significantly increasing for those with higher-level skills and significantly declining for the unskilled and poorly qualified. Low-cost competition from the East is compounding the problem for low-skilled workers in the West.

To extrapolate from the past however can be dangerous. Fifty years ago few people would have predicted the speed or direction of scientific and technical progress that has subsequently occurred or its impact on work and jobs.

Current advances in biotechnology, exemplified by the genome mapping project, are starting to enable mankind to control the basic building blocks of life itself, the information encoded in plant, animal, and human cells. Nanotechnology, an emerging technology based on the study of structures as small as a nanometer (one billionth of a metre), offers the potential for construction of vastly miniaturized devices with revolutionary possibilities in manufacturing, computing, medicine, and many other fields. Both these sets of technologies, particularly nanotechnology, are at an early stage of development. The advances in human knowledge which they already represent and the 'breakthrough' possibilities which that knowledge portends are however immense—further evidence that we are indeed in the midst of a knowledge revolution.

Someone once said that the only certainties in life are death and taxes. Doom-laden forecasts of a permanent workless underclass, the result of technological job replacement, have no greater claim to accuracy than the overly optimistic forecasts of a new, technologically driven, golden age. Clearly, however, countries which fail to adapt to the need to increase their national skill levels and build indigenous knowledge-intensive industries will end up both economically and socially impoverished. The risks of failure to adapt are likely to be severe, but the tools and technologies exist, to facilitate the transition process.

Careers versus Jobs

The principle of the division of labour popularized by Adam Smith, and later incorporated in Fordist production line principles, identified specialization by task as the optimum method of organizing labour. A particular task or set of tasks constituted the scope of a job. A worker was employed to perform a job, defined as one or more predefined tasks, on a repetitive basis and usually for a fixed wage.

The limitations of the Fordist approach began to manifest themselves in the 1970s and 1980s and are broadly acknowledged today. The 'one man one job' orientation is far too rigid and inflexible in an era of rapid change. The costs of middle management necessary to monitor large numbers of individually specified tasks have become unacceptably high. Workers' lack of identification with customers' needs and company goals, together with their susceptibility to manipulation by union pressure, have further exposed the deficiencies of too rigid a division of labour.

Greater flexibility now exists within firms to redesign tasks and processes and allocate responsibility for performing them. The fewer the physical resource dependencies involved and the greater the level of commonly shared knowledge in the firm, the greater the degree of flexibility possible in the design of production systems. By aggregating tasks formerly conducted by individual workers, economies of scale have been achieved, together with reduced monitoring costs, improved flexibility, and greater focus on the customer. Task orientation has given way to process orientation and (as later chapters will show) process orientation is now giving way to knowledge orientation.

These changes have gradually altered perceptions of what constitutes a job. A process worker/manager today is more likely to identify with the business process in which he or she is involved, rather than its individual tasks or components. Hammer points to a growing similarity between the attitude of those involved in process work and those involved in professions such as law or medicine.[31] The change in attitude is characterized most strongly by the way the work involved is referred to in terms of career specialization, e.g. 'the practice of medicine' as distinct from particular tasks involved in medical practice.

The shift from a job orientation to a career orientation is consistent with the generalization/standardization of previously specific knowledge mentioned earlier. Secretaries today find themselves more employable through their knowledge of industry *standard* word processing packages. Similarly programmers today find work through their knowledge of standard programming languages. Such trends are reducing the dependence of the average worker on firm-specific knowledge. In effect, careers owned by individuals will progressively replace jobs owned by firms. By the same token, firms are becoming less dependent on the idiosyncratic knowledge of particular workers, when the same/similar knowledge can be obtained more cost effectively, either through automation or on the open market. These changes imply a fundamental restructuring of the firm, of work, and of relationships between firms and workers—subjects that will be discussed in detail in later chapters.

KNOWLEDGE CAPITALISM

According to some schools of thought, an economy based on knowledge, rather than traditional forms of capital, could be seen to challenge the fundamental tenets of capitalism. This seems unlikely. Capitalism as we know it, and emerging Knowledge Capitalism, both thrive on capital accumulation, open market competition, free trade, the power of the individual, and the survival of the fittest. Since the overthrow of communism (i.e. state-controlled capitalism) free market capitalism is the only game in town.

Anyone who has watched old black and white movies of sporting events of the 1920s and 1930s will have been struck by the difference between the technical prowess and equipment used by the athletes in those days compared to today. Yet the rules of the game were much the same then as now. The difference in future is likely to be not so much the rules of the capitalist game, but the equipment used by the players. It is useful, however, to consider briefly how Knowledge Capitalism might affect current systems of capitalism.

Systems of Capitalism

Four regional systems of capitalism can be identified: the Anglo-American model, as practised in the USA, UK, Australasia, and Canada; social market capitalism—Germany, Sweden, Austria, Denmark, and the Netherlands; state capitalism as practised in France; and the Japanese model.[32]

According to Groenewegen, in the Anglo-American model the interests of the *shareholders* are central, management is controlled by various mechanisms that act for the shareholders, and the model is based on an individualistic value system in which the interests of risk capital are central.

In the social market/continental model, the interests of the principal *stakeholders* (shareholders and employees) are central, codetermination of the affairs of the firm means labour has a vote, and blocks of shares are held by stable shareholders. As a result the stock market has less influence than in the Anglo-American model.

State capitalism (as practised in France in particular) is similar in some respects to the social market model; however, labour unions and employer associations are not involved in strategic decision making. An elite comprised of politicians, bureaucracy, and the management of large firms control the economy.

In the Japanese model, a broader community of stakeholders controls the firm; they include shareholders, employees, suppliers, customers, and business groups. Transactions are largely internalized, i.e. performed within the firm or between the firm and its stakeholders, rather than in the open market. Contracts are relational (based on inputs) rather than transactional (based on achievement of outputs or results). Management of the firm has a high degree of autonomy and is ultimately responsible to stable shareholders (as in the social market model).

Each of these systems of capitalism has particular strengths. The Anglo-American model provides short-term flexibility, the continental model fosters long-term firm–worker relationships, and the state model is strong in guiding complicated technology projects such as public transport which can be isolated from the international market.

In terms of weaknesses, the Anglo-American model tends to maximize short-run efficiencies and to be weak where long-term efficiencies require relation-specific investments. The European models tend to induce rigidities in the short run and lock-in path dependencies in the long run, due to personal relationships. The Japanese model tends to suffer from the rigidities of the European model and also from time-consuming decision making.

In contrast to these regional variants, Knowledge Capitalism represents a *generic* new variant of capitalism, based more on the accumulation of knowledge than monetary or physical forms of wealth. It is not a system in conflict with traditional capitalism. Indeed, it shares the same fundamental belief in the free market and in the potential of the individual. Knowledge Capitalism is also capable of being moulded to the philosophies and traditions of different regions of the world. It corresponds closely with the Anglo-American model in relation to flexibility, but also stresses the importance of stakeholder not only shareholder interests. Suppliers of knowledge, rather than suppliers of financial risk capital, are central to the concept of Knowledge Capitalism. These are aspects of Knowledge Capitalism that will be discussed in detail in later chapters.

Knowledge Capitalism is also close to the current Japanese model, insofar as both models place considerable store on specific human capital.[33] Knowledge Capitalism, however, while emphasizing the centrality of the individual, acknowledges the role of organizations, products, processes, routines, and directives as capable of embodying and disseminating knowledge.

No single regional variant appears likely to become globally dominant—at least in the short term. Europe and Japan have borrowed from the Anglo-American model and vice versa. The current trend towards a global knowledge-based economy suggests that ultimately all these regional variants will become forms of Knowledge Capitalism. In the process, many of these regional differences can be expected to disappear.

SUMMARY AND CONCLUSIONS

The shift to a post-industrial, knowledge-based economy is progressively altering the role of the traditional factors of production: labour, materials, and capital. Symbolic resources are replacing physical resources, mental exertion is replacing physical exertion, and knowledge capital is beginning to challenge money and all other forms of capital. New symbolic goods, new services, new forms of manufacturing and distribution, and a boundaryless, global business environment are emerging, fuelled by information and driven by knowledge. The commercialization of information and communications technologies (collectively IT) has been largely responsible to date for this shift to the knowledge economy. IT, as Freeman and Soete put it, 'the biggest technological juggernaut that ever rolled', can be seen to have both positive and negative effects, both destroying and creating work opportunities.[34] The implications of such massive change are clearly grounds for despair or hope, dependent on the circumstances in which the firm or the individual finds itself.

It is already apparent from current trends that the organization of future work and the level of knowledge necessary to benefit from future work opportunities are going to alter dramatically and that worker skill levels are going to have to improve equally dramatically. It is also becoming apparent that ownership of the means of production in the emerging knowledge economy is going to be less straightforward than in the past. The firm's most valuable knowledge capital tends to reside in the brains of its key workers, and ownership of people went out with the abolition of slavery. Employment contracts are not much help either: people go home at night; they talk to each other; they change employment—all the time retaining a copy of that knowledge in their brains. This suggests that owning and organizing the means of production will become increasingly problematic. The implications of the knowledge economy for firm owners and investors will be just as profound as they are for employees. Future chapters will explore these wide-ranging and critical implications.

NOTES

1. A. Touraine (1969), *La Société post-industrielle*, Paris: Denoel. D. Bell (1973), *The Coming of Post-industrial Society*, New York: Basic Books.
2. M. Castells and Y. Aoyama (1994), 'Paths towards the Informational Society: Employment Structure in G-7 Countries, 1920–1990', *International Labour Review*, 133/1: 10–17.
3. J. B. Quinn (1992), *Intelligent Enterprise: A Knowledge and Service Based Paradigm for Industry*, New York: Free Press.
4. B. Russell (1973), *An Inquiry into Meaning and Truth*, Harmondsworth: Penguin Books Ltd.
5. R. M. Chisholm (1989), *Theory of Knowledge*, Englewood Cliffs, NJ: Prentice-Hall Inc.
6. G. N. von Tunzelmann (1995), *Technology and Industrial Progress: The Foundations of Economic Growth*, Aldershot: Edward Elgar Publishing.
7. J. Roos, G. Roos, N. C. Dragonetti, and L. Edvinsson (1997), *Intellectual Capital: Navigating the New Business Landscape*, Basingstoke: Macmillan Press Ltd.
8. T. A. Stewart (1998), 'Leading Edge: A New Way to Think about Employees', *Fortune Magazine*, 13 Apr.: 169–72.
9. M. Polanyi (1967), *The Tacit Dimension*, London: Routledge & Kegan Paul Ltd.
10. E. von Hippel (1994), 'Sticky Information and the Locus of Problem Solving: Implications for Innovation', *Management Science*, 40/4: 429–39.
11. W. M. Cohen and D. Levinthal (1990), 'Absorptive Capacity: A New Perspective on Learning and Innovation', *Administrative Science Quarterly*, 35/1: 128–52.
12. M. E. Porter and V. E. Millar (1985), 'How Information Gives you Competitive Advantage', *Harvard Business Review* (July–Aug.): 152.
13. C. Jonscher (1994), 'An Economic Study of the Information Technology Revolution', in T. J. Allen and M. S. Scott Morton (eds.), *Information Technology and the Corporation of the 1990's*, New York: Oxford University Press: 5–38.
14. SAP—Corporate Profile, *http://www.sap.com*.
15. J. Hibbard (1998), 'The Learning Revolution: The Web and Other Collaborative Technologies are Helping Companies Redefine Corporate Learning—and Do a Better Job of Training Employees', *Information Week* (9 Mar.). TechSearch *http://www.techweb.com/se/directlink*.
16. H. Saint-Onge (1996), 'Tacit Knowledge: The Key to the Strategic Alignment of Intellectual Capital', *Strategy and Leadership* (Mar.–Apr.).
17. I. Nonaka and H. Takeuchi (1995), *The Knowledge-Creating Company: How Japanese Companies Create the Dynamics of Innovation*, New York: Oxford University Press.

18. Interview, 18 Dec. 1998. Junnarkar referred to the often overly 'mechanistic' approaches which firms have taken and stressed the importance to effective knowledge management of 'interweaving technologies with people'.

19. N. Negroponte (1995), *Being Digital*, New York: Alfred A. Knopf.

20. Jonscher, 'An Economic Study of the Information Technology Revolution'.

21. T. Richards (1995), 'Banking without Borders, Forex without Frontiers', *International Banking on the Internet IQPC*, London.

22. Karl-Eric Sveiby (1996), 'Transfer of Knowledge and the Information Processing Professions', *European Management Journal*, 14/4: 379–88.

23. R. Ashkenas, D. Ulrich, T. Jick, and S. Kerr (1995), *The Boundaryless Organisation: Breaking the Chains of Organisational Structure*, San Francisco: Jossey-Bass Inc.

24. A. Smith (1776), *An Inquiry into the Nature and Causes of the Wealth of Nations*, London: George Routledge & Sons (1893 edn.).

25. L. C. Thurow (1996), *The Future of Capitalism: How Today's Economic Forces Will Shape Tomorrow's World*, New York: William Morrow & Company, Inc.

26. J. A. Schumpeter (1939), *Business Cycles: A Theoretical, Historical, and Statistical Analysis of the Capitalist Process*, New York: McGraw-Hill.

27. A. Gruebler (1995), *Time for a Change: Rates of Diffusion of Ideas, Technologies, and Social Behaviors*, WP-95–82, Laxenburg: International Institute for Applied Systems Analysis.

28. C. Freeman and L. Soete (1994), *Work for All or Mass Unemployment? Computerised Technical Change into the 21st Century*, London: Pinter Publishers.

29. C. Perez (1983), 'Structural Change and the Assimilation of New Technologies in the Economic and Social System', *Futures*, 15/5: 357–75.

30. M. Carnoy and M. Castells (1997), *Sustainable Flexibility: A Prospective Study on Work, Family and Society in the Information Age*, Paris: OECD: 13.

31. M. Hammer (1996), *Beyond Reengineering*, New York: HarperCollins Publishers, Inc.

32. J. Groenewegen (1997), 'Institutions of Capitalisms: American, European and Japanese Systems Compared', *Journal of Economic Issues*, 31/3: 333–47.

33. R. S. Ozaki (1991), *Human Capitalism*, Tokyo: Kodansha International Ltd.

34. Freeman and Soete, *Work for All or Mass Unemployment?*

Knowledge, the Firm, and the Market

Up to the time of the Industrial Revolution in the mid-eighteenth century, most economic activities occurred in the market. The discovery of the benefits of the division of labour led to the birth of the mass production economy and the rise of the modern business enterprise as the premier institution for organization of economic activities.

In 1776, Adam Smith wrote of the 'invisible hand' of market forces, which determined price and helped coordinate production of goods.[1] Within little over a century, the 'visible hand', as Chandler described it, of the modern business enterprise had emerged, having largely replaced market mechanisms in coordination and allocation of resources.[2] Instead of obtaining their factors of production when needed on the open market, firms began internalizing an increasing range of functions, perceiving this as an aid to efficiency and effectiveness. Labour was employed rather than hired; premises, plant, and equipment were leased or purchased, rather than rented. Capital intensity thereby increased. Firm hierarchies became more complex. The volume of transactions occurring within the firm grew exponentially as a result—often outnumbering transactions between the firm and its suppliers and clients.

Firms continued to grow, mainly through internalization and centralization, until, during the 1970s, improvements in computing and communications started to offer firms the opportunity to decentralize their operations, thereby saving costs and reducing administrative complexity. Large-scale centralized and monolithic organizations began to give way to distributed organizational structures. During the 1980s and 1990s, traditional Fordist and Taylorist methods of production and organization were further challenged. IT continued to play an enabling role, assisting the transformation of production inputs and outputs and improving their coordination. Organizations became even leaner and flatter and internalized functions tended to be hived off unless they could be shown to be necessary to the firm's core business. As a result, the commercial firm of the late 1990s is typically less inhibited by geographic, industry, or technical boundaries, employs fewer people on a full-time permanent basis, and often has fewer tangible assets. Nonetheless, it continues to generate ever-increasing returns for its shareholders.

The paradox of the simultaneously shrinking and expanding firm is not unexpected, given the changing nature of its factors of production already discussed. It prompts a number of fundamental questions, however, about the future of the firm as an institution for organizing economic activities. In the knowledge economy, what types of transactions will be performed in the firm, as distinct from the market? As the firm changes shape, how will patterns of ownership and control be affected? How will these trends affect the availability of work and thus jobs? In order to address these issues, it is useful to have a broad understanding of current economic theories of the firm. The next section therefore provides a brief overview of relevant theories in this area.

THEORIES OF THE FIRM

Why do firms exist? Why are all economic transactions not performed in the market? No single unified theory of the firm as yet exists. What we do have are a number of partial explanations for its existence, structure, and principles of operation from various different theoretical perspectives.

These theories provide a series of frameworks, some conflicting, others complementary, which can be used to model the effects of the changing nature of economic activities on the firm as an institution. Among the many theories which have been propounded, transaction cost economics, agency theory, resource-based theory, and (emerging) knowledge-based theory are particularly relevant to establishing how the firm is likely to evolve in the future knowledge economy. The overview that follows briefly describes key features of each of these theories.

Transaction Cost Economics

Transaction cost economics (TCE) builds on Nobel Laureate Ronald Coase's celebrated 1937 work 'The Nature of the Firm'.[3] Up to the publication of Coase's thesis, conventional economic theory had viewed the economic system as being coordinated impersonally by the price mechanism, but it also had acknowledged that the entrepreneur performed a similar coordinating role. Coase sought to bridge the gap between these apparently inconsistent theories. His conclusion was that the reason for establishing a firm is to avoid the cost of using the price mechanism, the most obvious cost being 'discovering what the relevant prices are'. Even if one could purchase that information from market specialists, the purchaser would still be faced with the cost of negotiating and completing a separate contract for each market transaction.

Based on Coase's earlier work, TCE views the market and the firm as alternative instruments for completing a set of transactions.[4] The choice of the firm or the market is determined by its relative efficiency. The human factors affecting choice of governance (i.e. firm or market) are assumed to be bounded rationality (limited ability) and opportunism (self-interest plus guile). The last assumption has been frequently criticized, but cannot be disproven. To assume otherwise can lead to unsustainable risk taking—akin to leaving the door of the office safe open all the time!

According to TCE, the firm provides certain advantages over the market in its ability to compensate for these perceived human limitations. Opportunism can be reduced in the firm through increased scope for monitoring, coupled with rewards such as promotion for positive compliance with firm goals. The limitations of bounded rationality can be mitigated in the firm by the pooling of knowledge resources which occurs naturally between co-workers and by the use of routines and directives which workers can follow, but do not necessarily need to understand fully.

The major external or environmental factors determining choice of firm or market are assumed to be uncertainty, small numbers bargaining, and asset specificity. Uncertainty refers to the inability of all parties to a transaction to predict all future contingencies that may affect their relationship. The existence of small numbers of parties to an exchange increases the chances of opportunistic behaviour in bargaining. Asset specificity occurs where transactions require the use of particular assets such as special machinery, individuals with unique skills, or materials that can only be obtained from a particular place. Capital-intensive production activities such as mining or manufacturing, for example, tend to be highly asset specific.

Since all transactions involving an exchange between two or more parties imply some form of contract, contractual complexity can be a critical factor. Writing and enforcing complete contracts which ensure a fair return to all the contracting parties may be impractical or too costly in the market. In such cases, the firm offers a framework within which the contracting process may be less complex, as in the case of employment contracts that are generally open ended and flexible, as compared to market hire contracts which tend to be more rigid and specific.

A desire to reduce cost and risk, improve quality, and leverage buying power has frequently encouraged firms to develop asset-specific relationships with a restricted number of suppliers. The specific assets involved are typically the systems and technologies favoured by the purchasing firm with which the suppliers are required to comply. For example, as Xerox progressed to new high-quality, just-in-time processes, it cut its supplier base from several thousand to a few hundred.[5]

Human factors interacting with the key properties of the transactions involved in any given circumstance determine whether the market or the firm is the most appropriate governance structure. In general, according to TCE, transactions that involve a high level of asset specificity, uncertainty, small numbers of contracting parties, and would require complex contracts if conducted in the market, are more likely to be conducted in the firm. In contrast, transactions which are simple, unambiguous, and where the productive assets involved are non-specific, as in the case of products and processes which use standard commodities, low-skilled labour, or widely available information, are likely to be conducted more efficiently in the market.

Agency Theory

The origins of agency theory lie in the legal authority relationship that formerly existed between master and servant, and was later seen to apply to the relationship between employer and employee. The orientation of agency theory as it has been developed in financial economics focuses on the effect of various factors in human contractual relationships that arise within the firm. These include information asymmetry, opportunism, adverse selection, and moral hazard. Adverse selection occurs where the principal recruits an agent who is not suited to the task, due to incomplete knowledge of the agent (an example of information asymmetry) or through misrepresentation by the agent (an example of opportunism). Moral hazard occurs where the agent fails to work to the agreed standard (shirking). This leads to the need for monitoring of the agent by the principal and, in some instances, bonding by the agent to the principal. Monitoring involves costs for metering or measuring the agent's input and output. Bonding involves costs for provision of information by the agent to satisfy the principal of non-shirking activity, such as the provision of accounting reports by management to the owners of a firm.

According to positive agency theorists, the firm emerged as a result of a need to combine and coordinate the inputs of multiple self-interested individuals in pursuit of a common goal. The common goal implicitly must include some productivity advantages over operating independently in the market, otherwise there would be no incentive for combined activity. The need for combined activity gives rise to cooperative behaviour or teamwork involving the individual input owners. Various consequences flow from the need for cooperative behaviour, which include the need for some party to coordinate the individual factor inputs and the need for controls to be established, to ensure that where individual self-interest is not congruent with group goals, it does not prevail.

According to such theories, the firm and its owner(s) evolved as a natural response to the need for and the need to coordinate such group behaviour. It follows that 'the firm' has no special authority over its workers. Any rights belonging to the firm or its workers must be embodied in contracts between them—just as in market contracts. The firm is in effect simply a type of privately owned market.[6] Rewards to individual input owners naturally need to reflect their individual contributions. This gives rise to the concept of metering to measure actual performance, to deter 'shirking' and control allocation of rewards.

Metering, however, is particularly difficult where joint inputs are required to achieve a common output. The cost of individual workers metering each other may also outweigh the benefits of cooperative activity. A central monitor is thus required, to overview measurement and control processes, and to ensure they operate most efficiently. The monitor however also requires to be monitored, leading to an infinitely recursive situation. To solve this, the monitor logically becomes the residual claimant: the 'owner', the person whose rewards are more closely aligned to corporate performance than anyone else in the firm.

The essential nature of the firm, according to Alchian and Demsetz, is thus 'a contractual structure with (1) joint input production; (2) several input owners; (3) one party who is common to all the contracts of the joint inputs; (4) who has rights to renegotiate any input's contract independently of contracts with other input owners; (5) who holds the residual claim; and (6) who has the right to sell his central contractual residual status'.[7]

Jensen and Meckling draw upon theories of property rights, agency, and finance to develop a theory of firm ownership structure which once again focuses on the contractual relationship between the parties involved in the firm. The notion of the firm is seen to be a legal fiction; all that exists is a 'nexus of contracting relationships'.[8] This concept of the firm as a collection of contracts is a useful way of highlighting that the relationships between the various stakeholders in the firm, including both those 'internal' and 'external' to it, are central to what we mean when we speak of 'the firm' as a definable entity. As the firm becomes an increasingly knowledge-based institution, these stakeholder relationships are being radically altered, as we will see in later chapters.

Resource-Based and Knowledge-based Theories

The foundations of resource-based theory (RBT) owe much to the work of Penrose, and her conceptualization of the firm as 'a collection of productive resources'.[9] This perspective implies that a firm's distinctive competencies are based on its resources and capabilities, which may be represented by tangible assets such as patented inventions, or intangibles such as reputation, brand image, or human skills. According to RBT, firms expand by utilizing these pre-existing resources. A proposition also advanced by many RBT theorists is that sustainable competitive advantage is mainly derived from the inimitability of a firm's resources.[10]

Studies in the strategic management field relating to innovation underscore the importance of protecting new inventions/products from imitation. Teece for instance provides a theoretical analysis of firm and industry characteristics which determine when *innovation* is likely to be more effective than *imitation*.[11] He cites the case of Cola and Diet Cola. These products were originally produced by RC Cola but, when both Coke and Pepsi released their cola-based products, RC Cola's sales were soon eroded. Teece argues that two sources of appropriability are critical to the success of an innovation strategy: legal instruments such as patents and the nature of the technology such as the degree of tacit knowledge involved.

Much recent research has centred on human capital resources, defined by Barney as 'the training, experience, judgement, intelligence, relationships and insight of managers and workers in a firm'.[12] This focus has been partially responsible for the development of an emerging knowledge-based theory of the firm. This emerging theory draws upon RBT and other research streams including epistemology, organizational learning, organizational capabilities, innovation, and new product development. Key assumptions involved in the emerging knowledge-based theory of the firm include:

- knowledge is the key productive resource of the firm;
- knowledge is acquired by and, in the case of tacit knowledge, stored by individuals;
- due to time and cognitive limitations of human beings, individuals need to specialize in the knowledge they acquire;
- production (value creation through translation of inputs into outputs) typically requires numerous different types of specialized knowledge.[13]

The primary role of the firm, according to knowledge theorists, is, therefore, the protection and integration of specialized knowledge. If two parties to a transaction in the market exchange knowledge, there is danger of expropriation or imitation. In the case of general or explicit knowledge these are not important issues; in the case of specialist knowledge, however, it may be critical. The firm in contrast can protect its knowledge resources in various ways.[14] It can for example, design jobs such that individual workers do not have to be experts in each other's fields, but can collectively benefit from the integration of their component skills. Firms can further protect knowledge by requiring their workers to sign non-disclosure agreements and by offering incentives to key knowledge workers to remain in the firm. Additionally they can design products and processes in ways that prevent access to the core knowledge that is embedded in them, even after the products leave the firm. For example, in the case of software packages, the software developer normally retains the source code and only the object versions, which perform limited functions, are licensed for use.

Legal protection in the market place is available for copyrights, trademarks, and trade secrets. Formal mechanisms used to achieve knowledge integration in the firm include routines and directives.[15] Such mechanisms also provide a degree of knowledge protection. Organizational routines enable members of an organization to exchange information on an as-needed basis. The CFO, for example, may need to know certain aspects of financial performance, the accounts department others, Directives, as mentioned earlier, include the provision of information in policies, procedures, and guidelines that enable workers to operate without having to understand the prior knowledge which gave rise to them. Examples typically include the provision of manuals or training which may enable individuals to maintain or operate specific items of equipment, or how to operate a business according to a predefined set of rules, as in the case of franchises (see Chapter 6) .'Embedding' firm-specific or tacit knowledge in routines and directives may thus not only assist integration, but also offer protection against unauthorized use or expropriation.

The firm's capacity to utilize its knowledge is largely a function of the relationship between its knowledge and its products or processes. Most knowledge in a firm is neither product nor firm specific, for example, knowledge of IT, the law, accounting, or finance. There is therefore usually some imbalance or lack of perfect congruence between what a firm knows and what it needs to know, which may imply learning and/or knowledge trading with other firms.[16]

Firm-specific knowledge in contrast may be either tacit or explicit. It may either provide the firm with a strategic advantage, or simply represent an idiosyncratic approach to 'how it does things'. A typical example of the former would be the secret formula for a successful perfume, and of the latter, the use of a firm-developed rather than a standard office automation system (unless of course such a system actually provided some strategic advantage). In practice, the distinction between these two different types of firm-specific knowledge is not always easy to make (see Chapter 8). The main point in the long run, however, is that only *tacit* knowledge, whether alone or in conjunction with explicit knowledge, can give a firm a sustainable competitive advantage. Such knowledge is always associated with people, whereas explicit knowledge is generally capable of being stored, processed, and communicated using (widely available) technologies.

These aspects of knowledge highlight the importance of firms understanding their role as 'knowledge integrators' not merely 'information processors'. They also illustrate the importance, as noted earlier, of firms maintaining an appropriate balance between their investments in different sources of knowledge (see Fig. 2.1).

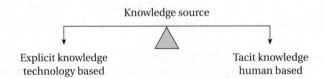

FIG. 2.1. Balance of knowledge

Theories of the Firm: Summary

According to transaction cost economics the firm represents a response to market failure. In a perfect market, all economic activities could be transacted impersonally between individuals and coordinated via the price mechanism. The firm is an alternative governance structure designed to economize on the costs that would otherwise be incurred through market contracting. Agency theory represents a spectrum of views of the firm, from an authority mechanism, to a structure designed to coordinate specialist inputs, to a nexus of contracts designed to economize on agency costs. Resource-based theory regards the firm as a bundle of resources, both tangible and intangible, whose characteristics determine the firm's core competencies, and may be used to determine growth and competitive strategies. The emerging knowledge-based theory of the firm draws on resource-based theory and other theories in defining the firm as a market-like structure, whose key resource is knowledge and whose principal activities are knowledge protection and integration.

Each of these theories represents a unique and largely complementary perspective on the nature of the firm. Their relevance to the questions at hand consists in their ability to model the implications of increasing knowledge intensification and predict its effects. The discussion that follows uses these theories to explore the dynamics affecting future choice of the firm, or the market, as alternative governance structures and also to predict changes in the structure of ownership and control of the firm.

THE FIRM VERSUS THE MARKET

What does the knowledge intensification of economic activities imply for the choice of the market or the firm as alternative governance structures? Knowledge-based theory predicts that economic activities containing high levels of explicit non-firm-specific knowledge, unless otherwise protected by the firm's structure or the exercise of its legal property rights, will move into the market (*externalization*). Conversely, those with high levels of tacit and specialized knowledge will remain in the firm (*internalization*). Firm-specific knowledge embodied in routine functions can be expected to reduce, due to automation. Routine firm functions requiring little firm-specific knowledge, such as office cleaning, equipment maintenance, and security, are already commonly outsourced.

Based on transaction cost economics, asset specificity, which favours the firm as a governance structure, appears likely to decline. Physical asset specificity can be expected to reduce as the materials, plant, and equipment used by firms to produce goods and services become increasingly standardized. The equipment needed to produce newspapers, make films, or run a telephone network used to be both functionally specific and highly capital intensive. Nowadays the same underlying production technologies are used for all these functions. Human asset specificity can be expected to reduce in overall terms as the idiosyncratic knowledge of particular individuals is superseded or reduced to explicit information which can be incorporated in organizational routines. As noted earlier, time and location specificity can similarly be expected to decline, as firms are able to use just-in-time production systems and global communication networks to trade across industry and geographic boundaries.

In order to gain the benefits of global connectivity, firms are having to reduce their use of non-standard firm asset-specific systems and methods. Thus we see a move away from proprietary EDI and messaging systems and proprietary networks to Internet-based electronic commerce, using standard tools and applications. These factors tend to imply an overall shift toward proportionately greater market-based coordination.[17]

The decline in specificity evidenced by these trends is likely to extend to a firm's suppliers and partners, where current ties are the result of asset-specific dependencies. As firms become more 'footloose' they will source their factors of production wherever it is most economically efficient. Vertical integration by acquisition should decrease and inter-firm collaboration increase as a by-product of these factors. Evidence of the trend towards greater inter-firm collaboration is shown by the rate of growth in alliances between US and international firms which by the early 1990s were recorded as having reached an average annual growth rate across all industries of 27 per cent.[18]

Whilst specificity of physical assets and explicit knowledge may be expected to decline in overall terms, the firm's dependency on its key knowledge resources and its tacit knowledge will become even more pronounced. Thus, while many transactions will become less specific and move out of the firm, others will become more firm specific and move closer to the core of the firm. Examples of the former type include many retail transactions, from selling videos and books to simple banking transactions and making travel reservations. Examples of the latter type include highly specialized or complex transactions involved in design, production, or other activities where the firm's specialized knowledge gives it a competitive edge.

Some argue that the desire by firms to protect what they regard as important intellectual property will drive large firms to become even larger. According to one scenario envisioned as part of the MIT Initiative on Inventing, 'The Organisations of the 21st Century', huge global conglomerates could as a result emerge. Such firms would form *keiretsu*-style global alliances between their operating companies and suppliers. In effect they would become 'virtual countries'. The opposing scenario envisions a world in which market-based transacting will become far easier and cheaper than today. In this scenario, the advantages of scale, speed, and flexibility offered by (virtual) networks of small firms and individuals will obviate the need for large firms.[19]

The rash of global mega mergers we have witnessed in the late 1990s, coupled with the tendency for small firms to become even smaller, suggests that in the short term, both these scenarios may eventuate, i.e. the market will polarize into mega firms and collaborating networks of micro firms. In the long term the relative efficiency of each organizational form will determine its survival. Key issues in the short term will revolve around what knowledge is worth retaining inside firms, and the cost and difficulties of market transacting. Knowledge protection and the protective mechanisms open to firms will also be critical. More on these topics later.

Technological improvements can be expected to reduce the uncertainty and complexity often associated with market contracting. Opportunism in the market, resulting from information asymmetries between contracting parties, can also be expected to reduce for the same reasons. As transactions move out of the firm into the market, the firm may be disintermediated totally, by the product market (consumers) dealing directly with the factors of production. Alternatively, the firm will retain a degree of involvement and possibly hierarchical influence by contracting both with the product market and with externally based factors of production. As an example, individual consumers in future may be able to purchase directly on line from a particular book publisher, who nowadays would only sell product to book retailers. Conversely, consumers may also be able to find the same product on the electronic bookshelves of major on line retailers like Amazon.com.

Even in those cases where for example an electronic service substitutes for a physical service, some downstream growth of work opportunities in the electronic services industry is likely to eventuate. Externalization therefore denotes a movement of functions and transactions out of the firm, not necessarily their total destruction. Where substitution occurs, some compensating increases in economic activities are likely. Physical disintermediation for example may be followed by electronic 'reintermediation', as in the case of electronic video stores replacing physical stores.

The sentiment of the share-buying public at present appears to be strongly favouring the fortunes of the new electronic intermediaries. How long this will last is an interesting question. Some would argue that electronic mediation will become big business, others would argue that the dizzying rise of Internet stocks is more a reflection of market belief in the future of electronic trading than in the stocks that happen to be currently available. Given intelligent agent software, which could trawl through the electronic warehouses of major suppliers, offer objective and expert recommendations as to the best buys, and even handle purchase and payment transactions, who would need electronic retailers, particularly for products which could be unambiguously represented electronically? Time will tell.

And the Winner Is . . . ?

Both knowledge and transaction cost perspectives support the view that transactions involving high levels of explicit, non-firm-specific knowledge will tend to move outside the firm, whereas those involving high levels of tacit or specialized knowledge will remain within it. The factors determining these movements are largely beyond the control of the firm. Despite, or because of, this inevitability, firms may exercise a conscious choice to adapt to their changing environments by deliberately externalizing non-core functions and in the process manage to retain a degree of hierarchical influence outside their borders. As a result, externalization involving inter-firm collaboration, outsourcing, subcontracting, franchising, and similar forms of contracting, between the firm and other firms or individuals in the market, will increase. Conversely, firms may take the view that they are going to protect their current physical and intellectual assets by more rather than less internalization.

In short, knowledge protection and integration of disparate specialized knowledge resources will become the primary function of the firm as an institution. A parallel process of internalization of key resources will mirror the externalization of the firm's non-core and explicit knowledge-based functions. Firms in the future are likely to be more aware of the value of their knowledge-based resources, and thus the resources which they do internalize will become more critical to their success.

OWNERSHIP AND CONTROL OF THE FIRM

Most productive activity has, over the last couple of centuries, gravitated from the market to the firm. Individuals, by and large, owe their careers and livelihoods to firms. Any significant changes therefore to the structure of ownership, or principles of control of the firm, will significantly impact all its stakeholders, not just its owners or investors. The following analysis examines how ownership and control of the firm will be affected by the transition to a knowledge economy.

The Nature of Ownership

Ownership of assets has been the subject of extensive definition and protection by way of property rights. Three distinct elements have been identified with property rights: the right to determine use, the right to bear the market value, and the right to exchange the rights to the first two elements.[20] Ownership is thus a bundle of rights. This bundle can be separated, however, and individual elements assigned. A firm owner may assign the rights to a manager to control plant or equipment—this does not mean the manager owns the plant or equipment, he or she merely has the assigned rights. Just as I might hand you the keys to my car, you can drive it, but that does not mean you own it!

Ownership is generally an imperfect or incomplete form of contract, due to the constraints and obligations carried with it. I may own a car, but I cannot park it wherever I like. Ownership therefore means having the residual rights of control over an asset, where such rights have not otherwise been legally defined or assigned. Despite the 'residual' nature of ownership, the right to exchange or trade the asset owned is of fundamental importance to its value. The value of any asset, be it your car, your house, or your firm, is diminished if you do not have the right to sell it. Specificity of ownership is also critical.

Where rights to ownership cannot be proven, as for example in the case of disputed land title, the market value of the asset decreases.

Ownership and the Firm

Ownership of the assets used in the firm has been subject to property rights as defined above. Ownership of exclusive knowledge has been defined by patents, real property by title deeds, and money by contracts with providers of capital. Following the abolition of slavery, labour could no longer be owned, but rights to its use have been gained by the firm through hire contracts and contracts of employment.

The imperfect nature of ownership applies equally in the case of ownership of the firm. The owner is the ultimate monitor, the individual or individuals whose rewards are most closely aligned with overall corporate performance (see Agency Theory above). As such, the owner is the residual claimant to the returns from the firm's activities after payment of staff, creditors, government taxes, and other contractual liabilities. The owner is also the individual who has the right to sell his or her ownership rights, for example, shares in a company.

Specificity of ownership has been as important to the firm as to individuals. Where production resources have been shared, as in the collectives of the former USSR, the farms and factories involved were generally less efficiently maintained and run than their western privately owned counterparts. Such examples are sometimes referred to as 'the tragedy of the commons', meaning that where owners are not identifiable, assets tend to be abused, since responsibility for the costs of abuse or the benefits of proper use cannot be specifically assigned.[21]

In the case of the classic entrepreneur or a small private firm, the identity of those holding specific ownership rights and those individuals to whom other rights have been assigned is usually readily apparent. In a public corporation, however, the situation is less clear cut. Stockholders have specifically limited rights; they cannot hire or fire the management team, they cannot determine strategy, and they cannot determine the dividends they will be paid. The directors are constrained in different ways; they can influence but not control the stockholders, who enjoy the rights of retention or disposal of their own shares. If the company is liquidated, the net proceeds flow to the shareholders. Managers and employees have even fewer rights, but these can be quite powerful. Managers run the business and directors and shareholders ultimately rely on them. Employees generally are in the majority and have the ability to contribute more or less effort and to hold up the firm's activities through strikes. Other parties may claim to have a stake in the firm such as the local community, major suppliers, or clients. Whilst these stakeholders may not be able to claim a financial interest, they may well have rights which the firm needs to acknowledge.

While stockholders legally own public corporations, it is apparent, therefore, that their ownership rights are actually quite limited. As Eugene Fama points out, the stock- or bondholders in a modern public corporation are the owners of its capital, but ownership of capital does not equate to ownership of the firm. The stock- or bondholders and the management function have between them absorbed the risk-bearing function of the classic entrepreneur. In the process, security, ownership, and control have been separated.[22]

Firm Ownership and Knowledge

The centrality of knowledge to the firm poses a new set of issues relating to the definition and attribution of property rights and has major implications relating to the separation of ownership and control and valuation of firm assets, as the following analysis describes.

Owning and Protecting Knowledge

Ownership of intellectual property poses some special problems relating to its definition and protection. Information can be protected by copyright and knowledge by patent, both of which confer property rights on the owners. Such property rights however are generally difficult to establish and once established are difficult to protect. If a patent is issued, it must define what it is that is being patented. By definition this allows some leakage of the knowledge which the patent is trying to protect. The problem is exacerbated by the concept of information as a public good which is already reflected in legislation, e.g. patents are for limited time periods.

Breaches of copyright are even more difficult to prove. Even minor changes to data can invalidate any claims of illegal use. Thurow cites the example of a decision by a judge that the 'look and feel' of a software program could not be patented. Thurow suggests that this ruling means effectively that any successful program could be legally copied. The copiers need to write their own code, but they start with the advantage of being able to see how the existing programs are structured, how the final product is supposed to look and feel, and the market for the product.[23]

To compound these problems, all data held electronically can be cheaply transformed and communicated just about anywhere in the world in seconds or minutes. Specific ownership of information and knowledge thus becomes very difficult to prove and, once proven, expensive to protect.

In the past such issues had little significance for most firms, since their competitive positioning was based on other factors such as market power, financial capital, or access to scarce physical resources. Ownership of these physical resources was not particularly difficult to define or protect. Progressively however this situation will change and firms must face the problem of defining and valuing their intellectual assets and determining how they should be protected—as well as coordinated and integrated.

Where intellectual assets are embedded in products and processes, rights to which can be clearly defined, traditional legal mechanisms such as patent and copyright protection may suffice. Where the resources are individuals employed by the firm, other approaches will be necessary, including job restructuring and special incentive schemes as mentioned earlier. For those key knowledge workers on whom the firm depends, and who singly or collectively are likely to be its key knowledge holders, greater participation in ownership of the firm may be expected to result. Other external factors affecting the level of protection offered to products once they leave the firm will typically include the degree of industry concentration and the time required by competitors to 'play catch-up'. The ramifications of these issues will be discussed in more detail later (see Part III). Fig. 2.2 provides a summary of the factors most likely to constrain imitation or expropriation of a firm's key knowledge assets or products.

As Fig. 2.2 indicates, most externally provided protection mechanisms are via the law. This situation poses a variety of problems insofar as access to justice nowadays is frequently time-consuming and expensive, laws vary consid-

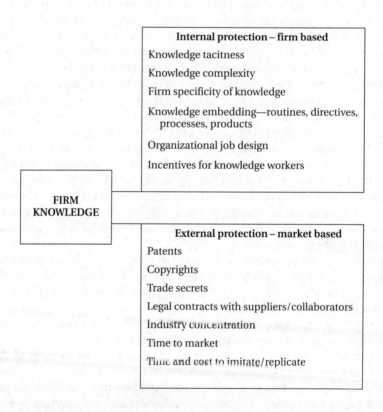

Internal protection – firm based

Knowledge tacitness

Knowledge complexity

Firm specificity of knowledge

Knowledge embedding—routines, directives, processes, products

Organizational job design

Incentives for knowledge workers

FIRM KNOWLEDGE

External protection – market based

Patents

Copyrights

Trade secrets

Legal contracts with suppliers/collaborators

Industry concentration

Time to market

Time and cost to imitate/replicate

FIG. 2.2.   Internal and external protection of firm knowledge

erably between countries, and intellectual property rights legislation appears to be in need of an overhaul, if not a complete redesign.

Such factors are likely to strengthen firms' bias towards using internal protection mechanisms wherever possible for valued intellectual property. Meantime firms with deep pockets and global coverage are at a distinct advantage when it comes to using (or avoiding the necessity to use) applicable local legislation. These are issues which clearly need attention at a supra-national, not merely a national level (see Chapter 11).

Non-tradability of Human Capital

As much of the preceding analysis has shown, the firm's most valuable knowledge will reside in the brains of its key knowledge workers. While ownership of the firm may confer legal rights on the firm's owners to bear the value of that knowledge, to use it, and to trade it, such rights may be difficult to enforce in practice, particularly after a key employee has left the firm.

Human capital being non-tradable, the principal opportunity for the firm to earn a return on its investment in people is therefore during the period of their employment. In order to achieve this return, however, firms typically have to make continuous incremental investments to protect and augment the knowledge represented by their key staff. Much of this is likely to involve training that is not necessarily firm specific, as for example in the case of most high-level management and technical training. Over the past few years, US corporations' investment in training staff has been growing at around 5 per cent annually and is now on a par with total US expenditure on secondary education. Most training in fact is likely to become less, rather than more, firm specific, as we will see later.

As training becomes an ever larger investment, and less firm specific, the risk for firm owners is that they will be investing, in effect, in a public good. This raises some interesting questions as to the most appropriate methods for balancing the reasonable expectations of the individual with those of the firm. What training should the firm expect to have to provide? What are the obligations of the employee to the firm in return for the training? Is there a case for the firm having a stake in the future economic rents received by the employee from the training received (after the employee leaves the firm) and how could such a system be enforced? These are questions to which we will return.

In general, it may be expected that investment in human capital, by way of salaries, non-wage benefits, training, monitoring, and infrastructure investments, will come under increasing scrutiny by stakeholders in the firm. This in turn is likely to influence the firm's criteria for selecting and employing staff and to cause it to review constantly the necessity to incur such investment costs. Externalization of resources through outsourcing and subcontracting represents a way of avoiding the problems posed by ownership of non-strategic or non-tradable assets. Such practices can therefore be expected to increase. Conversely, key knowledge workers may be expected to represent the firm's major assets. How to control such assets and how to retain and protect the firm against their loss will represent a different set of problems. Further internalization of such resources will occur as a result of these pressures, yet another factor favouring greater participation by core knowledge workers in the ownership of the firm.

Reconvergence of Ownership and Control

Sole proprietorships, small partnerships, and private companies involved in service activities and low-scale production generally have both their ownership and their decision making concentrated in a few key individuals. In such firms, therefore, ownership and control is typically united. In contrast, large public and private corporations, large partnerships, and other complex organizations nowadays tend to be characterized by decision rights diffused among many agents and separation of decision management from risk bearing. Thus in such firms, as noted earlier, ownership and control are generally separated.

The increasing intensity of knowledge in the firm as we move further into the post-industrial economy suggests that separation of ownership and control may not be as effective in the future as it has been in the past. Significant support for this view is provided by important economic theories regarding how decision rights are distributed in the firm, as discussed below. Increasing pressure to innovate and reductions in demand for financial capital, particularly among smaller, more highly knowledge-intensive firms, are additional factors favouring concentration of ownership and control.

Redistribution of decision rights. Jensen and Meckling examined the distribution of decision rights in the context of different types of knowledge transfer within organizations.[24] In this they built on the earlier work of F. A. Hayek, a Nobel Laureate who, writing about central planning in the post-war UK, described the infeasibility of first communicating all knowledge to a national planning board before integrating it and subsequently issuing orders back down the line.[25]

Jensen and Meckling developed this concept, demonstrating that in a firm, a system for assigning decision rights to those best able to use particular knowledge is required, together with a control system to motivate them to use the knowledge and decision rights properly. According to this theory, the costs attributable to inconsistencies where decision rights are distributed tend to increase with volume, as do the costs of transferring and using specific information where it is centralized. A trade-off between these factors therefore must determine the optimal arrangement. Perfection however cannot be attained—the firm will inevitably make suboptimal decisions, due to poor information and/or lack of congruence between the objectives of the central planners and those in the field.

Fifty years after Hayek's original observations, the concept of central planners making decisions based on information from operatives in the field has become less relevant. More capability exists at every level in the modern firm and the individual in the field is consequently better able to make informed decisions. Transferring information, both horizontally and vertically, in the firm is nowadays far easier and cheaper.

These factors all point to a reduction in the costs and risks of distributing decision rights within the firm. Such changes in turn imply higher levels of self-management among workers in the firm and reduced need for professional middle management—as evidenced by recent trends. The scene is thus set for a redistribution of decision rights within the firm and for the new decision agents, the firm's key knowledge workers, to take an increasing stake in its affairs.

Increasing innovation. Evidence suggests that public corporations that are diffusely owned, i.e. those in which ownership and control are separated, are less likely to be innovative than firms in which ownership and control is concentrated. The theoretical explanation for this is that professional managers, as decision agents, are more likely to choose low-risk strategies which tend to avoid innovative activities, since the penalties for failure are likely to be severe and the chances of success are uncertain (see also Chapter 8). In the knowledge economy, however, firms will have to innovate more frequently as new knowledge replaces old knowledge at an ever-increasing rate. Evidence of this trend can already be seen in the much shorter life cycles applying to 'pure knowledge goods' such as computer software, as compared to less knowledge-intensive goods such as cars or refrigerators. The need for continuous innovation involving constant cooperation and joint decision making by the key knowledge workers in the firm lends further support to the prediction that firm ownership and control will tend to converge among such workers. It also suggests that professional managers will need to find new roles—a subject we will return to later.

Reductions in capital intensity. The need for external funding often drives firms towards more diffuse structures, involving external bond- and stockholders. The less capital intensive the firm, the less the requirement for either debt or equity funding. As firms depend less on capital-intensive resources such as physical plant equipment and premises, one would expect to see more closely held organizations, with greater equity participation among the key decision makers, another reason for ownership and control to be rejoined.

Firm Ownership and Knowledge: Summary

Whilst ownership rights are normally imperfect, they have become central to the development of economic activity and maintenance of social order. Definition and attribution of property rights in the firm was a relatively straightforward matter in the era of the classic industrial entrepreneur. As the firm has grown, however, and acquired more factors of production, it has become more diffusely owned, leading to the current separation of ownership and control, typical of the modern corporation.

As the firm's focus shifts to coordinating specialist knowledge inputs and protecting and integrating knowledge, its ownership characteristics will change yet again. The major factors influencing this change as described above are: difficulties associated with defining and protecting intellectual assets, the non-tradability of human capital, and the reconvergence of ownership and control.

In an economy dependent on financial and physical resources, ownership of the firm has been concentrated in those individuals who owned such resources. As the economy shifts to dependence on knowledge, firm ownership will transfer to those individuals who own its knowledge resources. The implications of this change in the patterns of ownership are discussed in more detail later (see Chapter 9).

CONCLUSION

The knowledge intensification of economic activities was shown in Chapter 1 to be causing a progressive change in the factors of production: labour, materials, and financial capital. In this chapter, the implications of knowledge intensification have been discussed in relation to the institution which we have come to take for granted as the de facto organizing mechanism for production and the main source of work and jobs: the firm.

Barely two and a half centuries ago, the firm was a bit player in a pre-industrial economy organized largely in the market. The industrialization of the West made the firm pre-eminent as an organizer of mass physical resources. Since the 1970s, the commercialization of IT has been largely responsible for the growth of the post-industrial knowledge economy.

Just as the Industrial Revolution gave birth to the industrial model of the firm, so the Knowledge Revolution is replacing it with a radically new model (see Table 2.1). Dependent as most of us are on the firm as a source of livelihood, changes to its status and role must have far-reaching consequences. Understanding and planning for the ensuing changes thus becomes a vital necessity for all involved: investors, owners, workers, government, and society generally.

Naturally, the consequences flowing from these major shifts in the role and structure of the firm will tend to produce their own dynamics, generating a wide range of effects, some predictable, some less so. Succeeding chapters will develop these themes and explore the likely consequences for workers, owners, and other stakeholders in the firm.

Before moving on to analyse these issues, it is as well to underline the importance of questioning and, if necessary, jettisoning preconceptions and assumptions derived from older industrial economic models. Such preconceptions still unfortunately characterize much of the current debate on the symptoms of economic change we see all around us. Much attention, for

Table 2.1. *Towards the knowledge-based firm*

Trends in the transition to the knowledge economy	Major consequences for the firm
1. The principal functions of the firm will be knowledge coordination, protection, and integration.	• externalization of non-core functions • reduced investment in non-core assets (human, material, and financial) • reduced (financial) capital intensity • erosion of boundaries between internal functions, the firm and the market, industries and nations
2. Transactions involving high levels of specialized and tacit knowledge will be internalized.	• higher entry level requirements for employment • increased cross-functional teamwork • increased emphasis on learning • increased performance-based incentives • greater dependence on key knowledge workers • development of knowledge management
3. Transactions involving high levels of explicit knowledge will be externalized.	• reduction in average firm size • disintermediation of (some) physical channels • development of (electronic) markets • market contracts replace (most) employment contracts • careers replace jobs • increased inter-firm collaboration
4. Ownership and control of the firm will converge.	• increased ownership participation for key employees • reduced need for external equity investment • increased number of privately owned firms • organizational restructuring within the firm
5. The links between education, work, and learning will be redefined.	• increased opportunities for high-skilled workers • decreased opportunities for low-skilled workers • universal adoption of learning technologies • erosion of boundaries between academic and vocational training • convergence of academic and commercial interests

example, has been focused over recent years on the actions of firms in delayering, deskilling, and outsourcing functions previously conducted in-house. Firm owners have been both praised for their efficiency by shareholders and criticized for their habit of laying off workers by other sections of society. The truth is that the firm is as much sinned against as sinner. The processes referred to above as externalization and internalization are functions of a techno-economic paradigm which is outside the control of all of us, not just the firm. All firms can do, like any other organism affected by evolutionary forces, is to adapt to changing conditions. Whether the firm will eventually go the way of a dinosaur, or mutate into one or more different species, is a moot point. Meantime it has no option but to accept and work with, rather than against, forces outside its control. The same is therefore true for individuals, whether workers, owners, or investors.

NOTES

1. A. Smith (1776), *An Inquiry into the Nature and Causes of the Wealth of Nations*, London: George Routledge & Sons (1893 edn.).
2. A. Chandler Jr. (1977), *The Visible Hand*, Cambridge, Mass.: Harvard University Press.
3. R. Coase, (1937), 'The Nature of the Firm', *Economica*, 4: 386–405.
4. O. E. Williamson (1975), *Markets and Hierarchies: Analysis and Anti-trust Implications*, New York: Free Press.
5. R. Benjamin and R. Wigand (1995), 'Electronic Markets and Virtual Value Chains on the Information Superhighway', *Sloan Management Review* (winter): 62–72.
6. A. Alchian and H. Demsetz (1972), 'Production, Information Costs, and Economic Organisation', *American Economic Review*, 62: 777–95.
7. Ibid.
8. M. Jensen and W. Meckling (1976), 'Theory of the Firm, Managerial Behaviour, Agency Costs and Ownership Structure', *Journal of Financial Economics*, 3: 305–60.
9. E. Penrose, (1959), *The Theory of the Growth of the Firm*, New York: Sharpe.
10. R. Reed and R. J. deFillippi (1990), 'Causal Ambiguity, Barriers to Imitation and Sustained Competitive Advantage', *Academy of Management Review*, 15/1: 88–102.
11. D. J. Teece (1986), 'Profiting from Technological Innovation: Implications for Integration, Collaboration, Licensing and Public Policy', *Research Policy*, 15: 285–305.
12. J. Barney (1991), 'Firm Resources and Sustained Competitive Advantage', *Journal of Management*, 17/1: 99–119.
13. R. M. Grant and C. Baden-Fuller (1995), 'A Knowledge-Based Theory of Inter-firm Collaboration', *Academy of Management Best Papers Proceedings*: 17–21.
14. J. P. Liebeskind (1996), 'Knowledge, Strategy, and the Theory of the Firm', *Strategic Management Journal*, 17: 93–107.
15. R. R. Nelson and S. G. White (1982), *An Evolutionary Theory of Economic Change*, Cambridge, Mass.: Harvard University Press.
16. R. M. Grant (1996), 'Prospering in Dynamically Competitive Environments: Organizational Capability as Knowledge Integration', *Organization Science*, 7/4 (July–Aug.): 375–87.
17. T. W. Malone, J. Yates, and R. I. Benjamin (1994), 'Electronic Markets and Electronic Hierarchies', in T. J. Allen and M. S. Scott Morton (eds.), *Information Technology and the Corporation of the 1990's*, New York: Oxford University Press: 61–83.

18. J. R. Bleeke and W. Ernst (1992), 'The Way to Win in Cross-border Alliances', *Harvard Business Review*, 13/6: 475–81.
19. 'Two Scenarios for 21st Century Organisations: Shifting Networks of Small Firms or All-Encompassing "Virtual Countries"?', *http://ccs.mit.edu/21c.*
20. A. A. Alchian (1984), 'Specificity, Specialisation and Coalitions', *Journal of Institutional and Theoretical Economics*, 140/1: 34–49.
21. P. Milgrom and J. Roberts (1992), *Economics Organization and Management*, Englewood Cliffs, NJ: Prentice-Hall Inc.
22. E. Fama (1980), 'Agency Problems and the Theory of the Firm', *Journal of Political Economy*, 88: 288–307.
23. L. C. Thurow (1997), 'Needed: A New System of Intellectual Property Rights', *Harvard Business Review* (Sept.–Oct.): 95–103.
24. M. C. Jensen and W. H. Meckling (1995), 'Specific & General Knowledge & Organisational Structure', *Bank of America Journal of Applied Corporate Finance*, 8/2 (summer): 4–18.
25. F. A. Hayek (1945), 'The Use of Knowledge in Society', *American Economic Review*, 35 (Sept.): 35: 1–18.

Beyond Employment:
Towards a Model of Knowledge Supply

The increasing economic value of knowledge, as described in the last two chapters, suggests that relationships between firms as knowledge integrators and individual workers as knowledge suppliers are likely to shift in two polar opposite directions (see Table 2.1). Some individuals are likely to form stronger relationships with the firms for which they work, others are likely to move towards increasingly distant market-like contractual relationships. Clearly such fundamental changes cannot occur without profoundly altering both the nature of employment and its future role as a form of work arrangement. Equally, such changes imply that new work arrangements and new methods of sourcing and organizing knowledge supply will be needed.

Empirical evidence of changes to the character of employment is everywhere to be seen. In many OECD countries, on present trends, individuals in permanent full-time employment will soon represent less than half the total workforce.[1] Meantime, apart from the USA, full-time employment growth in the West is virtually at a standstill.[2] Even in the USA, however, the largest private employer in 1997 was not General Motors or IBM but Manpower the temporary employment agency.[3] Despite the underlying trend away from full-time employment, much political and media comment ignores or blurs the distinctions between different types of employment and between employment and other work arrangements. Thus we hear that employment prospects are improving, or that unemployment is static, that job opportunities are increasing or decreasing. Such terminology implies that employment and jobs are singular well-defined phenomena. We are constantly reminded that the unemployment rate is slowly declining—currently across the OECD nations to around 7 per cent. What is not revealed by this statistic is the massive shift which is occurring towards non-standard (i.e. not full-time, non-permanent, or non-employee status) work arrangements, and that the proportion of the workforce in such arrangements is growing rapidly. By the year 2000 at least 30 per cent of the American workforce are likely to be working under such non-standard arrangements. In some countries such as Australia, over half the workforce are already.[4]

The move away from regular, full-time employment is illustrated in the example of trends in non-regular employment in selected OECD countries between 1973 and 1993 (see Table 3.1 below).[5] The trend away from regular employment shown in Table 3.1 suggests that across the countries studied, approximately 39 per cent of all employment on average was non-regular by 1993. The data presented include a degree of overlap between categories (as noted) but omit wage-based homeworking and 'piecework' labour which would have otherwise increased the percentage of non-regular employment, so the estimate of 39 per cent is, if anything, conservative.

According to other independent research, Spain, the Netherlands, Australia, the UK, and France showed the strongest growth in non-regular employment over the two decades, whereas the USA only exhibited modest growth. Significantly, however, the incidence of low-paid jobs, defined as jobs with full-time earnings of less than two-thirds median earnings, ranged from less than 10 per cent of the workforce in Sweden and Finland to up to 25 per cent of the workforce in the USA.[6] This suggests that maintenance of relatively high levels of full-time employment in the USA has been at the expense of maintenance of full-time earning levels. Further evidence indicative of this trend in the USA can be found in the incidence of multiple job holding (i.e. workers with more than one job) which rose by 50 per cent between 1980 and 1989.[7]

Where the shift away from traditional employment practices has been explained, it has been generally attributed to a range of proximate causes, of which the most popular appear to be changing workforce demographics, globalization, technological change, or firms' need for greater flexibility, possibly reflecting some or all of the aforementioned factors.

Much of the current emphasis on 'flexible employment' owes its origin to research conducted in the UK in the 1980s by John Atkinson and subsequently reflected in Atkinson's Flexible Firm Model, popularly referred to as the 'Core Periphery' Model.[8] Writers such as Charles Handy have subsequently developed similar themes, pointing to the need for workers to come to terms with more flexible work arrangements and to develop 'portfolio lives' characterized by acquisition of multiple skills and shorter work engagements.[9] Some commentators, however, have taken issue with aspects of the Core Periphery Model, either from the perspective that it was normative (i.e. implied that such practices are acceptable) or that insufficient empirical evidence could be found to support the contention that firms were consciously pursuing such strategies.[10]

While offering many valuable insights, such approaches have not on the whole explained the relationship between the surface phenomena, i.e. changing work arrangements, and the deep underlying dynamics of change, occasioned by the growing economic value of knowledge. They have also (largely unintentionally) left the employment relationship enshrined in its traditional central role, its image if anything enhanced by the apparent modernity of the term 'flexible employment'. Similarly, much of the current literature on organizational learning and knowledge management reflects a traditional view of the firm's role and structure, including the centrality of the employment relationship. Fundamental changes to relationships between firms and workers, however, must redefine the context in which knowledge can be managed.

Table 3.1. *Non-regular forms of employment, selected countries, 1973–93*

	Self-employed (% of non-agricultural employees)		Part-time (% of total employment)		Temporary (% of total employment)		Total non-regular (% of total employment)[a]	
	1973	1993	1973	1993	1983	1993	1973	1993
USA	6.7	7.7	15.6	17.5	—	—	(22.3)	(25.2)
Canada	6.2	8.6	9.7	17.2	7.5	8.3	23.4	34.1
Australia	9.5	12.9	11.9	23.9	15.6[b]	22.4	(37.0)	(49.2)
Japan	14.0	10.3	13.9	21.1	10.3	10.8	38.2[c]	42.2
Austria	11.7	6.3[d]	6.4	10.1	—	—	—	—
Belgium	11.2	13.3	3.8	12.8	5.4	4.7	20.4[c]	30.8
Denmark	9.3	7.0	(22.7)[e]	23.3	12.5[f]	10.7	(42.5)	44.0
Finland	6.5	9.5	6.7	8.6	(11.3)[g]	13.5	(24.5)	31.6
France	11.4	8.8	5.9	13.7	3.3	10.2	20.6[c]	32.7
Germany	9.1	7.9	10.1	15.1	9.9	10.2	29.1[c]	33.2
Ireland	10.1	13.0[h]	(5.1)[e]	10.8	6.1	9.9	(21.3)	32.8
Italy	23.1	24.2	6.4	5.4	6.6	5.8	36.1[c]	35.4
The Netherlands	9.1[i]	8.7	(16.6)[e]	33.4	5.8	10.0	(31.6)	52.1
Norway	7.8	6.2	23.0	27.1	—	—	(30.8)	(33.3)
Portugal	12.7	18.2	(7.8)[e]	7.4	(13.1)[j]	8.6	(33.6)	(34.2)
Spain	16.3	18.7	—	6.6	15.6[b]	32.0	(31.9)	57.3
Sweden	4.8	8.7	(23.6)[e]	24.9	(12.0)[k]	11.9	(40.4)	45.5
UK	7.3	11.9	16.0	23.3	5.5	5.7	28.8[c]	40.9

[a] It is presumed that the part-time category refers to the percentage of regular wage and salaried employment. Many temporary workers would also be part-timers.

[b] For Spain, data for 1987; for Australia, 1984.

[c] This is based on the presumption for illustrative purposes of the 1983 figure for temporary as holding for 1973, so almost certainly giving an overestimate for 1973.

Those countries without estimates for temporary employment in one year (or in the case of Spain, part-time employment in 1973) are in parentheses. The data for Germany for 1993 refer to the whole of Germany. In most countries, the percentage in temporary employment refers to the share of paid employees only; in Belgium the share is lowered by being expressed as a share of all those working, including the self-employed.

[d] 1992.

[e] 1970.

[f] 1984.

[g] 1982.

[h] 1991.

[i] 1975.

[j] 1986.

[k] 1987.

Source: ILO and OECD; G. Standing (1997). 'Globalisation, Labour Flexibility and Insecurity: The Era of Market Regulation', *European Journal of Industrial Relations*, 3/1: 20. (Reproduced with the kind permission of the author.)

This chapter therefore presents a knowledge-centred perspective on the changing world of work and of relationships between firms and their knowledge suppliers. While acknowledging the many insights offered by the growing literature on new forms of work arrangement, it argues that demand for and supply of human skills and services need to be fundamentally reinterpreted in light of the growing importance of knowledge to the firm. The chapter takes as its starting point the implications of the changing factors of production and the organization of work discussed in earlier chapters and predicts the impact of these changes on employment and other forms of work arrangement. A typology of future knowledge supply is then described. The chapter concludes with an assessment of how demand and supply arrangements are likely to evolve and some critical implications for management, workers, and relevant government agencies.

THE CHANGING NATURE OF EMPLOYMENT

'What was it like, being employed?' This question is likely to be posed by the grandchildren of those currently entering the labour market. Being employed directly by a firm still seems as natural as birth and marriage, or perhaps as inevitable as death and taxes—dependent on one's age and point of view.

Employment is quite simply part of our way of life, so much so that we do not question its relevance. It was not always so however; 2,000 years ago most of us would have been slaves; in the Middle Ages we would have been serfs or bondsmen. Only in the last couple of centuries has mass production, and with it mass employment, become the norm. In the early stages of industrialization the employment relationship was rudimentary—the labourer simply exchanged what was virtually his sole capital, his labour, for money. As Marx characteristically put it, 'He who was before the money-owner, now strides in front as capitalist: the possessor of labour-power follows as his labourer. The one with an air of importance, smirking, intent on business; the other, timid and holding back, like one who is bringing his own hide to market and has nothing to expect but—a hiding.'[11]

Following the bitter struggles of the late nineteenth and early twentieth centuries, the representatives of organized (i.e. employed) labour gradually extended and refined the relationship between employer and employee into its current form. Not all of this progress can of course be attributed to the union movement; however, without their involvement, employment conditions today would doubtless be less favourable to the employee and rules and regulations governing employment relationships would be far less extensive.

Employment in the form we know it, i.e. regular, full-time, long-term, and direct, was largely a product of industrialization. We are now moving out of that phase into a post-industrial economy in which, as we have seen, fundamental changes are beginning to occur to the nature of economic activities, thus to the factors of production and to their organization. Our concern at this point is to understand how the parallel processes described earlier, of internalization and externalization, will impinge on the nature and practice of employment. In order to understand the nature of employment and how it is evolving, it is useful to consider the concept from several different perspectives: first as a form of legal contract, second as an element of corporate strategy, with particular reference to the traditional concept of the internal labour market, and finally as part of an emerging spectrum of work arrangements that characterize the knowledge economy.

A Comparative View of the Employment Contract

Jensen and Meckling (see Chapter 2) aptly described the firm as a nexus of contracts.[12] Such contracts commonly include sales contracts, contingent claims contracts, spot contracts, and employment contracts. It is useful to compare these different contractual forms, so as to appreciate how the employment contract differs from the other three.[13]

Sales Contracts

Sales contracts are typically complete and non-flexible, i.e. the deliverables are explicitly stated, as are the conditions of supply, costs, and all other relevant terms. Once finalized, the terms are usually left unchanged.

Such contracts are ideal for situations in which the supply of labour is not part of the contract, but merely a means to fulfilling it. The supply of a research report, for example, covering specific prior agreed topics on a particular date, may involve the use of labour, but the labour is embodied in the production of the report, not supplied separately. Similarly the supply of an office cleaning service may involve the use of labour, but the measure of service effectiveness is not who cleans the offices, but how well they are cleaned.

Key characteristics of sales contracts are that they are intended to be unambiguous and complete. A high level of certainty can be attached to the results of such contracts, but they are typically inflexible, restricted to specific transactions and of limited duration.

Contingent Contracts

Contingent contracts are those where the terms of the agreement may vary, dependent on some event or events which may occur in the future. Where permanent supply of labour is involved, this could involve highly complex contracts in which neither party to the contract is capable of envisaging all the possible future events. Such contracts are therefore generally impracticable for regular long-term employment arrangements. They are commonly used however in other types of work arrangement, such as those involving sales agents who are paid purely on results.

Spot Contracts

Spot contracts are characterized by the immediacy of the transaction, i.e. they are so called because purchase and supply arrangements are conducted 'on the spot'. Spot contracts are often used for the supply of labour in situations where the firm does not wish to commit to hiring labour in advance. Work which is infrequent, time critical, or simply difficult to anticipate has traditionally been handled in this way, such as agricultural crop picking, or, in days gone by, work on the waterfront.

The main benefits of spot labour contracting include elimination of fixed costs and overheads associated with other methods, plus access to a potentially broader range of resources. The main disadvantages are the costs of managing the transactions, the risk of failing to identify appropriate human resources, and loss of quality/productivity due to discontinuities in labour supply.

The Employment Contract

In simple terms, employment can be defined as the provision by an individual of his or her personal labour, to perform some predetermined work, for an agreed remuneration. The parties to the exchange are the supplier of labour (the employee) and the buyer of labour power (the employer).

The legal form commonly used to define this exchange, the employment contract, avoids the rigidity of the sales contract, the complexity of contingent contracting, and the short-term focus of spot contracting, by providing a more flexible framework. This framework provides for certain aspects of the worker's behaviour to be stipulated in the contract terms, certain other aspects to be placed within the authority of the employer, and still other aspects left to the workers' choice.[14] The degree of control which can be exercised by the employer and degree of choice by the worker can vary according to the individual contract, subject always to the governing laws of the country in which the employment contract originates.

Employment contracts are deliberately designed to be incomplete or imperfect, not only for simplicity, but also to permit ex post bargaining to occur between the parties. Such an arrangement can provide the benefit of flexibility, for example, the exact amount of a future rise in salary or precisely how a job should be performed can be left open to an extent for future negotiation.

Transactional and Relational Contracts

Contracts can also be broadly divided into either transactional or relational.[15] Transactional contracts are typically rigid, narrowly focused, explicit, and of limited duration. Sales contracts and spot market contracts tend to be transactional. Relational contracts by contrast are typically flexible, open ended, dynamic, broad in scope, and contain a mixture of explicit and implicit promises. Employment contracts tend to be of this latter type. Another relevant method of classification relates to performance measurement. Transactional contracts tend to be output or results based, whereas relational contracts tend to be input or effort based.

Categorizing contracts this way can be useful, but has its limitations. Frequently repeated spot contracts, and some contracts between firms and independent contractors, may contain relational elements. Likewise employment contracts involving casual, temporary, and, to a lesser extent, permanent employees often contain transactional elements. Sales staff for example are commonly employed under a relational contract having a strong transactional element, which typically relates a significant proportion of remuneration to the achievement of sales targets.

In practice, employment contracts are becoming less relational and more transactional. Evidence of this trend can be seen in the increasing use of output-based performance monitoring. Results, rather than time spent on the job, are becoming the principal measure of performance. Whether an employee attends the office or works from home is decreasingly relevant. The results-based component of most work is increasing as a percentage of total remuneration, rendering other measurements less critical.

These factors are gradually altering the nature of employment, from fundamentally relational to a hybrid of relational and transactional forms.[16] From low-skilled workers through to sales staff and even middle management, the move to transactional measurement is likely to be focused on personal results. For the core knowledge workers in the firm, the focus will increasingly be on team or firm performance.

The trend from relational to transactional contracting is thus likely to widen the gap between those close to the core of the firm and other employees. Those workers in the core group, or closely associated with it, will be incentivized to act as a team, thus assisting their identification with collective corporate goals. The balance of employees (the majority) will be incentivized to maximize personal productivity for personal gain—thus tending to dissociate them from corporate goals and influence their progression towards arm's-length, market-based contractual relationships.

Many leading firms in the USA and other countries, including many formerly career-oriented employers such as IBM, AT&T, and Hewlett-Packard, are reportedly hiring increasing numbers of managerial and professional staff from outside and making employment contracts contingent on the fit between people's competencies and business needs. Jack Welch, CEO of General Electric, is reported as saying that GE offers its people a 'one-day contract'.[17]

Implicit Contracts

Employment arrangements generally contain promises and expectations on both sides that are not explicitly stated. These nevertheless may constitute a legally binding agreement and hence are often referred to as forming an implicit contract.

In transactional contracts, the parties generally ensure that non-explicit promises are minimized; for example, if you sell your house or your car, neither you nor the purchaser would accept a contract that is not fully explicit. Relational contracts, however, by their very nature, tend to involve implicit promises. Calculation of bonuses, expectations of training and promotion, acceptability of styles of conduct, quality, and reliability standards, ethical standards, and more may be part of the implicit contract in an employment relationship. This 'fuzziness' may occasionally lead to the need for third party arbitration. In the case of third party interpretation of implicit contracts, they are usually guided by individual precedent and prevailing social norms of reasonableness.

The great majority of implicit contracts involving employers and employees are of course never subject to third party interpretation, because it is in the interests of both parties to reach a mutual accommodation. To this extent, implicit contracts have traditionally been self-enforcing. As firms have downsized, delayered, and casualized staff during the 1990s, however, implicit contracts have been put under pressure. The public nature of these events has contributed to the mood of job insecurity among remaining employees, attested to by many attitudinal surveys. During the late 1980s and early 1990s, IBM, AT&T, Kodak, Xerox, and other firms who formerly provided guaranteed employment to all their regular employees gradually abandoned their no-layoff policies. IBM was one of the last to do this, in 1993. When an IBM employee asked a spokesperson for IBM's new chairman at the time what was to replace the old social contract at IBM he was advised, 'We don't know yet.'[18]

On current trends, employers and employees will be increasingly wary of entering into agreements which contain implicit guarantees or promises. This lack of mutual trust will continue to weaken the value of the employment contract as a form of work arrangement and move the employment relationship away from its relational context towards a more explicit transactional model. The implications of the changes in the employer–employee relationship will vary, depending upon whether the employee is destined to remain in the firm or move outside it. For those destined to stay in the firm, their motivation will be increasingly driven by alignment of rewards with achievement of firm goals. This will push the employment relationship in the direction of greater mutual interest between employer and employee. Conversely, for those not in the core group, implicit guarantees by the firm will steadily reduce. Key among these will be reduced guarantees of long-term employment prospects, training, and internal promotion. As implicit promises are reduced, work arrangements will be expected to move further towards the transactional model and to arm's-length contracting, rather than employment.

It is important to note that these trends away from direct employment are a natural consequence of the knowledge intensification of the factors of production, and thus the nature and organization of the firm. Firms are not in control of these dynamics and therefore, while they have a degree of choice in how they react, they cannot 'turn back the clock'. Employees need to recognize these economic realities and act accordingly. Actions by workers or unions to try to slow the tide of economic change will merely delay the inevitable and make the problems of adjustment for workers even more difficult. A more positive approach is needed, involving cooperation between firms and workers, rather than confrontation.

It is interesting to note that over the past two decades, as firms have adopted more explicit, transactional work arrangements internally, they have been simultaneously building stronger links with individuals and firms in the market. Thus, downsizing and internal disaggregation into ever-smaller, autonomous business units has been accompanied by a rash of alliances, joint ventures, and preferred supplier arrangements, as firms have sought to strengthen relationships with external suppliers.

These parallel shifts in the firm's internal and external relationships are tending to reduce the role of asset specialization as a determinant of firm or market governance.[19] For example, in a climate of 'rightsizing' and increasing market-based alliances, firms are as likely to look favourably on buying specialist knowledge externally as on developing it in-house.

In summary, firms are becoming more 'market-like' internally, while at the same time seeking to extend their hierarchial influence beyond their borders. These trends underline the importance of viewing future knowledge supply as involving a spectrum of relationships from 'deep inside' to 'far outside' the firm.

Internal Labour Markets

Long-term employment has become a defining characteristic of advanced economies. In the early 1980s, the average US worker was in a job that would last about eight years, with a quarter of the total workforce in jobs that were anticipated to last over twenty years. In the UK, jobs lasting over twenty years were even more common than in the USA. In Japan the practice of lifetime employment, 'nenko', has been a distinguishing characteristic of national employment practices.[20]

The incidence of long-term employment can be largely attributed to the steadily increasing size and complexity of the firm throughout this century which, as we saw in Chapter 2, appears to have peaked around the late 1970s and has subsequently started to decline. Prior to the late 1970s, as workforce levels increased, so did the management hierarchy. The stability and continuity of management and key staff thus became increasingly important to the firm as it grew in size.

In order to maintain stability and continuity, firms developed internal labour markets from which they hired, trained, and promoted key staff. Access to certain jobs within the firm was restricted or closed to outsiders. The implicit contracts between the firm and its key staff were thereby strengthened. Gradually improving job prospects and a career within the firm thus became the norm.

Doeringer and Piore developed an economic theory of internal labour markets. According to this theory, firms used an internal labour market for 'primary sector' jobs, which included most skilled blue-collar, professional, technical, and white-collar managerial jobs.[21] Jobs in the 'secondary sector', i.e. low-skilled blue- and non-managerial white-collar jobs, were generally handled through the external labour market.

Features of internal labour markets which distinguish them from external labour market practices include long-term employment, internal promotion, and limited 'ports of entry', i.e. restrictions on the types of job opportunity that would be available to candidates from outside the firm. Another important distinguishing characteristic has traditionally been pay by the job, rather than by results or according to ability. A range of advantages has been identified in support of these practices. First, pay by the job, rather than ability or productivity, has been found to discourage wage bargaining, encourage internal competition, and improve firm control. Limited ports of entry and internal promotion have provided the employee with the advantage of closed rather than open competition and the employer with a longer period to evaluate the potential merits of competing employees—the latter practice possibly compensating for potential inequalities arising from pay by the job.

Internal labour markets have been and continue to be used by many types of organization, not just commercial firms. Religious institutions tend to promote from within—one never sees a job advertisement for a bishop, far less a cardinal or a pope! Public enterprises have become noted for their practice of favouring internal rather than external appointees. Academic institutions have similarly tended to appoint from within.

The practice of regular full-time and long-term employment, which has been facilitated by these various internal labour market practices, has been seen as desirable for a variety of reasons. The firm has the opportunity to invest in training and provision of on the job experience to improve its firm-specific human capital and thus obtain superior productivity. Stability and continuity of key staff offers firms greater flexibility in organizational planning and ability to react to sudden changes in the external competitive environment. Specialist and tacit knowledge is more likely to be retained in the firm if key staff remain within it.

The advantages of firms' internal labour markets can already be seen to be diminishing for lower-skilled workers. In the USA, for example, men without a high school diploma saw their job tenure drop by nearly a third in the period 1983–91 while the tenure of those with four or more years of college increased by 9 per cent.[22] Collective wage bargaining and payment by the job are giving way to individual work contracts and payment by results. Loyalty is only at a premium among key knowledge workers and a range of incentive options are available to firms to motivate such workers without resorting to protecting them from market competition. Again these trends need to be recognized as a natural and inevitable consequence of the growing importance of knowledge, including human skill levels, rather than a deliberate strategy by firms to achieve greater levels of flexibility.

From Control to Coordination

The notion of the owner/employer as an authority figure and the worker/employee as acting in a subordinate capacity is now firmly embedded in our collective subconscious. We speak of an employee working *for* rather than *with* an employer. Opportunistic behaviour is normally associated with employees, rather than employers, as is the notion of shirking. Social protocols normally require deference to be shown by employee to employer, not the other way about. Formal hierarchies imply that control is exercised within organizations from the top down, not the bottom up. The concept of employment as an authority relationship would therefore seem, on the face of it, to be unchallengeable.

The role of authority in the employment relationship has however declined as the nature of economic activities has started to change. In the days of Marx the employment relationship was obviously authoritarian. Firms were highly vertically organized with power centralized at the apex of the organization. In the 1990s firms are flatter, thinner structures, with decision rights increasingly assigned out to key workers. In the heyday of the mass production factory, workers were defined by the task they did—jobs were more important than people. In the 1990s people define jobs by how they do them. The notion of the employee as 'team member' and the employer as 'team co-ordinator' would have seemed bizarre to the average factory owner or labourer in Queen Victoria's day. Today in the West, the notion of the employer as an authority figure wielding control over a servile and compliant workforce would be considered equally out of touch with the times. As hierarchies have collapsed, so have many of the distinctions between owners as employers and core knowledge workers as employees. Teams are replacing hierarchies and the boss is fast becoming the coach, particularly for those workers close to the core of the firm.

As the nature of the firm's activities continues to evolve towards the model of a knowledge-based enterprise, so authoritarian command and control structures will continue to lose relevance. Flatter, thinner hierarchies, composed of workers with increasingly similar skill levels, will replace the old vertically organized bureaucracies. Interdependency between core knowledge workers will increase as the success of the firm becomes ever more dependent on how well they integrate their knowledge to produce innovative products and services. In such an environment, coordination will progressively replace subordination as the jobs performed by subordinates are either automated or externalized.

FROM EMPLOYMENT TO KNOWLEDGE SUPPLY

The firm is an institution that has evolved to make most efficient and effective use of the factors of production—traditionally labour, money, and materials. These factors of production are being transformed by the increasing importance of knowledge in economic activity. As the factors of production change, so too must the nature of the firm.

The modern firm's requirement for unskilled labour is rapidly decreasing, while its demand for human skills and other forms of knowledge is rapidly increasing. *Knowledge supply* rather than *labour supply* is fast becoming the critical issue. Employment and other forms of work arrangement are simply artefacts that the firm may use in future to access knowledge.

Unfortunately we are still hampered by outdated models of the economy, which place undue emphasis on the role of labour and of employment.[23] Current typologies of work arrangement used by statisticians and reflected in economic and social policies are almost universally 'employment centric'. Such arrangements are described in terms of variations on a theme of regular, full-time, salaried employment of individuals by firms. Commonly accepted definitions of these variations for statistical purposes include part-time employment, temporary employment, casual employment, contingent employment, atypical employment, and alternative work arrangements. These types of employment will be discussed in more detail in later chapters. Suffice to say for now that they all reflect the traditional assumption that direct full-time employment is the ideal benchmark against which other forms of work arrangement are to be compared. By implication, all other arrangements which fall short of full-time employment tend to be considered abnormal or less than ideal.

These assumptions regarding the centrality of labour and employment are often reflected in the contextual nature of political or social debates in which non-full-time employment and associated typologies are mentioned. Such discussions tend to focus on how to return to full-time employment, implicitly rejecting other arrangements as less desirable. The firm in such discussions tends to be referred to as if it were still a mass production, labour- and capital-intensive institution. In contrast, as we have seen, the character of the firm is radically changing and with it the dynamics of firm–market relationships, including firm attitudes to hire of people and other services. Firms are already using a variety of supply arrangements for functions and processes formerly conducted in-house. Outsourcing and employee leasing schemes, for example, are being used to substitute for whole departments or divisions of many firms. Franchising is being used as a means to grow and expand businesses with minimal additional investment in human capital. Such arrangements represent powerful alternatives to any form of direct labour supply. Rather than being planned, most of these supply arrangements have evolved as an adaptive response to changing market conditions. In this sense, there are no good or bad arrangements, and to idealize any particular arrangement is to risk second-guessing the operation of the market.

It is evident that we need a more inclusive and accurate model of how the firm will access and interact with the knowledge resources it needs in future. The model proposed here—the *Knowledge Supply Model*™—seeks to do this by incorporating employment-centred relationships, less traditional work arrangements, and other forms of knowledge supply, including various services (see Fig. 3.1).

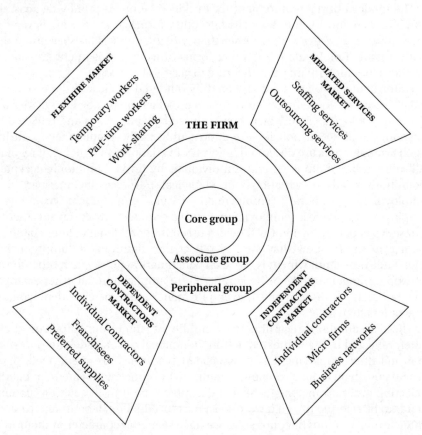

FIG. 3.1. Knowledge Supply Model™: seven sources of knowledge supply

Knowledge Supplier Classifications

As shown in Fig. 3.1, seven primary classifications are used in the model, each representing a major source of knowledge supply to the firm.

Three of the primary classifications of knowledge supplier are internal to the firm and four are external to the firm. The following notes briefly describe each primary classification in terms of the characteristics of the knowledge supplied, and the contractual relationship between the firm and the knowledge supplier.

Internalized Suppliers

The *Core Group*, comprising the firm's most senior knowledge workers, are responsible for its high-level knowledge integration functions and for planning, coordinating and controlling the firm's activities. Such functions demand high levels of both explicit and tacit knowledge and firm-specific knowledge. The core group's knowledge is also of high value in terms of its impact on the firm's operations.

The *Associate Group* provides the knowledge required for controlling the main operational functions of the firm, such as Finance, Marketing, Production, and R&D. Such functions require high levels of tacit and explicit knowledge but this knowledge is typically more narrowly based than in the core group. Similarly this group's level of firm-specific knowledge tends to be restricted to their areas of specialization.

The main focus of the *Peripheral Group* is on managing the interface to external suppliers and customers, and supporting internal functions where the level of firm-specific knowledge involved prevents them being externalized. Such functions will require high levels of firm-specific knowledge in terms of detailed knowledge of the firm's day-to-day operations, but generally low levels of tacit or specialized knowledge. The value to the firm of the knowledge provided by this group largely depends upon their levels of idiosyncratic/firm-specific knowledge gained through experience on the job.

Externalized Suppliers

Flexihire workers will supplement workers employed in the peripheral group within the firm. These workers typically support administration, maintenance, security, and similar functions requiring moderate to high levels of firm-specific knowledge, but low levels of tacit or explicit knowledge. The value of their knowledge to the firm is generally low.

Flexihire as a classification covers part-time, casual, and temporary workers involved in direct employment relationships with firms. Workers involved in work-sharing schemes are also defined as flexihire workers, since they are working on a part-time basis. Flexihire, as defined here, *excludes* hire of self-employed individuals, or hire of staff via mediated services providers.

Flexihire workers are usually dependent on one, or at most a few, firms for income. Firms on the other hand usually have a large pool of such workers to choose from. Although contractual arrangements between firms and flexihire workers are usually based on employment contracts, they are nevertheless defined as being 'external'. This is because the knowledge which flexihire workers supply is only required by firms on an occasional basis, and the relationship between firm and supplier is more likely to weaken than to strengthen over time.

Mediated Services will also supplement workers in the peripheral group and handle outsourced administration, maintenance, security, and similar infrastructure support functions. Firms currently use mediated services for functions similar to those handled by flexihire workers, but where the level of firm-specific knowledge required is not as high. In such cases, the firm generally does not need access to the same individual worker on each hiring occasion.

A distinguishing characteristic of mediated services is that the services of workers are delivered to the firm with the assistance of, or directly by, an independent intermediary agency. The two major subclassifications are staffing services and outsourcing services.

- *Staffing Services*, also known as Personnel Supply Services, Personnel Agencies, or Recruitment Services, comprise all those services included in the supply of workers to firms by independent intermediary organizations.
- *Outsourcing Services*, on the other hand, comprise the direct replacement of functions that would otherwise be carried out within the firm, thus often referred to as being 'contracted out'. Outsourcing must be considered in concert with other human resource options because it is merely another method of gaining access to knowledge.

Dependent Contractors handle functions requiring medium to high levels of firm-specific knowledge. The value of the knowledge supplied in terms of its impact on the firm's operations is high. The levels of explicit and tacit knowledge possessed by this group also tend to be higher than those of flexihire workers. The functions involved are typically those which require knowledge which the firm does not wish to internalize because it does not fit with its core knowledge base, or because of other constraining factors such as lack of financial resources or the need to grow quickly.

Dependent contractors may include self-employed individuals (both incorporated and non-incorporated), micro firms (employing one or a few workers), and small businesses. They are dependent on a relationship with one or a few firms for the majority of their income. Examples of members of this group include individual contractors, franchisees, and preferred suppliers.

Independent Contractors provide support for functions requiring high levels of tacit and/or explicit knowledge, but low levels of firm-specific knowledge. Such support typically involves technical, professional, and speciality services. The value of the knowledge provided by this group, in terms of its potential impact on firms' operations, is high. The frequency of demand by the firm for such knowledge is typically lower than for that supplied by dependent contractors.

Members of this group include self-employed individuals (both incorporated and non-incorporated), micro firms, and small businesses. They are usually not dependent on any particular firm for their major source of income. Members of this group frequently form independent business networks comprising a mixture of individuals and firms.

Firm-Supplier Selection and Matching Criteria

From the firm's perspective, many factors may be involved in the decision processes involving selection of a particular knowledge supplier. Equally, from the supply side, a broad range of factors will determine whether individuals or firms fit better in one classification or another. Some suppliers may fit into more than one classification and many will undoubtedly move from one to another over time. The real world is never as neat and predictable as theoretical models of it tend to imply!

It is also obvious that knowledge-related factors are unlikely to be sole determinants of decisions regarding sourcing and supply. For the firm, sourcing decisions are likely to be influenced by organizational size and structure, geographic location, type of business activity, volatility of market demand, and a host of other factors. Equally for the supplier, personal or organizational motivation will play a significant role, in addition to other factors. In the final analysis, such factors interacting with the knowledge characteristics of the transactions involved will determine suppliers' choice of markets and firms' choice of suppliers.

While acknowledging the complexity of decision making in the real world, the Knowledge Supply Model™ suggests that three key factors are likely to be critical in shaping firms' choice of particular suppliers and suppliers' fit with particular classifications.

  (i) *Level of Knowledge of Supplier*: the relative depth or breadth of knowledge characteristic of each supplier group, e.g. independent self-employed individuals will tend to exhibit higher levels of knowledge than flexihire workers.
  (ii) *Firm Specificity of Knowledge*: the degree to which the knowledge required is specific to functions or activities which are restricted to one or a few firms, e.g. knowledge of an office system designed by a firm for its own use that does not make use of a standard software package.
  (iii) *Value of Knowledge to the Firm*: the importance of the particular knowledge supplied to the business activities of the firm, e.g. its 'mission criticality'.

Demand Side Preferences

The main combination of factors influencing demand side preferences for particular supplier classifications will be their levels of firm-specific knowledge, coupled with the value of their knowledge to the firm. The knowledge

Firm specificity of knowledge

		HIGH	LOW
	HIGH	Dependent contractors	Independent contractors
Value of knowledge to the firm			
	LOW	Flexihire workers	Mediated services

FIG. 3.2. Firm specificity of knowledge and value of knowledge to the firm

characteristics of internal suppliers were described earlier; those of external suppliers are illustrated in Fig. 3.2.

As shown in Fig. 3.2, functions supported by suppliers in the top left quadrant of the matrix are typically those such as franchise arrangements, which tend to require highly firm-specific knowledge, reasonably high levels of knowledge/human skill, and are critical to the operations of the firm. Functions supported by suppliers in the top right quadrant similarly are also critical to the firm's performance, but the knowledge required tends to be non-firm specific, e.g. professional, technical, or other specialist skills. (Naturally these examples assume the skills involved are not part of the firm's core knowledge domain.)

Functions handled by suppliers in the bottom left quadrant tend to involve high levels of firm-specific knowledge, such as, for example, knowledge of a firm's suppliers, but the value of knowledge involved will tend to be low. Functions traditionally handled by suppliers in the bottom right quadrant, the traditional market for 'temping' and outsourcing services, are those which neither require firm-specific knowledge nor are particularly critical to the firm's operations. (This picture is changing, however, as we will see later.)

Supply Side Preferences

The combination of factors likely to determine the external supplier groups to which individual workers belong is the firm specificity of their knowledge, coupled with their personal knowledge levels, as shown in Fig. 3.3. This shows that dependent contractors in the top left quadrant tend to exhibit high average skill levels as compared to flexihire workers, as well as being highly dependent on firm-specific knowledge.

Firm specificity of knowledge

	HIGH	LOW
HIGH	Dependent contractors	Independent contractors
LOW	Flexihire workers	Mediated services

Supplier knowledge level

FIG. 3.3. Firm specificity of knowledge and supplier knowledge level

Suppliers in the top right quadrant tend to have high general or specialist skills but will be less dependent on firm-specific knowledge. Suppliers in the bottom two quadrants tend to have lower average levels of knowledge than those in the top half and the flexihire group have more firm-specific knowledge, as noted earlier.

Predicting the Direction of Change

As well as providing a classificatory framework, the Knowledge Supply Model™ can be used to explore and predict the direction of change, involving internalization and externalization of different types of knowledge and knowledge workers.

Internalized Supply

The predicted direction of internalization is one of continuous distillation or refinement, characterized by a gradual erosion of the peripheral group, constant renewal of the associate group, and gradual expansion of the core group. The proportion of workers employed in each category will naturally vary between industries and between individual firms. The more knowledge intensive the individual firm's activities, the higher will be the proportion of workers in the associate and core groups.

Highly knowledge-intensive firms, such as many of those in the IT industry, in other 'cutting edge' technologies, and in the professions generally, all exhibit a relatively high proportion of workers in the associate and core groups.

Externalization

Flexihire arrangements will continue to grow strongly in the short term, as firms continue to shed full-time employees from the peripheral group. As the size of the flexihire workforce increases, however, and firms' peripheral functions are increasingly standardized, staffing and outsourcing services are predicted to make inroads into the flexihire market and to a lesser extent to attract independent contractors who require assistance in marketing their own services. Mediated service suppliers will offer firms the advantages of economies of scale, and both firms and workers the benefit of their ability to match supply and demand.

A degree of overlap between staffing and outsourcing services also appears inevitable, as major mediated service providers compete for market share. Signs of competitive overlap are already becoming apparent, as staffing services providers take on increasingly large and complex projects and outsourcing providers take on ever larger numbers of firms' former employees. These trends underscore the importance of viewing *knowledge* as the key resource to be supplied and its method of supply (labour or services) as secondary.

Contracting is expected to grow at the expense of all forms of direct employment, with dependent contracting growing faster than independent contracting in the short term. The main reasons for the latter prediction are that fewer individuals are likely to have the capability or inclination to operate fully independently and also that firms are more likely to foster relationships in which they retain a degree of control. In the longer term, however, growth of independent contracting is predicted to catch up, as dependent contractors begin to see the benefits of greater autonomy.

SUMMARY

The firm is an institution that has survived because of its ability to make best use of the available factors of production. As those factors change, so must the nature of the firm. Knowledge, rather than labour, materials, or money, is becoming the most important resource in the firm. The role of labour in particular has been transformed; from a source of physical energy, to a source of know-how and information. Labour however is not the only source of knowledge. Standardizing and embedding explicit, reusable knowledge in routines and systems can replace the need for human provision of the same knowledge. From the firm's perspective, this means that hiring labour via employment contracts or other work arrangements is merely one of its options for gaining access to knowledge (see Fig. 3.4).

Traditional labour market models and strategies aimed at more flexible forms of employment thus simply miss the point. The employment contract, an artefact of an older industrial era, is ill designed to suit the rapidly changing

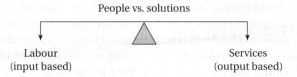

FIG. 3.4. **Knowledge supply options**

patterns of knowledge demand in the modern economy. Firms do not necessarily need to employ labour directly to gain access to the knowledge they
require. Outsourcing services, franchising, contracting, and staffing services
are just a few of the options available to the firm in addition to employment.
The fundamental difference between the old world and the new is that now
firms need knowledge not labour. Knowledge supply has replaced labour supply.

In practice, the structure of work arrangements is already starting to change
in response to these economic realities. The traditional relational employment
model is becoming a hybrid of relational and transactional arrangements with
the emphasis moving from labour inputs to outputs or results. For key knowledge workers these trends imply a closer association with the firm and its
goals, with personal rewards being geared ever more closely to collective performance—witness the proliferation of stock options as a form of incentive for
CEOs. For other workers, personal productivity is likely to become the basis of
reward, which in turn will push such workers into increasingly market-like,
commercial relationships with firms. Once started, this process will tend to
become self-reinforcing—the majority of workers drifting ever further away
from the firm's gravitational field, the minority being pulled ever closer to the
firm's centre of gravity. The predicted effects of these trends may be summarized as follows:

- Firms will regard labour supply as secondary to knowledge supply and
  will adjust their resourcing strategies accordingly.
- Non-employment-based work arrangements, based on market contracting, will grow at the expense of employment-based contracts.
- Employment-based relationships in general will tend to become more
  explicit and transactional, involving fewer implicit promises and greater
  emphasis on outputs or results, rather than inputs.
- In the longer term, only key knowledge workers will remain in direct full-
  time employment and they will move progressively towards mutual ownership of the firm.
- An intermediary group of knowledge workers, the associate group, will
  divide the core knowledge workers from those on the periphery of the
  firm. This intermediate group will comprise workers with high levels of
  participation in firm decision making and firm performance-related
  rewards. Such workers will be selected and incentivized to move either *up*
  or *out* of the firm.

- Full-time employment on the periphery of the firm will diminish over time, as more workers leave the firm than progress to the associate group. The functions involved will largely be automated or externalized.
- Direct part-time, temporary, and casual employment of individuals by firms (flexihire) will continue to increase in the short run, at the expense of full-time employment. Flexihire will be progressively replaced, however, by externally mediated staffing and outsourcing services, as firms find direct employment of low-skilled and non-core workers to be impractical and inefficient.
- Staffing services involving personnel supply, such as temporary help and employee leasing, will grow strongly and tend to converge with outsourcing services as supply contracts between service providers and firms become increasingly output/results based.
- Self-employment will increase faster than direct employment by firms, leading to growth in single owner operators and micro firms, which will increasingly form business networks. Dependent forms of contracting will tend to increase faster than independent forms in the short term. In the long term, however, the benefits of autonomy will attract more workers to independent modes of operation.

IMPLICATIONS

How does a better understanding of the role of knowledge in the firm and, in particular, the dynamics affecting its supply help firms' management, workers, and other stakeholders? A few key points are worth highlighting at this stage. Later chapters will expand on these and a range of associated issues.

Management

Rather than pursue individual departmental strategies based on often conflicting views of what work and resources should be internalized or externalized, firms' management now have the opportunity to develop a broad, unified perspective of knowledge demand and also the range of options available in terms of knowledge supply. Rather than insource, or outsource whole functions, more sensitivity can be applied to sourcing strategies, based on the knowledge characteristics of the work involved, not merely the functions performed. Similarly, more intelligence can be applied to systems of remuneration, and incentives and rewards for performance, based on calculations as to which activities and which human skills are likely to be required in future.

Firm organizational structures based on traditional functional lines, such as Finance, Production, Information Systems, or Human Resource Management, can be re-evaluated from a knowledge perspective, noting the intersections and overlaps between different knowledge domains. Structures and agencies needed to facilitate knowledge sharing and teamwork in the firm can then be better identified and organized. Relationships with customers, suppliers, and partners can similarly be re-evaluated and if necessary reorganized. Corporate initiatives aimed at improving business processes or product/service quality can be rationalized and integrated within a holistic framework for nurturing and managing knowledge.

Understanding the knowledge-based dynamics of internalization and externalization should help management develop a more selective approach to external sourcing. Strategically planned relationships with dependent and independent contractors may offer firms the opportunity to develop large networks of skilled suppliers or distributors, without the costs and risks often associated with employment. Better forecasting of demand should help firms make better decisions as to when to hire directly and when to use staffing or, alternatively, outsourcing providers.

The implications are however not all positive, or at least not immediately so. Decisions regarding whether to retain or externalize staff or functions will tend to involve a more complex range of considerations. Management itself will be affected. Managing knowledge is not the same as managing people—despite the obvious overlap. Professional 'people managers' may have to learn new skills or find themselves redundant.

Workers

From the perspective of individual workers, the implications of knowledge supply replacing labour supply should help them to face the future and plan for it in a more realistic way. Rather than view firms as employers, individuals need increasingly to view them as customers, or partners in a knowledge-based exchange. Individual workers will, as a result, need to consider more carefully the characteristics of knowledge demanded by firms, in exactly the same way as firms will need to evaluate their knowledge supply options.

Having dispensed with the mental model of employment as an ideal form of work arrangement, individuals will be able to focus on the style of work arrangement which best suits them. For some this may mean professional 'temping', for others taking up a franchise or developing an independent micro business. For those retained in the firm, their contribution is likely to be measured, not so much by functional role or position, but by how their skills contribute to growing the firm's knowledge base.

For all concerned, a more realistic appraisal of future knowledge demand should help identify what additional skills and training may be required to develop a successful and (largely) self-managed career.

Government

Governments need to create a social and business climate which understands and accepts the implications of the knowledge economy on work and employment, and which can therefore assist firms and workers to capitalize on the strategic opportunities represented by more appropriate forms of work arrangement. To create this climate of understanding and acceptance, governments everywhere need first to advise their citizens of economic reality, instead of beguiling them with visions of an unattainable future, based on gradually improving levels of regular full-time employment. Secondly, governments have to accept the realities of flexihire and other non-traditional forms of work arrangement, and stop requesting that firms act contrary to their best economic interests by maintaining rigid conditions of employment, including wage and non-wage benefits.

Exhorting firms to act as good corporate citizens is appropriate insofar as all citizens may be expected to live up to some societal ideals, but firms should not be unreasonably singled out. Legal requirements on firms to maintain and increase unemployment benefits are a sure way to drive firms even faster towards externalized work arrangements.

Governments can positively assist a transition strategy by providing tax breaks and other incentives to businesses that offer workers low-cost access to training facilities, career counselling, and outplacement services. For workers, governments need to reduce the real cost of retraining by offering full tax deductability of personal expenditure on approved learning activities. Furthermore, governments could assist by linking payment of unemployment benefits to worker participation in transition schemes involving retraining.

CONCLUSIONS

It has become conventional, as noted earlier in this chapter, to ascribe the trend away from full-time, permanent employment to a spectrum of factors. Typically these range from demographic change to globalized competition, technological job replacement, or a desire by firms for greater flexibility. As this and the preceding chapters have hopefully illustrated, many of these factors are themselves symptoms of the shift from an industrial to a knowledge-based economy.

Technological progress, as we have seen, is both driving and driven by this shift. Globalized business for example was a dream only fifty years ago; it is a present and growing reality largely due to advances in knowledge and knowledge-based industries. Similarly, an ageing and increasingly active population can attribute their longevity and thus their ability to continue working and learning to the power of (medical) knowledge. Women's capacity to take on an increasingly significant role in the workforce has certainly been enabled by cultural acceptance of gender equality and economic pressure on the family unit, but it has also been assisted significantly by improved access to education.

As for the often-cited flexibility imperative, the question remains as to what is driving firms' undoubted need for greater flexibility. Clearly, uncertainty as to the type of knowledge and human skills they will require in future is playing a significant role in firms' decisions to opt for more flexible work arrangements. In short, the driving force behind much of what we attribute to other causes can be seen to be the shift from one type of economy to another, from physical resources to knowledge.

Having argued the case for a knowledge-centred view of the world of work, we now need to move on to look at the issues and opportunities facing firms and their stakeholders, in organizing and managing knowledge supply. In Part II we will look outward beyond the firm, at each of the four major classifications of externalized supply. This will be followed in Part III with a look back inside the firm and an analysis of the implications of internalized supply.

NOTES

1. G. Standing (1997), 'Globalisation, Labour Flexibility and Insecurity: The Era of Market Regulation', *European Journal of Industrial Relations*, 3/1: 7–37.

2. OECD (Organization for Economic Co-operation and Development) (1997), *Employment Outlook*, Paris: OECD (July).

3. T. W. Malone and R. J. Laubacher (1998), 'The Dawn of the E-Lance Economy', *Harvard Business Review* (Sept.–Oct.): 145–52.

4. J. Connell and J. Burgess (forthcoming), 'Workforce and Skill Restructuring in Australia', *International Employment Relations Review*.

5. Standing, 'Globalisation, Labour Flexibility and Insecurity: The Era of Market Regulation'.

6. OECD, *Employment Outlook*.

7. J. F. Stinson Jr. (1997), *Monthly Labor Review*, Washington: Bureau of Labor Statistics (Mar.): 3–15.

8. J. Atkinson (1984), 'Emerging U.K. Work Patterns in Flexible Manning: The Way Ahead', Report 88, Brighton: Institute of Manpower Studies.

9. C. Handy (1996), *Beyond Certainty: The Changing Worlds of Organizations*, London: Arrow Books Ltd.: 13–31.

10. A. Pollert (1988), 'The Flexible Firm: Fixation or Fact', *Work Employment & Society*, 2/3: 281–316.

11. K. Marx (1867), *Capital: A Critique of Political Economy*, i: *The Process of Capitalist Production*, New York: Moore & Aneling (1967 edn.).

12. M. C. Jensen and W. H. Meckling (1976), 'Theory of the Firm, Managerial Behaviour, Agency Costs and Ownership Structure', *Journal of Financial Economics*, 3: 305–60.

13. O. E. Williamson (1985), *The Economic Institutions of Capitalism*, New York: Free Press.

14. H. Simon (1951), 'A Formal Theory of the Employment Relationship', *Econometrica*, 19: 293–305.
15. I. R. MacNeil (1985), 'Relational Contracts: What we Do and Do not Know', *Wisconsin Law Review*: 483–525.
16. D. M. Rousseau and J. McLean Parks (1992), 'The Contracts of Individuals and Organizations', *Research in Organizational Behaviour*, 15: 1–43.
17. P. H. Mirvis and D. T. Hall (1996), 'Psychological Success and the Boundaryless Career', in M. B. Arthur and D. M. Rousseau (eds.), *The Boundaryless Career: A New Employment Principle for a New Organisational Era*, New York: Oxford University Press: 237–55.
18. D. Q. Mills (1996), 'The Changing Social Contract in American Business', *European Management Journal*, 14/5: 451–6.
19. G. Walker and L. Poppo (1994), 'Profit Centres, Single-Source Suppliers, and Transaction Costs', in T. J. Allen and M. S. Scott Morton (eds.), *Information Technology and the Corporation of the 1990's*, New York: Oxford University Press: 298–319.
20. P. Milgrom and J. Roberts (1992), *Economics Organization and Management*, Englewood Cliffs, NJ: Prentice-Hall Inc.
21. P. Doeringer and M. Piore (1971), *Internal Labour Markets and Manpower Analysis*, Lexington, Mass.: D. C. Heath.
22. R. W. Judy and C. D'Amico (1997), *Workforce 2020: Work and Workers in the 21st Century*, Indianapolis: Hudson Institute Inc.
23. P. D. Sherer (1996), 'Toward an Understanding of the Variety in Work Arrangements: The Organization and Labor Relationships Framework', in C. L. Cooper and D. M. Rousseau (eds.), *Trends in Organizational Behaviour*, iii, New York: John Wiley & Sons Ltd.: 99–120.

PART II

NAVIGATING KNOWLEDGE MARKETS

This sphere [the market] . . . is in fact a very Eden of the innate rights of man. There alone rule Freedom, Equality, Property and Bentham. Freedom, because both buyer and seller of a commodity, say of labour-power, are constrained only by their own free will. They contract as free agents, and the agreement they come to, is but the form in which they give legal expression to their common will. Equality, because each enters into relation with the other, as with a simple owner of commodities, and they exchange equivalent for equivalent. Property because each disposes only of what is his own. And Bentham because each looks only to himself.

(Karl Marx (1867), *Capital: A Critique of Political Economy*, i: *The Process of Capitalist Production*)

4

From Jobs to Careers

This chapter is the first in a series of four chapters which will explore issues and trends in the sourcing and provision of knowledge from outside the firm, involving the four major external sources of supply: flexihire, mediated services, dependent contractors, and independent contractors. The subject of this chapter is the flexihire market, which as described earlier (see Chapter 3) covers direct relationships between firms and workers, including temporary, part-time, work sharing, and similar forms of non full-time employment.

Flexihire represents a natural starting point for exploring knowledge supply markets beyond the boundaries of the firm since, from a contractual perspective, it marks the first step away from traditional full-time employment. For many firms and many workers, flexihire will also mark the first stage on an evolutionary path towards an increasing variety of work arrangements, and (for workers) multiple shorter engagements with particular firms.

Part of the reasoning behind this prediction derives from the nature of the knowledge supplied in flexihire arrangements (see Fig. 4.1). As Fig. 4.1

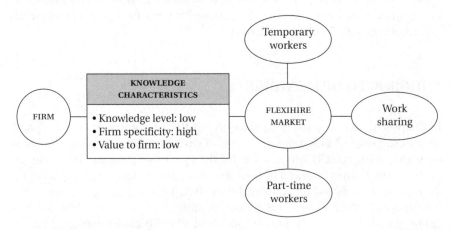

FIG. 4.1. Knowledge Supply Model™: flexihire market

indicates, firms' use of flexihire is clearly linked to their need to have access (albeit on a limited basis) to particular individuals who have specific knowledge of their business processes. This firm-specific and often task-specific knowledge gives flexihire workers an advantage over individuals provided by staffing agencies who would generally lack such knowledge.

As firms standardize their routine functions, however, the degree of firm-specific knowledge required to manage and operate the processes involved tends to reduce. A knowledge of Microsoft Office nowadays, for example, is a more valuable passport to work than knowledge of a particular firm's office system. This is not to imply that the level of general or specialized knowledge required to operate standard systems is less than that for non-standard or firm-specific systems. Use of modern software packages such as MS Office may require more not fewer skills than the systems they replace.

As knowledge specificity reduces, firms are less likely to need the services of particular flexihire workers. Add to this the management overhead implied in directly controlling an ever-growing externalized workforce and other supply options, such as outsourcing or staffing services, start to look increasingly attractive. Meantime, from the perspective of flexihire workers, increasing uncertainty over future work prospects is likely to reduce their loyalty to their employer.

Flexihire, therefore, despite the fact that it currently accounts for approximately 30 per cent of the total in employment in the western world, appears unlikely to remain as popular in the long term. While firms are likely to continue to deal individually with some flexihire workers, a variety of mediated services are likely to make major inroads on the flexihire market. A number of important consequences flow from this conclusion, which will be discussed in the course of this chapter and Chapter 5.

The chapter opens with a look at the evidence of growth in major forms of flexihire, including part-time employment, temporary/contingent employment, and work sharing. This is followed by an analysis of trends in flexihire arrangements and a discussion of their implications for management, workers, and other stakeholders in the firm.

THE GROWTH OF FLEXIHIRE

In Chapter 3, we discussed the decline in full-time employment and the parallel shift to various 'non-standard' forms of work arrangement which has been occurring across OECD nations now for the past three decades (see Table 3.1). Further details are presented here of the size, growth, and composition of the flexihire market, based on statistical snapshots from various countries. While international comparisons are rendered difficult by country differences in defining and classifying various components of the flexihire market, a picture of the market as a whole emerges fairly clearly.

Part-time Employment

Part-time employment represents the largest single employment classification after full-time employment and is the largest component of the flexihire market.

Comparative Growth Trends

In the USA approximately 22 per cent of those in traditional work arrangements and 42 per cent of those in non-traditional arrangements were recorded as part-timers in 1995. In the EU, growth accelerated in the 1991–5 period. In the UK, for example, two-thirds of all new jobs created in 1995 were classified as part-time. Partly as a result of government policies favouring non-traditional work arrangements, the Netherlands recorded by far the highest incidence of part-time working in the OECD: 36 per cent of the workforce in 1996. Nine out of ten recently created jobs in the Netherlands have been part-time.[1] In Japan, part-time employment increased to 17 per cent of total employment by 1992 and is currently estimated to have risen to over 20 per cent.[2] By 1990, 41 per cent of the total labour force in Japan were women, of whom over 25 per cent were in part-time employment, mainly in the manufacturing, wholesale and retail, and services sectors.

Growth of Casualization

Along with the shift to part-time employment, a significant percentage of those in part-time work tend to have diminished access to the non-wage benefits such as paid sick leave and annual leave to which they were previously entitled as full-time employees. The reduction in such non-wage benefits, although sometimes accompanied by higher hourly wage rates, represents a further distancing between employer and employee and heightens the impermanent or casual nature of the relationship. Among OECD countries, Spain, Portugal, and Australia in particular have all evidenced strong growth over recent years in casualized work arrangements. In Australia, for example, casual employment, as a percentage of the total workforce, grew from 13.3 per cent in 1985 to 22.1 per cent in 1996.[3] According to Burgess, part-time casual employment is growing at approximately twice the rate of non-casual part-time employment in that country.[4]

Industry Sectors, Demographics, and Occupations

Consistent with the general pattern of employment by industry sector, part-time employment in the services sector as a proportion of total employment in Europe was nearly three times that of major goods-producing sectors in 1992 and grew twice as fast as employment in those sectors in the period 1983–92.[5]

Women currently make up over two-thirds of the part-time workforce in OECD member countries. The relatively high level of female participation appears to have been maintained for some years and is generally attributed to a greater propensity for women to accept part-time work as a way of reconciling conflicting demands of work and family life. Youth and retirees make up a large proportion of the remaining one third of part-timers.

Based on a sample of EC countries, part-time workers appear to be relatively unskilled, with part-timers' qualifications generally found to be fewer than those for full-timers.[6] The growth of part-time working and its association with low-skilled occupations is generally consistent with the trends predicted in Chapter 3. Workers with low skill levels are also likely to be first to leave full-time employment and to find it more difficult to re-enter the workforce, other than through casual/part-time work arrangements.

Temporary and Contingent Employment

The US Bureau of Labor Statistics (BLS) describes jobs where there is not an explicit or implicit contract for long-term employment as 'contingent'. In the EEC, work is generally classified as 'temporary' if objective conditions for its termination are referred to in the contract between the parties. Otherwise it is assumed that an implicit contract exists, implying permanency or at least an open-ended and potentially long-term relationship. These definitional differences need to be borne in mind when considering the various trends detailed in this section.

Growth of Temporary and Contingent Employment

Temporary employment has evidenced even faster rates of growth than part-time working in most countries—albeit from a smaller base. Across the EU, temporary employment grew from approximately 4 per cent of total employment in 1983 to over 9 per cent by 1991. In the UK, temporary employment growth, which was relatively flat in the period 1983–92, subsequently accelerated from 5.5 per cent to 7 per cent by 1995, representing 464,000 jobs or a 43 per cent increase in the size of the temporary workforce.[7]

In Japan, temporary employment is also on the increase. Toyota is reported as forecasting in 1995 that it aimed to raise the percentage of temporary workers from 10 per cent to 20 per cent whilst reducing its regular workforce by 20–30 per cent.[8] In the same year, temporary employment agencies in Japan were forecasting an increase in business of 10 per cent.[9]

In the USA the BLS used three different measures of contingency in their 1995 survey, according to which the total of contingent workers ranged from 2.2 per cent (approximately 2.7 million), to 4.9 per cent (approximately 6 million), of all those in employment. Those in alternative work arrangements, defined as independent contractors, on-call workers, temporary help agency workers, and workers provided by contract firms, as well as those in traditional full-time work arrangements, were all found to contain a proportion of contingent workers. This ranged from as low as 3.6 per cent for those in traditional work arrangements to 3.8 per cent for independent contractors, 19.8 per cent of workers provided by contract firms, 35.2 per cent of on-call workers, and 66.5 per cent of temporary help agency workers. The balance in each case were classified as *non-contingent*.[10]

Occupations

In the EU, 63 per cent of those in temporary employment were found to be in low-skilled jobs, whereas in the USA the distribution of contingent workers by skill was more uniform, reflecting the broader composition of the workforce involved in the contingent category. Both these findings are in fact consistent with the predicted trend to externalization of low-skilled workers. The main difference between the EU and the USA appears to be that low-skilled workers in the latter country have taken a pay cut in order to stay employed (see Chapter 3).

In the UK, apart from the teaching profession, most temporary work has historically been concentrated in clerical, secretarial, and other generally low-skilled occupational groups. The picture is rapidly changing however in the UK, with one in seven 'professional' employees in 1996 being temporary versus one in ten in 1992.[11] There is also evidence that workers with higher skill levels are more likely to be engaged by firms on longer-term temporary contracts.[12] The trend among professional workers to undertake temporary work may of course be associated with various factors, including a propensity for younger workers in particular to travel and to job-hop in order to increase their earnings, while gaining experience and a trackrecord. These findings are however also consistent with the Knowledge Supply Model™, as described in Chapter 3, i.e. that firms will enter into different forms of work arrangement with suppliers, dependent upon their particular levels of knowledge, the perceived value of that knowledge to the firm, and the specificity of that knowledge relative to the firm's processes. Extending the length of temporary contracts also suggests that firms place a higher value on the job-specific and/or high-level skills of particular professional workers and are seeking to reduce the risk of losing them prematurely.

Demographics

In the EU over 27 per cent of young workers (aged 15–24) are in temporary employment, which is three times the average for all age groups. In the USA contingent workers were almost twice as likely as non-contingent workers to be aged between 16 and 24. The demographics of temporary employment are consistent with the dynamics of knowledge demand discussed earlier. Young people are those least likely to have the job- or firm-specific experience that firms are looking for in flexihire workers—a 'catch-22' situation.

In the USA by the late 1990s, according to the BLS, contingent workers were only slightly more likely to be women than men. In the EU the rate of temporary employment was also slightly higher among women than men. In the UK women again outnumbered men; however, the rate of male temporary employment in the 1992–5 period grew twice as fast as for women. This trend possibly reflected the growth in fixed-term temporary contract work and the slower growth in secretarial and clerical temporary jobs, where women have been more highly concentrated. As clerical and secretarial work has become largely computerized and based on standard software packages, firm-specific and occupation-specific knowledge has become less relevant. Anecdotal evidence suggests that much of this work has been absorbed within organizations, by other workers who now have the necessary knowledge and (keyboard) skills to undertake such work, or hived out to external agencies. Since the great majority of clerical and secretarial temporary work has traditionally been performed by women, a drop in demand for firm-specific and occupational-specific skills would have reduced opportunities for such work.

Other Factors

Factors traditionally found to be associated with firms' use of temporary workers include firm size, industry, geographic location, organizational characteristics, level of non-wage benefits provided to full-time staff, level of unionization, volatility in demand for the firm's products, and need to access specialist external resources. In this context a study of the use of directly hired temporary workers in the USA based on data collected in the early 1980s produced some interesting findings.[13] According to this study, the cost of provision of non-wage benefits was not mentioned by many employers as a reason for using temporary staff. Whether this was a reflection of lack of such motivation or merely reticence by employers is a moot point. Volatile or cyclical demand for the firm's products had a significant positive effect on temporary worker use. Where the firm was likely to be particularly subject to government oversight, the use of temporary working was significantly lower. Unionization tended to favour greater use of temporary workers, but not significantly. Large firms were less likely to use temporary workers than small firms, probably due to incompatibility between strong internal bureaucratic practices and use of 'outsiders'.

Significantly, although knowledge characteristics of firms' operations were not specifically studied (other than in relation to the demand for specialist resources), the research findings still appear consistent with the predictions made in Chapter 3. The greater the informational or technical complexity of the work, for example, the less likely it was to be outsourced. Since the study did not specifically analyse the knowledge characteristics of the work in relation to the knowledge demands and priorities of the firm, it would not have been possible to distinguish those types of activities which, although informationally or technically complex, might still have been outsourced. Work which demanded strong interpersonal skills (implying tacit but not firm-specific knowledge) was as likely to be performed by temporary workers as by in-house staff.

Work Sharing

The notion of work sharing as a means of generating jobs whilst maintaining current levels of employment was promoted in Europe, particularly by certain sectors of the union movement, in the late 1970s and early 1980s. At that time it met with little success. In the early 1990s, however, it was reintroduced with government support in several countries, notably France, Germany, Belgium, and the Netherlands.

Germany has recently introduced one of the biggest work-sharing framework arrangements, covering 3.7 million workers in the West German metal-working industry. This scheme provides for a reduction in working time to thirty hours per week, with workers accepting pro rata reductions in wages subject to certain conditions. The agreement is set against a background of negotiations for a shorter working week across Germany, covering ten industry sectors, involving specific provisions for 'employment-securing working time reduction'.

Volkswagen in Germany introduced a similar arrangement in the early 1990s, in the face of massive falls in sales volumes, threatening over 30,000 jobs at the time. The agreement centred on a 20 per cent cut in average weekly working hours, accompanied by a 16 per cent reduction in annual gross income. The agreement was subsequently successfully renegotiated in 1995. Daimler-Benz later cut its working week by one day and reduced wages by 10 per cent in order to save jobs in its car division.[14] France has recently introduced a reduced official 'full-time' working week of thirty-five hours, which reflects a general European trend towards reduced annual working hours. Such schemes may be viewed as the national equivalent of work sharing, albeit in a different form.

Whether work sharing has any significant future remains highly debatable. Its main advantage consists in spreading the pain of redundancies or layoffs. Where firms are going through a 'bad patch', work sharing may be desirable, but as a long-term response to changing patterns of demand for human skills and knowledge, it has little to offer by way of benefit to the firm, nor is it of long-term benefit to the employee unless tied to an upgrading of skills.

The weaknesses in the concept of work sharing can clearly be seen by reference to the Knowledge Supply Model™. Most of the industries and occupations which are the subject of work-sharing arrangements are those where investments in standardization and automation have been highest—typically older manufacturing industries and production line jobs. Most of the workers employed in such occupations are typically those which would fall into the peripheral group in the firm. The main strength of this group, like the flexihire group, has been their firm-specific/process-specific knowledge. As firms automate and standardize such work, they become less dependent on the knowledge of their workforces. At this point, some firms may transfer the work to another lower-cost country, introduce work sharing, or simply outsource the production processes to a third party supplier, as Ford for example has done in the USA.

The key to long-term survival for workers caught in such situations is clearly to upgrade their skill levels. The problem is that, with little time, opportunity, or motivation to acquire new knowledge, workers may fail to do so or may acquire knowledge which is not in demand by the time they have acquired it. In the short term such workers, in common with many others employed in various flexihire arrangements, will also be seeking career counselling, retraining, and psychological and financial support (see Implications below).

'GOOD' VERSUS 'BAD' FORMS OF EMPLOYMENT

Whereas many individuals entering self-employment can be shown to have exercised some degree of personal preference for that mode of working, as can many 'professional temps' working for temporary agencies, the motivational picture is not so clear when it comes to various types of flexihire. Demand and supply side factors affecting temporary employment, for example, have been traditionally assumed to be weighted on the demand side, i.e. the employer. The high incidence of young people in temporary employment is a case in point. Researchers have assumed that, given the option, young workers would prefer to be employed on a regular full-time basis. Factors outside the firm's control have popularly been dismissed or ignored.

An analysis of the degree of choice exercised by workers entering into contingent work arrangements in the USA by Polivka, reported by the BLS, suggests, however, that from a motivational perspective the picture is not so clear cut and that supply side preferences are also involved. According to the results of this research, less than a third of all contingent workers stated a preference for their arrangement, clearly indicating that the majority found it less than ideal. There were however striking differences between the subgroups involved. The highest level of dissatisfaction was evidenced by those searching for a (full-time) job and the next highest by those who had been full-time employed before taking a contingent job. In contrast, excluding those in school, those who were engaged in non labour market activities prior to taking the contingent job were more satisfied—90 per cent of those actually *preferred* contingent arrangements. Of those in school prior to taking a contingent job, approximately 80 per cent expressed satisfaction with being in contingent employment.[15]

As these research findings indicate, attitudinal responses are largely conditioned by past experience. In an employment-centric world it is natural to wish to be employed, just as a couple of centuries ago it was considered equally normal and even desirable to pursue a lifetime of subordination as a servant to one master.

SUMMARY

The statistical evidence of a decline in full-time employment and growth in flexihire supports the arguments presented in Chapter 3 and reflected in the Knowledge Supply Model™. This evidence together with related conclusions and predictions may be summarized as follows:

- The evidence of the past three decades shows a progressive and now rapid trend towards flexihire throughout enterprises large and small, in both the public and private sector and throughout the West. Those workers most affected are uniformly the lowest skilled. While many firms are consciously taking advantage of this situation to improve efficiency, it is apparent that the dynamics of change are beyond the control of firms.
- Part-time work continues to grow at the expense of full-time work, with part-timers, mostly women, now representing approximately 25–30 per cent of the employed workforce in leading OECD countries by the late 1990s. Growth of part-time work however is slowing and much of this slowdown can be attributed to a decline in the dominant occupations, mainly (female) secretarial and clerical work. This decline is consistent with the automation and standardization of the processes involved, leading to internal efficiencies and reduced dependency on firm/task-specific knowledge.
- Temporary work in its various forms also continues to grow and more recently to outpace the growth of part-time work. Approximately 9–11 per cent of the total workforce of the OECD nations appears to have been in some form of temporary employment at the end of 1996. The recent surge in temporary employment across the West is consistent with the prediction that employers will find managing flexihire work increasingly onerous. Temporary employment arrangements enable firms to put specific end points on their relationships with workers and to move from a relational to a transactional model, based more on achievement of results. Such practices take firms and workers one step closer to using mediated services, or to dependent or independent contracting arrangements (see Chapter 5).
- Work sharing, as a form of collective part-time working, continues to grow, particularly in certain countries such as Germany and in the shape of a reduced national 'working week' in many countries. Work sharing however is unlikely to provide significant long-term advantages to firms or workers, unless combined with education and training programmes.

- For workers, flexihire typically implies being 'squeezed', first out of the traditional employment relationship and then into a dependent work arrangement, usually with a single firm. Such arrangements, typically characterized by shorter hours, and fewer non-wage benefits, are likely to become increasingly unattractive as a long-term proposition for most workers. Exceptions to this are likely to be some women, young people, and retirees who, for one reason or another, seek more flexible work arrangements and are prepared to accept dependency on a single firm for that employment.

- For firms, managing increasingly large part-time and temporary work-forces is likely to become equally unattractive. The explosive growth of the staffing services industry, and the popularity (in the USA at least) of services such as employee leasing, suggests firms are already reacting to these problems by moving from direct to indirect hiring, particularly of less-skilled workers (see Chapter 5). Standardization of low-skilled corporate functions is fuelling this trend. If, as seems likely, this trend continues and spreads to other countries, a slowdown in the growth of the flexihire market will occur.

- Attitudes of workers to flexihire, while generally negative, indicate that prior experience of employment/unemployment has a marked effect on preferences. Meantime, the flexihire market itself is restructuring, moving from part-time to temporary work and in the direction of dependent or independent forms of contracting. Much of the residual flexihire market appears likely to be absorbed by providers of mediated services in the short to medium term. The debate about good or bad forms of employment therefore needs to move on and to be replaced with a more forward-looking vision of work arrangements which takes account of the dynamics of knowledge supply.

IMPLICATIONS

The decline of full-time employment and the growth of flexihire present workers, firms, governments, and other stakeholders with a variety of challenges.

Management

Anticipating the need to externalize work arrangements, as noted earlier, will be easier in some cases than others. The major onus on management will be to advise the workforce as far ahead as practicable of its intentions. Many firms are already adopting the practice of advising new employees that there is no guarantee of long-term work—all contracts are thus defined as temporary from the outset.

There is a risk that if firms do not take the initiative, governments may step in and in doing so probably create even greater inefficiencies. Work sharing and other transition arrangements will need to be combined with retraining if they are to be of long-term value. This is an area where joint cooperation involving firms, unions, industry bodies, and government will be essential (see Chapter 11).

Within limits, flexihire will continue to play a useful role, but maintenance of a large external workforce on this basis, as noted earlier, is likely to prove inefficient. Management will therefore need to improve corporate links to staffing services and other external service providers. Conversely, a strategic opportunity exists for staffing agencies, outsourcing specialists and employee leasing firms to align themselves with firms in anticipation of future change.

Workers

For workers still in full-time employment, particularly those in the peripheral group, the key issues will involve planning for a transition to different work arrangements of which flexihire is the most likely short-term prospect. Short-term tactics may involve taking a second job whilst still employed, or acquiring skills which are likely to broaden the range of work opportunities for which they are suited. Longer-term strategies will require more explicit knowledge development plans. Such plans will need to identify the type of knowledge, qualifications, and work experience that will be needed to achieve career objectives. Once longer-term goals and objectives are established, flexihire may then be used as a bridge, providing time and income to assist the pursuit of strategic goals, which are most likely to be based around a programme of skills acquisition. Many flexihire workers will require assistance to develop such plans. Expert independent advice from career guidance specialists may be needed to help them in this process.

For those workers with higher skill levels, who anticipate a prolonged period of flexihire with one particular firm, it will be advisable either to enter into a long-term contract which provides some security of tenure, or to seek to broaden their range of future work opportunities. The latter course is likely to involve dealing with one or more intermediary agencies in order to gain access to more varied temporary work, or alternatively to consider some form of dependent or independent contracting.

Government

Western governments have traditionally viewed flexihire as a variant of full-time employment, whereas it can now be seen as the first stage on the road away from employment-centred work. Just as an understanding of the role of flexihire may act as a catalyst for firms, so such an understanding should help governments to revise their active labour market programmes, which have been traditionally geared to getting workers back to full-time employment.

Once the notion of production and work is divorced from traditional institutional and organizational settings and the changing role of knowledge accepted, flexihire can be seen for what it is, and strategies developed to help firms and workers in dealing with it. Retraining schemes for workers involved in, or likely to enter, the flexihire market clearly will be important. Given the rate of technological change, a key issue will be how to ensure that whatever training is given actually fits workers for the rapidly changing workplace.

Other Stakeholders

In addition to assistance with career planning, flexihire workers are likely to need access to financial support, training, and placement services, plus peer group support from workers from similar educational and occupational backgrounds.

Laubacher and Malone suggest a modern-day equivalent of the workers' guilds of medieval times as a possible answer to this dilemma for externalized former employees.[16] In the days before it was customary to be employed, such guilds provided many of the non-wage benefits that are provided today by employers to their full-time staff. According to Laubacher and Malone, modern guilds could be formed by workers having particular affinities with each other, for example via common trade or professional qualifications, through having shared similar experiences, or because they live in the same area. Such guilds, in addition to offering peer group support, could provide sufficient collective buying power to obtain tailored health insurance and other benefits. Similarly they might be able to assist with job placement, career consulting, and training.

Since around two-thirds of flexihire workers today are women, groups oriented towards the advancement of women's rights, women's business networks, and similar organizations would seem to offer a potential starting point for supply or referral to these types of collective self-help services. Other demographic groups which would tend to fit with the profile of flexihire workers are youth organizations and those supporting mature-age workers and retirees. Unions, employer groups, and staffing services may also be in a position to offer such services to flexihire workers, as well as others in non-traditional work arrangements. Professional and trade associations, many of whom are already involved in implementing workforce transition strategies, could play an enlarged role in determining and publishing industry strategies which reflect future industry knowledge requirements and training needs. Workers involved in transition flexihire arrangements would then be able to take advantage of such information to plan their own career strategies.

CONCLUSIONS

Classifications such as part-time employment and temporary employment reflect the employment-centred view of work, which, as this and preceding chapters have hopefully illustrated, is a relic of a fast-disappearing industrial era.

While firms are undoubtedly still using flexihire to supplement their full-time workforce, it is clear that the 30 plus per cent of the western workforce now involved in such arrangements are ultimately headed away from their current flexihire employer, not back into the firm. It is equally apparent that they are unlikely to remain in the limbo of flexihire with the same firm for long, unless the expertise and know-how they supply is specifically relevant to that firm's activities. Such situations are of course rare. Flexihire therefore needs to be recognized for what it is: a transitional stage on the road from jobs owned by organizations to careers owned by individuals.

Viewed in this way, flexihire, despite its limitations, could be used as part of a transition strategy, one of the many bridges leading from the old world of work to more productive and efficient forms of work arrangement. This takes us to the next chapter, which focuses on what is shaping up to be one of the boom markets of the early twenty-first century, the market for mediated services.

NOTES

1. J. Visser (1998), 'Two Cheers for Corporatism, One for the Market: Industrial Relations, Wage Moderation and Job Growth in the Netherlands', *British Journal of Industrial Relations*, 36/2 (June): 269–92.
2. J. Benson (1996), 'Change and Continuity: Contemporary Employment Practices in Japan', *International Employment Relations Review*, 2/1: 21–31.
3. J. Connell and J. Burgess (forthcoming), 'Workforce and Skill Restructuring in Australia', *International Employment Relations Review*.
4. J. Burgess (1996), 'Workforce Casualisation in Australia', *International Employment Relations Review*, 2/1: 33–53.
5. OECD (Organization for Economic Co-operation and Development) (1996), *Technology Productivity and Job Creation*, ii: *Analytical Report*, Paris: OECD: 161.
6. D. Meulders, O. Plasman, and R. Plasman (1994), *Atypical Employment in the EC*, Aldershot: Dartmouth Publishing Company Ltd.
7. K. Purcell (1996), 'Employment Flexibility', in *Review of the Economy and Employment 1996/7: Labour Market Assessment*, Warwick: Institute for Employment Research, University of Warwick: 25–49.
8. J. R. Lincoln and Y. Nakata (1997), 'The Transformation of the Japanese Employment System: Nature, Depth, and Origins', *Work and Occupations*, 24/1 (Feb.): 33–55.

9. Benson, 'Change and Continuity: Contemporary Employment Practices in Japan'.
10. A. E. Polivka (1996), 'Contingent and Alternative Work Arrangements, Defined', *Monthly Labor Review*, Washington: Bureau of Labor Statistics (Oct.): 3–9.
11. F. Sly and D. Stillwell (1997), 'Temporary Workers in Great Britain', *Labour Market Trends*, London: Office for National Statistics (Sept.): 347–54.
12. Purcell, 'Employment Flexibility'.
13. A. Davis-Blake and B. Uzzi (1993), 'Determinants of Employment Externalisation: A Study of Temporary Workers and Independent Contractors', *Administrative Science Quarterly*, 38: 195–223.
14. P. Blyton and R. Trinczek (1997), 'Renewed Interest in Work-Sharing? Assessing Recent Developments in Germany', *Industrial Relations Journal*, 28/1: 3–13.
15. A. E. Polivka (1996), 'Into Contingent and Alternative Employment: By Choice?', *Monthly Labor Review*, Washington: Bureau of Labor Statistics (Oct.): 55–74.
16. R. J. Laubacher and T. W. Malone, 'Flexible Work Arrangements and 21st Century Workers Guilds', Working Paper 004 Initiative on Investing the Organisations of the 21st Century, Sloan School of Management, MIT (http://ccs.mit.edu/21c/21CWP004.html).

Mediators of Knowledge Supply

In the previous chapter we saw how access to the specific knowledge of particular workers on convenient and cost-effective terms fuelled the growth of flexihire. We also saw these advantages beginning to erode, as firms standardize
their routine operations and seek to offload the responsibilities associated
with managing a growing externalized workforce. As the playing field levels
out, opportunities are opening up for the mediators of knowledge supply,
principally staffing and outsourcing services, to make major inroads on the
flexihire market and the firm's peripheral functions.

The results-focused orientation of modern business is further enhancing
the appeal of those suppliers who can provide large-scale substitution services
for entire workforces or complete departmental functions. The mediated supply market is thus developing parallel streams of services, which can be
broadly segmented as supply of people and supply of solutions (see Fig. 5.1).

As can be seen from Fig. 5.1, mediated services tend to be low on firm-
specific knowledge, but the level of knowledge supplied and its value to the
firm can cover a wide spectrum of needs. Rather than choose multiple service
providers to satisfy their diverse knowledge requirements, it can be expected
that some firms, particularly the larger players, will increasingly seek single
sourcing arrangements involving both people and solutions. This in turn is
predicted to lead to competition and a degree of convergence between
staffing and outsourcing providers.

The growth and diversity of the mediated services market implies that it will
encroach not only on flexihire and the peripheral group in the firm, but also to
a degree on the independent contractors market. In this context its major
appeal is likely to be to those individuals who wish to pursue an independent
workstyle, without the attendant responsibilities of marketing themselves and
administering their own businesses.

The purpose of this chapter is to provide an overview of the rapidly expanding market for mediated knowledge supply and to discuss its implications for
the firm and its stakeholders. The chapter opens with a profile of the staffing
services industry, including comparative growth statistics from various countries, followed by an analysis of trends and a discussion of some of the key

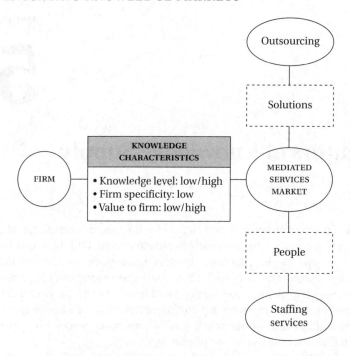

FIG. 5.1. Knowledge Supply Model™: mediated services market

issues and opportunities which are emerging from a knowledge-based perspective. A similar profile and analysis is then provided in relation to outsourcing, including a discussion as to how firms insourcing/outsourcing
decisions can be improved by explicit recognition of the knowledge characteristics of the functions involved. This is followed by a summary of the evidence
regarding staffing and outsourcing trends and some pointers to future developments. The chapter ends with a review of the implications of the growth of
mediated knowledge supply for management, workers, service providers, and
other stakeholders.

STAFFING SERVICES

In the USA, employment in business services from 1972 to 1988 grew at the
rate of 6.9 per cent annually and from 1988 to 1996 by 5.8 per cent annually. Of
the eight industries comprising business services, four accounted for over 85
per cent of all employment in the group. Two of these—personnel supply services (staffing services) and computer services—recorded the highest average
annual employment growth rates of 11.4 per cent and 10.7 per cent respectively since 1972, five times the rate of growth of the total US economy (see

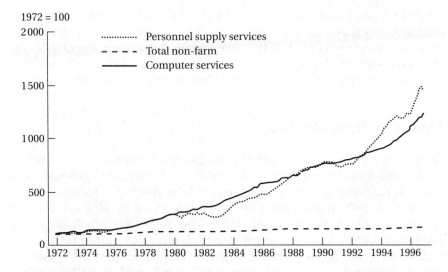

FIG. 5.2. Employment index of total non-farm, personnel supply, and computer services, 1972–96
Source: A. Clinton (1997), 'Flexible Labor: Restructuring the American Workforce', *Monthly Labor Review*, Washington: Bureau of Labor Statistics (Aug.): 5–6.

Fig. 5.2).[1] Despite some differences in the classification of 'services' particularly between Europe and the USA, similar trends to those reported for the USA are apparent across most OECD nations.

The main subclassifications of staffing services are *employment agencies*, specializing in permanent placements; *temporary agencies*, specializing in temporary placements; and *employee leasing*, which to date has been largely a US phenomenon. *Internet-based recruitment* and placement services have demonstrated explosive growth, both from within the ranks of existing staffing service providers and from outside them in the shape of services such as TMP Interactive's Monster Board. Such services are potential 'category killers' with the potential to revolutionize the operations of the staffing industry. *Internet-based recruitment* will thus be treated as a fourth classification for the purpose of this analysis. The following profile presents some statistical snapshots of the growth of these four types of staffing service in various countries.

Employment Agency Services

Traditional *permanent* placement services supplied by employment agencies throughout the West are declining, consistent with the decline in permanent full-time employment. In the USA in 1996, despite buoyant economic conditions, employment agency services growth was flat; in Australia permanent placements actually declined by 14.5 per cent between 1995 and 1996, a period of strong economic growth in that country.[2] The future role of such services in most countries will be increasingly tied to recruitment of workers in the associate group and to a lesser extent the core group in the firm.

Temporary Agency Services

Temporary agencies have been the fastest-growing component of the staffing services industry since the early 1980s. Between 1975 and 1987 the number of temporary agencies in the USA tripled from 3,133 to 10,611.[3] Manpower Inc., one of the world's largest temporary agencies, has been growing at around 20 per cent per annum since the early 1990s. With 2,776 offices in 48 countries, Manpower had become the largest technical 'employer' in the USA by the mid-1990s.[4] Other major temporary agencies such as Adecco, Kelly Services, Interim Personnel Services, and Olsten similarly exhibited strong growth during the 1990s. Many of the major temporary agencies are reportedly aiming to create global services and some are already physically exporting workers. Randstad, the Netherlands-based firm, for example, is reported as having sent aircraft engineers from the Netherlands to temporary jobs with Boeing in Seattle.[5]

In the USA, at the end of 1996, over 2.3 million workers were employed by temporary agencies.[6] While temporary agency work has grown rapidly in the USA and most other western countries, some countries, including Italy, Greece, France, and Germany, originally banned such agencies in order to protect full-time workers. These barriers are now being lifted as the move to non-employment-based work arrangements takes hold around the world.

In the UK, temporary work arrangements are customarily divided into 'fixed contract arrangements', 'contract for a fixed period', 'fixed task', and other temporary work which is 'not permanent in some way'. Combined placements for both fixed contract and other temporary work by agencies in the UK jumped by 32 per cent during 1993–4 and grew by a further 15 per cent between 1995 and 1996.[7]

The available evidence suggests that in the USA around 93 per cent of temporary workers in 1985 were hired directly by firms. By 1996, however, that figure had reduced to around 80 per cent, a very significant drop in such a short space of time and one that is consistent with the predicted trend from flexihire to mediated services. UK figures are similar. In the UK by mid-1996, 17 per cent of temporary workers in the private sector and 6 per cent in the public sector were hired via temporary agencies rather than directly by firms.[8]

Employee Leasing Services

Employee leasing services, sometimes referred to as staff leasing services or professional employment organizations (PEOs), are a relatively recent phenomenon, having started in the USA in the 1980s, over sixty years after the first temporary employment service appeared.

Official statistics on the incidence of employee leasing suggest a few hundred thousand workers are involved in the USA. According to NAPEO, a national association representing professional employment organizations in the USA, however, the industry already has between 2 and 3 million workers on its payroll and is growing at over 30 per cent annually.[9] Based on NAPEO's figures, employment by professional employment organizations is at least on a par with employment by temporary agencies in the USA.

From a knowledge-based perspective, employee leasing offers firms the benefits of flexihire without the problems. The main advantage of flexihire to firms, as we saw earlier, is that it enables firms to gain flexible access to workers with firm/job-specific knowledge, a service that temporary agencies are ill suited to provide. The main disadvantage of flexihire, however, is that it leaves the firm with the responsibility of recruiting and managing an externalized workforce, which as it grows is likely to prove increasingly onerous. Employee leasing services, unlike temporary agencies, provide firms with access to their current workforces, thus preserving access to firm/job-specific knowledge. At the same time, they undertake the responsibility for workforce management, thus freeing the firm of a potential burden.

From a more cynical perspective, employee leasing could be viewed simply as a device to enable the firm to avoid administrative costs, while it remains in effect the 'true employer'. Whatever the motivations prompting firms to use employee leasing, its growth is consistent with the predictions of the Knowledge Supply Model™ described in Chapter 3. By subcontracting the management of its entire workforce to another organization, a firm is externalizing the management of functions and resources which, by implication, it no longer sees as its business. The firm as a result is left free to concentrate on 'doing what it knows best'. If trends in the USA are any guide, firms will increasingly see management of large low-skilled workforces as a function better handled externally by organizations with the necessary focus and expertise.

Industry, Occupational, and Demographic Trends

The distribution of agency-supplied temporary workers by industry, occupation, and demographic characteristics appears to be broadly consistent with that for temporary employment as a whole. According to research conducted in the USA by the National Association of Temporary and Staffing Services

(NATSS), at the end of 1996, 70.5 per cent of temporary agency workers were assigned to low-skilled/semi-skilled work. Of the balance, 14 per cent were assigned to technical work, including computer programming, systems analysis, engineering, and similar skilled activities. A further 6.3 per cent were engaged in professional work, ranging from legal and accounting work to professional sales, marketing, and management activities. Health care (excluding home health care personnel) accounted for a further 5 per cent. The balance of temporary staff, just under 5 per cent, were engaged in marketing and miscellaneous other activities. The strongest increase apart from the 'other' category occurred in the high-skilled professional segment, which nearly tripled in the same period, albeit from a small base.[10]

Anecdotal evidence suggests the major area of growth in employee leasing and similar externally managed, large-scale workforce supply has been in the low-skilled/semi-skilled manufacturing sectors. Ford Motor Corporation for example has outsourced its US production workforce to a number of major staffing service providers. According to research by Segal and Sullivan, possibly up to half the decline in the size of the US manufacturing workforce between 1991 and 1993 involving 403,000 workers may have been attributable to increased use of temporary agency workers and employee leasing.[11]

Other research in the USA indicates that all industries increased their use of staffing services between 1977 and 1993. The finance, insurance, and real estate services sector was the major purchaser, recording an eightfold increase in usage over the period compared with a fourfold increase by industry generally.[12] Similar growth in this sector occurred in the UK and Europe. The disproportionate use of staffing services in this sector may be in part attributable to their heavy use of technology to standardize basic business functions, which would have reduced the levels of firm-specific knowledge required of workers.

In terms of demographics, according to the BLS 1995 survey, 25 per cent of all temporary agency workers in the USA were likely to be under 25, compared with 15 per cent for workers in this age group in traditional work arrangements. These figures match those for the EU where around 27 per cent of young workers were reportedly in temporary employment (see Chapter 4). Male temporary workers in the USA were even younger on average than female temporary workers with nearly one third aged under 25. The relatively high proportion of young workers using temporary agencies may be attributed to lack of firm-specific knowledge as well as their general lack of experience in the job market. By seeking work via agencies, young workers stand a better chance of finding positions with firms requiring their generic/academically acquired skills.

An interesting and different perspective on the use of staffing services emerges from a recent study of 'flexible employment' in Silicon Valley.[13] This shows that in the Santa Clara County, which is dominated by Silicon Valley, employment in temporary help service agencies (temporary agencies) grew by 70 per cent between 1990 and 1995, far outstripping percentage growth in flexihire work over this period in the whole of California. That this strong growth occurred in an area associated with high-skilled rather than low-skilled jobs is interesting and contrasts markedly with the traditional profile of temporary work as representing occupations with even lower levels of skill than part-time work.

From a knowledge-based perspective, however, the growth of temporary agency services in a fast-moving hi-tech environment such as Silicon Valley is not unexpected. The knowledge characteristics of work in Silicon Valley would involve high levels of explicit knowledge regarding generic and leading edge technologies. As a percentage of any given firm's recruitment needs, demand for firm-specific knowledge would be low, compared with demand for high-level specialized skills. On the supply side, individuals would be motivated to hone their skills (and their incomes) in a variety of settings, thus motivating them to job-hop, but not necessarily to wish to market their own talents.

Such a scenario implies that firms would be either unwilling or unable to attract such workers into full-time employment. Flexihire would be inappropriate, since firm-specific knowledge is not the issue. Dependent contractors would be equally inappropriate, since firms are seeking access to high-end, up-to-date specialist knowledge, rather than longer-term dependent relationships. This leaves independent contractors or mediated services as the most likely options. In the fast-moving environment of Silicon Valley, temporary agencies capable of matching knowledge demand with knowledge supply currently seem to have the edge over other supply options.

The rapid increase noted earlier in the incidence of occupations with traditionally high knowledge levels now being handled by staffing services suggests that the Silicon Valley example is by no means exceptional. According to Carl Camden, Executive Vice-President Operations at Kelly Services, reputedly the largest supplier of legal professionals, the number of disciplines for which Kelly supplies workers is increasing by three or four each year. Camden says, 'there will soon be no position from the mailroom clerk to the CEO that we cannot supply from our free agent pool.'[14]

In summary, the stereotype of the traditional 'temp' as a female clerical worker is clearly out of date. Clerical temporary work, while still the largest component of temporary work, is only just ahead of low-skilled manufacturing temporary work and declining while the latter continues to grow. The ratio of female to male temporary agency workers is approaching 1 : 1. Meantime, although around 70 per cent of the temporary market still comprises low-skilled clerical and production work, the incidence of workers in traditionally high-skilled occupations such as lawyers, accountants, and IT professionals using temporary agencies is rapidly increasing.

Internet-based Recruitment

Electronic (largely Internet-based) services are being used increasingly by traditional temporary agencies as well as by newcomers to the staffing services industry. A cursory glance through the Internet sites of various agencies providing staffing services (a by no means exhaustive list) revealed the following types of service on offer, many from the same agencies:

Traditional Temporary
Temp-to-Full-Time
Contract to Hire
Staff Leasing
Contract Consulting
On-Site Management
Outsourcing
Government Contracting
National Marketing
Payroll Services
Human Resource Management

Services for candidates typically included: job fairs, job relocation assistance, career counselling, training, and advice on the tax and legal implications of self-employment. Other services also on offer included the traditional range of job search, candidate evaluations, profiling, and matching services conducted on behalf of firms and candidates. On-line databases are typically used to store advertised positions and job seekers' résumés. Increasing use is also being made of intelligent electronic agent software to search, filter, and match individuals' profiles to work opportunities.

The dramatic growth of Internet-based recruitment advertising and job-matching services is illustrated by the phenomenal growth of services such as the Monster Board, provided by TMP Interactive. The Monster Board, which provides a Web-based virtual marketspace for job advertisers and job seekers, recorded around 60 million visitors in 1998 and, according to Jeff Taylor, CEO TMP Interactive, expects to pass the 200 million mark by the year 2000. As the number of Internet users in the USA starts to exceed the nation's combined newspaper readership, the writing appears to be on the wall for print media recruitment advertising. Use of Internet-based staffing services is also likely to change the behaviour of both knowledge buyers and suppliers. Says Taylor: 'the whole job announcement strategy is going to go away.' According to Taylor, in future firms will not need to advertise positions, they will simply be able to search through the electronic résumés of job seekers, identifying the best match to their current needs. Individuals will leave their biographies on-line with services like Monster Board, updating them with details of lifetime experience and credentials achieved.[15]

Traditional staffing service providers, such as Adecco, are also making extensive use of the Internet and have made significant investments in their own proprietary systems for screening and matching candidates. According to Adecco CEO John Bowmer, while use of the Internet will grow, the major value provided by staffing services lies in their ability to screen and match candidates accurately to firms' requirements. Says Bowmer, 'the human resources function cannot possibly screen everything that comes in over the Net and so a lot of them put it back to us to check, because that's our job'.[16]

The Future of Staffing Services

The traditional image of the temporary agency is typically a small business catering for firms' peaks and troughs. Today's temporary agency is a long way from that stereotype. Major 'temp' agencies are multibillion-dollar global players offering an ever-widening range of services.

The word 'temporary' can be expected to fade progressively from the literature as permanent placements continue to decline in importance and as temporary agencies seek to develop their image as the 'natural' providers of staffing and associated human resource services. Adecco, now reputedly the world's largest 'temp' agency, plans to remove the word 'temporary' altogether from its literature. These trends reflect the emergence of mediated staff supply as a mainstream service: a direct alternative to employment by firms, particularly for those functions currently performed by firm employees in the peripheral group. Future growth trends forecast by the key players in the industry include specialization in supply of services such as candidate sourcing/job matching; employee leasing; sophisticated candidate screening services; and the provision of a widening range of non-wage benefit packages. Supply of professional, technical, and other more highly skilled staff is tipped to grow strongly, and the range of disciplines and corporate functions covered to continue to increase, until only the key associate and core groups in the firm remain as full-time employees.

Other factors causing an upsurge in demand for staffing services include reduced job tenure and the ageing of the population. Jobs that previously lasted twenty years are now lasting two or three. Today's worker is likely to work for five or even ten times as many firms as his or her parents did. The massive 'churn' effect caused by this phenomenon reinforces the appeal to firms of using external agencies to supply staff.

In 1900 one in twenty-five Americans was over 65; by 2040 according to some forecasts the figure will be one in four or five.[17] As the baby boomer generation starts to retire in the first decade of the twenty-first century, demand for goods and services for the elderly is forecast to skyrocket.[18] This demand is likely to fuel demand by firms and the elderly themselves for (mainly) service workers of all types, which in turn is likely to increase their use of staffing services.

Use of Internet-based and other IT-based services can be expected to replace many of the more labour-intensive functions provided by agencies and to fuel the growth of new services and new entrants to the industry. Since the technologies involved are commonly available, however, they seem unlikely to provide a source of sustainable competitive advantage for particular agencies over others. A degree of industry restructuring seems likely, though, as some agencies fail to recognize the competitive necessity of adopting new technologies and suffer the consequences.

Looking further ahead, electronic services could conceivably lead to the disintermediation of the staffing services industry itself and the establishment of open electronic markets where knowledge buyers and suppliers interact directly. According to one scenario, individuals would leave their résumés permanently on-line via their personal Web pages and firms would use sophisticated software agents to make contact directly with the knowledge suppliers most appropriate to their needs. Global electronic directory services, possibly provided by the multimedia conglomerates of the future, could assist the search process.

Such scenarios however tend to ignore the potential for staffing service providers themselves to take pre-emptive action, by constantly value-adding or even completely remaking their own services. It also assumes that firms would be prepared to reabsorb the task of identifying, screening, and recruiting staff which, for reasons discussed earlier, appears unlikely. Future electronic 'talent banks' and 'knowledge exchanges' will still need to be managed, which points to a continuing role for staffing services.

OUTSOURCING SERVICES

Outsourcing is the second major category of mediated service. Outsourcing invariably involves the hiring of people by the service supplier but the contractual relationship between the supplier and the firm is essentially concerned with the delivery of the *results* of productive activities, not the provision of staff as such. The terms commonly used to describe such services are *contracting out* and *outsourcing*. Either term may be used to refer to the provision of a service by an external supplier in substitution for a function, process, or collection of tasks formerly conducted by a firm using its own resources. Unfortunately they are both also used (particularly outsourcing) to refer to other bought-in services of various types, which may involve new or additive services as well as substitution of existing in-house functions. Both terms are also frequently used to describe what would be defined here as flexi-hire, or other services that do not involve functional substitution.

Despite, or perhaps because of, the 'fuzziness' of outsourcing as a concept, the term has permeated daily use. The media frequently report on the latest 'outsourcing deals'. Leading accounting, consulting, and IT firms regularly pronounce on the future of outsourcing. Large numbers of trees have been sacrificed in the production of reports and books on the subject, yet however interesting they may be, outsourcing remains ill defined and therefore difficult to measure. The rest of this section reviews some research findings which may shed some light on the incidence and characteristics of contracting out and outsourcing.

Evidence from Growth in Services Industries

According to the BLS, of the 14.3 million jobs 'added' to the US economy in total between 1988 and 1996, *business services* and *engineering and management services* generated 3.1 million jobs or 22 per cent of them. During this period, business services (including personnel supply/staffing services) grew by 18.3 per cent. Similarly business services hired about 44 per cent of all new helpers in the lower-skilled and most labour-intensive occupational grouping. Business services also accounted for over 1 in 3 systems analysts and over 8 out of 10 programmers recruited since 1983.[19]

As discussed earlier in this chapter, there is an obvious connection between the growth in services generally and the growth of outsourcing services. Shift-share analysis provides an insight into patterns of replacement. Table 5.1 illustrates the *increasing* share of certain occupations in business services and engineering and management services recorded in the USA between 1983 and 1995, in parallel with a *declining* share of the *same* occupations in other industries. A share index of more than 1 or less than 1 indicates faster or slower than average growth for that occupation in the selected industry than the average growth for the same occupation in other industries.

As can be seen from the chart, the strong growth in cleaning and building services in business services is paralleled by a lower than average growth rate in every other industry. This is consistent with often reported trends in the outsourcing of cleaning and building maintenance. Likewise more computer programmers were employed in business services than any other industry. This implies that growth in external programming services was far higher than that of in-house programming staff, which is consistent with reported trends in outsourcing of IS functions. Overall, occupational employment in business services grew faster in five out of the eight specific occupational groups and the 'other' category. These analyses strongly support the anecdotal evidence of strong growth in outsourcing and contracting out by firms, in parallel with growth in their use of staffing services.

An interesting aspect revealed by occupational shift-share analysis is that the increase in the percentage of occupations represented in business services, and to a lesser extent engineering and management services, has not only been at the expense of the goods-producing sector, but has occurred between industries in the services sector. In other words, services firms are themselves making increasing use of external services. These data provide further support to the contention that we are witnessing, not merely a shift from goods to services, but the externalization of work—irrespective of whether the work involves production of goods or services.

Table 5.1. *Wage and salary employment share indexes by industry division and occupational group, 1983–95*

Occupation	Administrative	Cleaning and building services occupations	Computer engineers scientists and systems analysts	Computer programmers	Engineering and science technicians	Engineers	Helpers, labourers, and material movers	Managerial and administrative	All other occupations
Business services	1.78	1.43	1.60	1.62	1.06	1.39	2.52	1.83	1.88
Engineering and management services	1.10	.64	1.68	1.25	1.48	1.36	1.00	1.51	1.03
Agriculture	1.29	.83	.15	.28	.52	1.96	.71	1.07	.89
Mining	.45	.54	.24	.46	.75	.53	.46	.45	.48
Construction	1.06	.48	.62	.55	1.33	.75	.97	1.36	1.00
Manufacturing[g]	.75	.59	1.01	.66	.93	.89	.80	.81	.78
Industrial machinery and equipment	.69	.54	1.40	.58	.82	.78	.91	.84	.78
Electronic and other electrical equipment, instruments, and related products	.66	.50	1.34	.57	.96	.86	.67	.80	.69
Transportation equipment	.70	.53	.87	.72	.84	.98	.94	.77	.81

Transportation and public utilities	.91	.89	.82	.70	.82	.84	1.15	.99	.98
Wholesale trade	.90	.75	.68	.63	1.16	1.56	.95	.89	.97
Retail trade	.94	.88	1.66	1.27	1.17	1.24	.96	.75	1.11
Finance, insurance, and real estate[a]	.93	.91	.82	.98	.80	1.13	.62	1.03	1.00
Depository and non-depository institutions	.82	.63	.66	.71	.70	1.26	.56	.74	1.02
Services, except business services and engineering and management	1.16	.98	1.03	.83	1.80	1.37	1.40	1.22	1.07
Health services	1.22	.85	1.16	1.07	1.02	1.30	.95	1.27	1.12
Government	.89	.97	.65	.76	.98	1.01	.91	.98	.92

Note. An occupational share index greater than 1 represents faster than average occupational growth; a value less than 1 represents slower than average growth.

[a] Includes other industries not shown separately.

Source. A. Clinton (1997), 'Flexible Labor: Restructuring the American Workforce', *Monthly Labor Review*, Washington: Bureau of Labor Statistics (Aug.): 10.

Contracting Out

According to the 1995 BLS survey of alternative forms of work arrangement in the USA, about 650,000 workers worked for contract companies at that time. Contract companies were defined as those which were used to provide a variety of services which client companies preferred to have performed by contract staff rather than in-house employees, i.e. they were outsourcing specialists. Services frequently contracted out were building security, cleaning, construction, and computer programming and systems analysis.

This study found that the profile of contract workers as defined differed from that of temporary agency workers in several respects. They tended, as may be expected, to have been engaged on the current assignment longer than the average temporary worker—1.1 years versus 0.3 years. They were also more likely to be male, white, and under 35 years of age, and better educated than their temporary counterparts. The largest single occupation was security guards (15 per cent) followed by construction trades and computer occupations (12 per cent each). A large percentage also worked in the public sector.[20]

In order to distinguish contracting companies from other service providers, the definition used in the BLS study required that to be classified as a contract company worker, individuals had to be assigned to work for only one customer at a time and that the work had to be done on the customer's premises. Identification was based on self-categorization by the workers involved, rather than by the firm to which they had been assigned. Due to these factors the 650,000 figure can be regarded as a conservative estimate.

IS Outsourcing

One of the most fertile markets for both contract staff hire and outsourcing has been firms' information systems (IS) functions. Estimates of the size of the IS outsourcing market vary considerably. In the UK the IS outsourcing spend for 1993 was estimated at £800 million, forecast to rise to £1.72 billion by 1998.[21] In the USA, IS outsourcing was forecast to grow from an estimated $US10 billion in 1991 to $US26.5 billion by 1997.[22] Other estimates generally are higher than these. According to some research, 20 per cent of Fortune 500 firms in the USA, for example, were expected to have signed IS outsourcing contracts by the end of 1994. According to other research, 50 per cent of all firms with annual IT budgets over $US5 million are either already outsourcing or actively considering it. This figure rises to 85 per cent among banking and finance firms.[23] In addition to the private sector, significant growth in IS outsourcing is coming from the public sector, with many national and local government bodies round the world hiving off their routine IS functions.

Some IS outsourcing companies are beginning to reconceptualize their businesses and to diversify. EDS, originally founded by Ross Perot and famous for concluding the (then) world's largest IS outsourcing contract with General Motors, has subsequently diversified into management consulting (A. T. Kearney), systems and technology services, business process management, and electronic business. Systems and technology services (mainly IS outsourcing) accounted for 83 per cent of EDS's 1997 revenues of nearly $US16 billion. The size of the global market for systems and technology services was estimated by EDS Vice-Chairman Gary Fernandes at $US320 billion in 1997 and growing at 8.3 per cent, suggesting a market of some $US477 billion by 2002. Says Fernandes, 'in fact, this market is so strong that we've introduced a high value-added outsourcing offering that we call CoSourcing Service'.[24] The concept of CoSourcing in the case of EDS appears to reflect an integration of its traditional and new services and a deepening involvement in the risks and rewards associated with delivering results to certain of its customers.

CSC, another large US-based IS outsourcing specialist with 1997 revenues of $US6.6 billion, has coined the term CSC Fusion™ to describe its methodology for aligning and merging business and IT strategies to derive results. Like EDS, the focus appears to be on moving from arm's-length functional outsourcing to a closer relationship with customers and to an increasingly diverse range of services and solutions, from large-scale consulting and project management work to customized services for healthcare, financial services, and other industry groups.[25]

As a generic strategy, the shift from 'arm's-length' functional outsourcing to a range of knowledge- and people-intensive services, and towards closer customer relationships, is consistent with the trends predicted earlier, of a growing convergence between supply of solutions and supply of people. Such trends also signal that outsourcing is becoming a more complex business, involving an ever-wider spectrum of knowledge domains and a mix of relational and transactional contracts with customers.

THE FUTURE OF MEDIATED SERVICES

The statistical evidence presented in this chapter shows that mediated services are in general growing strongly. Temporary agency services and employee leasing services are among the fastest growing (if not *the* fastest growing) of all business services. Temporary staff hire growth has totally eclipsed permanent placements, which are stagnant or declining, consistent with the predictions made earlier of a decline in full-time employment. Temporary hire is also growing significantly faster than direct hire of temporary staff by firms via flexihire—again in line with the predicted trend.

Employee leasing, in the USA in particular, has been adopted by some of the largest employers of low-skilled workforces. If this trend continues, employee leasing will become very big business indeed. Its long-term success however will obviously depend on being able to offer its acquired employees new career development paths, or the leasing industry will simply drown in its own labour.

Internet-based recruitment is taking off rapidly and beginning to replace current methods based on physical branch offices and press advertising. The recent $US330 million bid by US Internet recruitment specialist TMP Worldwide for Australian personnel company Morgan & Banks is a sign of things to come.[26]

Outsourcing, despite the problems of defining it as an industry, is clearly growing strongly. Based on the occupational shift-share analyses described above, its growth seems to be on a par with that of staffing services. In many ways its future looks even rosier than staffing services. This is because, as firms begin to rely more upon mediated services, they will seek economies of scale through contracting with one rather than multiple suppliers. It also seems likely that they will tend to favour services that provide outputs or solutions rather than merely inputs.

Outsourcing however is an inherently riskier business than staffing. Outsourcing specialists make their profits from the marginal advantages they possess over their customers in terms of knowledge, financial, and physical resources. Retaining these advantages in an era when knowledge is becoming the pre-eminent resource presents an ever-growing challenge. A second problem traditionally inherent in outsourcing contracts is the 'cost-minus' rather than the 'cost-plus' nature of many deals. Customers are generally well aware of the costs of their internal functions. Outsourcers are usually faced with the challenge of performing the same functions at lower cost.

In contrast, staffing has traditionally been a cost-plus business; firms have accepted the need to pay a premium for not having to recruit, train, manage, and motivate temporary staff. Staffing is also inherently a simpler business than outsourcing. The knowledge supplied in the shape of a temporary secretary or temporary crane driver is generally explicit; thus the firm is usually in a good position to identify any obvious knowledge deficiencies and to compensate for them from within its existing resources. In the case of outsourcing, such deficiencies may not be as obvious to the firm (or the outsourcing specialist), due to the complexity or scale of tasks being performed. When deficiencies are identified the firm is less likely to be in a position to compensate for them, particularly where complete functions are being outsourced, since it may lack the relevant in-house resources.

The move by some outsourcing providers to diversify their service portfolios raises further issues relating to knowledge acquisition and transfer. The failure of many diversification strategies by large firms in the 1960s and 1970s can be traced to their inability to acquire, and integrate within their existing businesses, the specialized and often tacit knowledge of the industries they were entering. Firms ignore issues of stickiness and absorptive capacity at their peril (see Chapter 1, also Chapter 8).

Finally, the tendency for some outsourcing providers to get even closer to their customers through undertaking joint projects suggests that effective and efficient knowledge transfer between the parties will become even more critical. Where this is explicitly recognized and mechanisms adopted to achieve it, the resultant 'partnership' may well be highly successful. The risk however is that the hoped-for synergies will be less than expected, leaving both parties in a complex relationship that is difficult to unravel.

A hierarchy of mediated services may emerge with the major staffing service providers and the major outsourcing specialists interposing themselves between the firm and other mediated service providers as master vendors or prime contractors. Whichever type of supplier takes on prime contract responsibility, it can be expected that it will itself outsource responsibility for the specialist functions which it does not normally provide. Anecdotal evidence suggests this trend is already becoming widespread among leading mediated services providers.

Looking further ahead it seems that most workers currently employed on the periphery of the firm will be more likely to move from direct employment straight to some form of mediated service provider, rather than to flexihire. The explosive growth of electronic agencies is indicative of a shift in this direction. This trend may be partly attributable to the reduction in knowledge specificity caused by automation and standardization (see Chapters 2 and 3). Overall the growth of mediated services is likely to have a continued downsizing and fragmenting effect on firms as they accept that many of their currently internalized functions can be better handled externally.

The growth of staffing and outsourcing suggests that, as predicted in Chapter 3, firms are beginning to switch from flexihire to mediated services— although flexihire can still be expected to grow. Mediated services can also be expected to encroach to a lesser extent on the independent contractors' market (see Fig. 5.3).

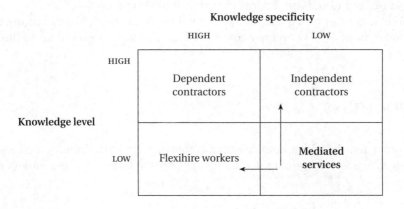

FIG. 5.3. Mediated services expand into new markets

SUMMARY

In summary, the future direction of the trends discussed in this chapter are seen as follows:

- Externally mediated supply of people and services will progressively replace the majority of flexihire-based employment.
- Permanent placements will continue to decline, both in absolute terms and as a percentage of labour hired via staffing services.
- Growth of the staffing service industry will result in greater market acceptance of employee leasing and similar schemes, which in turn will lead to further contracting out of workforce management.
- National/political barriers to staffing services will reduce as governments recognize the impracticability of preserving direct employment in the firm and as they seek to privatize public employment services.
- Internet-based services will progressively replace traditional methods based on physical agency branches and press advertising by firms and agencies.
- More sophisticated outsourcing deals can be anticipated, involving closer client–supplier relationships, greater diversity of knowledge, and more complex knowledge transfer processes. The risks and rewards inherent in such arrangements will be commensurately increased.
- The occupational composition of the mediated services market will continue to be dominated by low-skilled workers, mainly involved in clerical and production activities, but workers with higher skills will represent an increasing proportion of this market.
- Firms will increasingly demand results-based arrangements. This will tend to place larger suppliers at an advantage. Cooperation between outsourcing and staffing services providers is likely to increase.
- Workers employed on the periphery of the firm are more likely in future to move from direct employment to mediated services, rather than to flexihire.

IMPLICATIONS

The predicted shift from both full time employment and flexihire to mediated labour hire and outsourcing will affect the firm's stakeholders in a variety of ways.

Management

Issues for management will include determining when to hire staff, when to outsource, and how to avoid over-dependence on intermediaries. Where a total function can be effectively provided from an external source, as in the case of many non-core functions, then it will probably prove advantageous to outsource rather than hire staff. For many firms, for example, hiring individual maintenance, security, or cleaning staff has already proven less effective than contracting out the entire function. This is because firms are more interested in the *outputs* of such services (well-maintained, clean, secure premises) than their *inputs* (well-qualified, experienced maintenance, cleaning, or security personnel).

Rather than make decisions based solely on functional or operational attributes of systems or processes, however, firms will need to pay equal if not greater attention to their knowledge attributes. For example, a particular IS development project could demand low firm-specific knowledge, high levels of explicit knowledge which the firm happens not to possess, and be non-critical to the firm's operations. For such an application, outsourcing may be the best answer. Another IS project however may be similar in respect of knowledge specificity and knowledge levels, but its success or failure may be highly critical to the firm's operations. The best answer in this case may be a combination of externally sourced expert development staff working under the direction of in-house management.

Many projects of course may not be so easily categorized, implying much finer judgements. The key requirement for firms' management will be an ability to take decisions based on an assessment of all the knowledge factors which can be identified and measured. This process necessarily entails having a methodology in place to categorize and measure the value of knowledge in the firm (see Chapter 8).

The availability of ever more sophisticated staffing and outsourcing services as well as other externalized services will challenge firms to reinterpret and reconceptualize their core businesses. For some airlines, for example, outsourcing the provision and maintenance of aircraft could cause them to focus more on the customer experience involved in having a comfortable and entertaining journey.[27] The issue in all cases is to match the demands of the target market with the core knowledge and other resources of the firm. Again this brings us back to being able to identify and measure knowledge in the firm.

Workers

The majority of full-time employees on the periphery of the firm and those in flexihire arrangements will need to consider seeking work via temporary agencies or outsourcing service providers. Such workers will need to adjust to an 'assignment-driven' workstyle involving frequent changes of state between work, learning, and leisure. They will also need to acquire or develop higher levels of self-sufficiency involving self-organization and self-direction. Most of these issues imply acquisition of new or additional skills.

A critical issue for most workers will be the degree to which they depend upon any particular service provider to facilitate their career needs. Workers in such situations may regard themselves as free agents, but, as noted earlier, freedom is a relative term.

Career development needs will include not merely finding the next work assignment, but engaging in a continuous programme of learning. Many leading staffing services are now providing Internet-based educational courses and links to career counselling services to assist workers in these areas.

Other Stakeholders

Whilst individual workers will have to become more responsible for their own career development in future, trade unions, trade and professional associations, and the education sector all have a vested interest in the availability of a more highly skilled and flexible workforce. It can be expected that greater cooperation will occur in future between these other stakeholders, along with firms, intermediaries, and government bodies, to develop and link educational and labour market programmes. The development of industry-specific (rather than firm-specific) training and accreditation schemes will need to be high on the agenda for such programmes (see Chapter 10).

Apart from continuous learning programmes, workers will need access to financial, health, and other benefits programmes that are geared to a non-employment-based, 'free agent' workforce. Providers of such benefits today are unfortunately still geared to workers being full-time employed. Private housing finance for example is usually difficult for young first home buyers to obtain without proof of regular employment income. Similarly availability of insurance and a host of other services are often geared to workers spending a certain length of time with a particular employer. All this will have to change. Those service providers who are first to identify and match the needs of a free-wheeling, increasingly independent workforce will reap the benefits.

CONCLUSIONS

From one perspective, it would seem that the mediators of knowledge supply will tend to hold the balance of power in the new economy. The firm has, so to speak, been stripped down to the equivalent of a living brain, its life support systems only available to it through the good offices of (hopefully skilled) intermediaries. Out in the market are the providers of those life support systems, notionally free agents but actually dependent on the same intermediaries to hook them into the patient. In this rather uncomfortable scenario, intermediaries are the power brokers of the knowledge economy. While the prospect outlined may sound far fetched, it may not be so far away from reality. Service providers today dominate the world economy, increasingly mediating the supply of physical goods and services from producers to consumers. Why should this dominance not be increased even further in the knowledge economy?

An opposing scenario is suggested by the nature of technological progress. As we saw earlier, traditional (physical) staffing agencies are rapidly going electronic and some are making a financial killing in the process. The same technologies available to such agencies are however available, or soon will be, to the average citizen. The cost of providing all citizens with personal Web sites/résumés, and all firms with access to global directories and electronic search agents, is basically trivial. At that stage Internet-based staffing agencies could become redundant—electronic knowledge supply could be managed in the market. The same fate could befall outsourcing specialists as firms unpick the fabric of relationships binding them to their suppliers and adopt more selective sourcing strategies.

On balance, neither of these two rather extreme scenarios appears likely to eventuate. On the one hand, mediated knowledge supply is certainly poised to be a major global business. On the other hand, firms and individuals in the market will have access to the same explicit knowledge embodied in communications and information technologies. In the end, the market and knowledge will determine the winners and losers.

NOTES

1. A. Clinton (1997), 'Flexible Labor: Restructuring the American Workforce', *Monthly Labor Review*, Washington: Bureau of Labor Statistics (Aug.): 3–17.
2. National Association of Personnel Consultants (1996), 'Survey Results: Industry Activity and Revenues', Melbourne: RCSA.
3. M. Carnoy, M. Castells, and C. Benner (1997), 'Labor Markets and Employment in the Age of Flexibility: A Case Study of Silicon Valley', *International Labor Review*, 136/1 (Spring): 27–50.
4. Manpower Inc., 'Fourth quarter and Year-End 1997 Report', *http://www.manpower.com.*
5. R. L. Rose and M. du Bois (1996), 'Temporary-Help Firms Start New Game: Going Global', *Wall Street Journal Interactive Edition, http://wsj.com* (16 May).
6. NATSS (National Association of Temporary and Staffing Services) (1977), 'Temporary Help Services 1996 Performance Review', Alexandria, Va.: NATSS.
7. K. Purcell (1996), 'Employment Flexibility', in *Review of the Economy and Employment 1996/7: Labour Market Assessment*, Warwick: Institute for Employment Research, University of Warwick: 25–49.

8. F. Sly and D. Stillwell (1997), 'Temporary Workers in Great Britain', *Labour Market Trends*, London: Office for National Statistics (Sept.): 347–54.
9. NAPEO (National Association of Professional Employer Organizations) (1997), 'PEO Industry Information', Alexandria, Va.: NAPEO, Nov. (*http://www.podi.com/peo*).
10. NATSS, 'Temporary Help Services 1996 Performance Review'.
11. L. M. Segal and D. G. Sullivan (1995), 'The Temporary Labor Force', *Economic Perspectives*, Chicago: Federal Reserve Bank of Chicago (Jan.–Feb.): 2–18.
12. Clinton, 'Flexible Labor'.
13. Carnoy, Castells, and Benner, 'Labor Markets and Employment in the Age of Flexibility'.
14. Interview, 6 Jan. 1999. Camden reports that firms are becoming increasingly selective about the type of specialist knowledge they seek from staffing services: 'it used to be "send us a patent attorney" today it's "send us a patent attorney who is a specialist in computer hardware and who has filed patent applications in the area of disk drives". So instead of trying to retain the intellectual capital inside their own firms, they are aware that it resides in many places in a network of free agents and they look for us to bring to them sets of intellectual capital or knowledge from the workforce.'
15. Interview, 30 Dec. 1998. Taylor says: 'Monster Board is more than an advertising medium, it's a community, we provide the community where buyers and sellers interact.'
16. Interview, 12 Jan. 1999. Bowmer says: 'people are not like dollar bills, it's very easy to transfer money [electronically] because one dollar bill is like another, but people are unique . . . at the end of the day, clients will be much more likely to take a candidate sight unseen from us as we clearly have proven skills in screening, selection, and recruitment.'
17. P. G. Peterson (1996), 'Will America Grow up before it Grows Old', *Atlantic Monthly* (May): 55–86.
18. R. W. Judy and C. D'Amico (1997), *Workforce 2020: Work and Workers in the 21st Century*, Indianapolis: Hudson Institute Inc.
19. Clinton, 'Flexible Labor'.
20. S. R. Cohany (1996), 'Workers in Alternative Employment Arrangements', *Monthly Labor Review*, Washington: Bureau of Labor Statistics (Oct.): 31–45.
21. L. Willcocks, M. Lacity, and G. Fitzgerald (1995), 'Information Technology Outsourcing in Europe and the USA: Assessment Issues', *International Journal of Information Management*, 15/5: 333–51.
22. V. Grover, M. Cheon, and J. T. C. Teng (1994), 'An Evaluation of the Impact of Corporate Strategy and the Role of Information Technology on IS Functional Outsourcing', *European Journal of Information Systems*, 3/3: 179–90.
23. M. Johnson (1997), *Outsourcing . . . in Brief*, Oxford: Butterworth-Heinemann.
24. 'EDS: Past, Present, Future'. Address by EDS Vice-Chairman Gary Fernandes to the Goldman-Sachs Technology Conference, New York, 10 Feb. 1998. Fernandes says, 'CoSourcing brings together all of our offerings to help clients rapidly achieve competitive repositioning. It is our premier offering, and it's a joint endeavour that combines expertise from EDS, A. T. Kearney, and our clients.'
25. CSC Annual Report, *http://www.CSC.com/investor/annual_98/solutions/fusion.html*.
26. M. McGuire (1998), '$330m US bid for Morgan and Banks', *Australian*, 19 Aug: 25.
27. B. J. Pine II and J. H. Gilmore (1998), 'Welcome to the Experience Economy', *Harvard Business Review* (July–Aug.): 97–105.

Dependent Entrepreneurs

In the last two chapters we explored the rationale for firms' use of flexihire workers and mediated services. Critical factors involved in firms' selection of one or other type of supplier were seen to include the characteristics of the knowledge involved in the transaction, and the form in which the knowledge was to be supplied, i.e. as a human input or as a service/business solution.

The relational characteristics of each type of supply arrangement were also shown to be different insofar as flexihire workers are hired directly by firms, whereas individuals working for staffing or outsourcing providers enjoy a more distant relationship with the end users of their services. In practice, this situation has meant that flexihire workers have become highly dependent on their employers, whereas the relationship between a mediated service provider and its workers is more akin to that between a talent agency and the actors it represents. This chapter discusses a third major market for knowledge supply: the dependent contractors' market (see Fig. 6.1).

Dependent contractors, as described in Chapter 3, are, in the majority, self-employed individuals who are dependent on one or a few firms for their

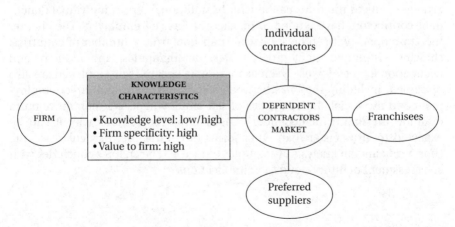

FIG. 6.1. The dependent contractors' market

income. Some micro firms and small businesses also fit within the dependent contractor definition. As shown in Fig. 6.1, the type of work likely to be handled by dependent contractors involves functions which are mission critical to the firm and require high levels of firm-specific knowledge, but which the firm does not wish to internalize, typically because of cost constraints, because the firm wishes to grow quickly, or because that knowledge does not fit with the core knowledge base of the firm.

The degree of risk associated with outsourcing such functions to external suppliers on a strictly arm's-length commercial basis is likely to be regarded by many firms as too great, given the damaging consequences for production inefficiencies, loss of quality, or unauthorized use of corporate knowledge. A further problem is likely to arise in relation to control of the firm's value chain. Once firms lose contact with the interfaces to their suppliers and customers, they may not be able to regain them. While firms may wish to distance themselves from suppliers or customers, they still need to maintain some links.

These factors imply that while firms will seek to benefit from externalizing the routine aspects of mission critical functions, it may not be readily obvious how to achieve this goal without losing strategic control. Flexihire arrangements are unlikely to represent a viable option, since such workers are unlikely to have the necessary skills or experience. While outsourcing or employee leasing may be the best answer for large-scale centralized production functions, decentralized production and distribution functions will demand a more flexible approach. Arm's-length relationships with independent suppliers would imply an unacceptable loss of control. Developing a *dependent* network of skilled, experienced contractors, however, may represent an attractive arrangement for firms seeking to leverage their knowledge assets and to grow, without incurring significant incremental costs or risks.

The purpose of this chapter is to analyse the characteristics of dependent contracting, and to explain how both firms and contractors can use such arrangements to their mutual benefit. In traditional terms, individual dependent contractors have tended to be classified as self-employed. The chapter therefore opens with some statistical snapshots from a number of countries, showing self-employment growth rates, demographics, and industry and occupational breakdowns. The reasons people become self-employed are also discussed, including the links between self-employment and direct employment and the social characteristics of self-employment. We then move on to examine the nature of dependent contracting, the reasons why it can be expected to grow faster than other forms of contracting, particularly in the short term, and an analysis of examples of its use. The chapter concludes with an assessment of future trends and implications.

SELF-EMPLOYMENT

The statistical definition of self-employment tends to vary somewhat between countries, but most commonly includes individuals in business on their own account, who organize their own work and own or control the means of its production. Home workers and on-call workers, whilst often classified separately, tend to include a high percentage of self-employed workers. Similarly, some part-time and temporary workers may also be self-employed.

Distinctions are sometimes made, as in the USA for example (see below), between those self-employed workers who have incorporated themselves and pay themselves a wage or salary and those who are unincorporated. Similarly distinctions are sometimes made between self-employed workers who contract out their services as consultants, freelance workers, or contractors, and those who are engaged in some other type of production activity such as farming, manufacturing, operating a shop or restaurant. Whilst acknowledging the distinctions involved, all of these classifications are assumed to be types of self-employment for the purpose of this overview.

Rates of Growth

Across the eighteen selected countries discussed earlier in relation to part-time and temporary employment trends, self-employment, excluding the farm sector which has traditionally had the highest incidence of self-employment, averaged 11.2 per cent of total employment in 1993, up from 10.3 per cent in 1973 (see Chapter 3).

Therefore, while self-employment grew more slowly in most countries than either part-time or temporary employment, it still represented a significant component of total non-regular employment. In Finland, Sweden, and Italy, self-employment actually grew faster than part-time employment. This may have been related to the strength of small independent business networks in Italy and government encouragement of small business development in Sweden and Finland over the period. In the UK, the rate of growth of self-employment appears to be increasing strongly, so much so that self-employment is expected to reach about 14 per cent of the workforce by 2001, compared to just 9 per cent in 1981.[1]

In the USA individuals in self-employment have traditionally been counted separately from those who have incorporated and pay themselves a wage or salary, the latter group being classified as wage and salary earners, rather than self-employed. Based on this definition and excluding the farm sector, self-employment grew from 6.7 per cent of the workforce in 1973 to 7.7 per cent in 1993. During approximately the same period, self-employment in the farm sector fell from 50.5 per cent to 43.3 per cent, reflecting the declining productivity of small-scale agriculture.

Adding self-incorporated businesses to the US totals for self-employment raises the figure for 1993 by about 3 per cent, giving a combined total of self-employment excluding the farm sector of approximately 10.7 per cent in 1993. A rapid increase occurred in business incorporations in the late 1980s and appears to have occurred again in the late 1990s, so self-employment from business incorporations may be increasing more rapidly than from individuals who decide to 'go it alone' without incorporating.

The growth profile of self-employment is broadly consistent with the model of externalized knowledge supply. The largest proportion of transactions in the firm have traditionally been those requiring the least knowledge. These transactions and associated functions have been the first to leave the firm, hence the early growth of flexihire and more recently mediated services.

Over the past decade, however, firms have started to move up the hierarchy, externalizing work that has traditionally involved higher levels of knowledge, but which does not fit into their core knowledge domains. Examples include legal, financial, IT, engineering, and other expertise which some firms have decided they only need on an occasional basis. Outside the areas of non-core scientific or professional expertise, firms have also flattened their hierarchies, removing the necessity for many middle management, whose role had been to monitor the workers under their control. Many middle managers and highly skilled specialists have, as a result, found themselves outside the firm. Self-employment for these workers has frequently proved the only viable option. The firm 'push factor' in self-employment has thus been a relatively recent phenomenon that may account for its slow early growth and its more recent growth spurt.

Demographics

Self-employment as a percentage of total employment tends to be mainly skewed towards older workers. In the USA in 1994, whereas only 2.5 per cent of individuals aged between 20 and 24 were self-employed, 9.2 per cent of those in the 35–44 age range, 14.2 per cent in the 55–64 age range, and 26 per cent of those aged 65 and older were self-employed. These figures exclude those in self-incorporated businesses. The reasons for the disproportionate percentage of older workers can be attributed to the effect of mid-career downsizings, lack of skills and financial resources among younger workers, and the tendency for some of those in retirement to start a second career.

In the EEC between 1983 and 1990 self-employment among women, including the farm sector, decreased as a percentage of total employment in Germany, Greece, Portugal, and Spain, but increased in all other countries, notably the Netherlands, the UK, and Italy. The decline in Greece, Portugal, and Spain may have been partially attributable to the overall decline in employment in the farm sector in those countries. In other countries the growth of female self-employment was predominantly in service industries.

Industry and Occupational Characteristics

Most of the growth in self-employment appears to have been in white-collar occupations in the services industries. Most of the decline has been in the farm sector for the reasons mentioned earlier. Outside the farm sector, home-based working, involving both directly employed and self-employed workers, is on the increase. According to an analysis of the US 1990 Population Census, published by the US Bureau of Labor Statistics, 20 million non-farm employees did some work at home in 1991, of whom 1.518 million worked entirely at home. Of the latter group, a high proportion (63 per cent) were self-employed. Over 70 per cent of all home-based workers were in service industries (mostly personal services), compared to 35.1 per cent for all workers. Managerial and professional speciality occupations were also more highly represented than for the average of all of those in employment (32.7 per cent versus 27.5 per cent). Women represented 67 per cent of all home-based workers.[2]

Self-employment has traditionally been associated with particular industries, such as the construction and engineering industry and more recently the IT industry. In the four largest towns in Silicon Valley, for example, the number of single employee business licences granted grew by 44 per cent between 1989 and 1995. This growth compares with an average growth rate of approximately 15 per cent for self-employment in the USA as a whole over the previous two decades.[3] The Silicon Valley example is also arguably characteristic of the microelectronics and IT industry worldwide and other hi-tech industries, where the culture of direct employment is not as strong as in more traditional industries and alternative forms of work arrangement are generally more prevalent.

Direct Employment and Self-employment

From a traditional economic perspective, lack of opportunities for direct employment has been seen as likely to stimulate self-employment. Immigrant groups of different cultural and racial origins have frequently been discriminated against when seeking direct employment, thus causing them to select self-employment. Many of these workers have succeeded in business despite having low levels of education. Their success, incidentally, is a reminder that high levels of explicit knowledge are not the only passport to being successfully self-employed. Tacit knowledge, often gained on the job, plus hard work have often compensated for more formally acquired skills.

Women reaching the so-called 'glass ceiling' of advancement within organizations may choose self-employment as an alternative. Older-age workers have traditionally found it more difficult than younger workers to obtain full-time direct employment and anecdotal evidence suggests that many of these workers have taken up self-employment as an alternative to part-time or casual work.

Table 6.1. *Motivations of New Zealand business founders*

Principal motivation	Previous study		1985–6		1990–1	
	No.	%	No.	%	No.	%
To make the most of a commercial opportunity	176	39	48	33	46	33
To give the founders their independence	153	34	46	32	37	26
To create wealth for the founders	46	10	25	17	19	14
To avoid unemployment or the threat of this	30	7	15	10	30	21
Other	43	10	11	8	8	6
TOTAL	448	100	145	100	140	100

Source: L. Lawrence and R. T. Hamilton, 'Unemployment and New Business Formation', *International Small Business Journal*, 15/3 (1997), 80. (Reproduced with permission.)

Table 6.2. *Unemployment and the decision to become self-employed*

Period	Number influenced by unemployment	%	NZ unemployment rate (%)[a]
1970–1	14	11	1.4
1975–6	30	20	2.1
1980–1	44	26	4.5
1985–6	40	31	6.8
1990–1	58	47	10.2

[a] The unemployment rates relate to the later of each pair of years. The rates for 1971 to 1986 were taken from the *New Zealand Official Yearbook*, 1990 (tables 12.1 and 12.6) and the 1991 rate was taken from the 1995 *Yearbook*, 322.

Source: L. Lawrence and R. T. Hamilton, 'Unemployment and New Business Formation', *International Small Business Journal*, 15/3 (1997), 80. (Reproduced with permission.)

Research in New Zealand into the motivations and aspirations of business founders points to a strong positive association between the decline in direct employment and the rate of self-employment in that country (see Tables 6.1 and 6.2).[4] According to this research, during 1970–1, when the New Zealand unemployment rate was a mere 1.4 per cent, only 11 per cent of those sampled gave unemployment as their main reason for being self-employed. In 1990–1, with the unemployment rate at 10.2 per cent, this figure had jumped to a staggering 47 per cent.

Another factor that has been shown to be positively associated with self-employment has been the availability of necessary resources, often obtained through business networks such as those in various European countries, e.g. Mondragon in Spain and Prato in Italy. Access to the necessary financial, human, and material inputs to start a business is generally a prerequisite for becoming self-employed.

The self-employed show a marked reluctance directly to employ others. Of the 10.4 million self-employed persons in the USA in early 1995 (excluding incorporated self-employed) only 21.4 per cent had any paid employees. Among the 2.2 million with employees, 33 per cent had only one employee and only 14 per cent had six or more employees. Of the 2.1 million who held second jobs in which they were self-employed, only 6.9 per cent hired employees.[5] Attempts by governments in the EEC and elsewhere to promote small business as a means to induce greater levels of direct employment thus appear to be based on a misconception. In the UK there has been reportedly 2 per cent growth since the 1980s in the number of small firms with employees, compared to an increase of 125 per cent in the number of self-employed without additional employees.[6] From this, one can also infer that many of the newly self-employed are dependent or independent contractors or freelance workers rather than traditional 'small business' operators such as restaurateurs and small manufacturers, who are more likely to require staff in addition to themselves in order to operate successfully.

Social Characteristics

Other factors often associated with self-employment include many of the elements noted above which, when interpreted in a social context, have been shown to give rise to greater levels of autonomy. New organizations are typically started by entrepreneurs who themselves have close networks of social relationships. Family support is probably one of the strongest factors involved in stimulating and sustaining levels of self-employment. Entrepreneurs have often been found to come from families where one or both of the parents were themselves self-employed. It is notable that the countries recording the largest percentages of self-employed in the EEC in 1990, Greece, Spain, Portugal, Italy, and Ireland, are also those with particularly strong traditions of family loyalty and family businesses—thus also family knowledge is of value to the budding entrepreneur.

Personal Characteristics

Characteristics of self-employed people have tended to be discussed in terms of personal, psychological development. Individual psychological traits long thought to be associated with self-employment, such as achievement orientation, independence, and willingness to take risks, have not stood up well, however, to empirical testing.

Research into factors influencing career choices, on the other hand, have yielded some relevant and interesting evidence, suggesting that early family experience, education and training, and workplace experience all influence entrepreneurial activity.[7] Studies of existing entrepreneurs have shown that many of them believed early encouragement to entrepreneurial activity shaped their future career choice. Empirical studies of business start-ups also show that those who have started one business are more likely to start another—an example of 'learning by doing'.

In the 1990s, the 'second career' entrepreneur has become far more common than hitherto. Some estimates indicate that up to one in six 'corporate cast-offs' in the USA choose to start up a business. Many of these are experienced workers at or near retirement age; others have been laid off in mid-corporate career.

For many such people, loss of full-time direct employment has been involuntary and, if not unexpected, has left little time for planning a career change. Interestingly, however, evidence from the USA (BLS 1995 survey) revealed a far more positive attitude among self-employed workers than any other group, with 80 per cent of independent contractors saying they preferred their workstyle, whereas the majority of on-call and temporary workers would have preferred more traditional work arrangements.[8] The level of satisfaction shown by the self-employed could be attributable to their generally higher levels of skill—as in the case of many retrenched middle management. Such workers may not have chosen to be self-employed but were well equipped to capitalize on their skills once they got over the initial shock of being externalized.

DEPENDENT CONTRACTING

Dependent contracting represents a style of self-employment that, from the supply side, is characterized by reliance on one or a few firms for income. For firms, it is characterized by relationships that offer greater influence than they would normally exercise in totally arm's-length trading relationships, e.g. with independent contractors or temporary agencies.

Dependent contracting is more likely to be the result of 'firm push' as opposed to 'market pull'. As a result it often characterizes relationships between firms and individuals who have recently become self-employed, after having left their previous employment involuntarily. Factors causing the growth of dependent contracting include:

- firms seeking to externalize strategically important functions through the use of externalized resources, in a way that preserves a high degree of control over the resources used;
- growth in the number of involuntarily externalized workers who cannot find alternative forms of direct or mediated employment and who lack the knowledge and other personal attributes required to operate self-sufficiently in a fully independent mode (probably the majority of workers);
- growth in the number of mature-aged workers who either cannot, or do not wish to, find alternative forms of direct employment, and/or who have some financial capital to invest and do not wish to risk it in a wholly independent venture;
- growth in the number of externalized workers who have knowledge that is more likely to generate returns if allied with other resources which firms are likely to have, e.g. knowledge of retailing.

The profile of the typical dependent contractor is likely to be a mature-aged person of above average education, with some business experience. Such an individual will also be reasonably self-sufficient and willing to invest significant personal resources (time and money) in acquiring the specific knowledge needed from the firm to create a semi-autonomous business. Firm specificity of knowledge thus can be seen to correlate with dependency on the firm by the worker who needs access to that knowledge (see Fig. 6.2).

Three rapidly growing and relatively distinct forms of dependent contracting include contracting in via leasing arrangements, franchising, and certain preferred supplier arrangements. Whilst many other hybrid organizational

		Supplier dependency on firm-specific knowledge	
		HIGH	LOW
Supplier knowledge level	HIGH	**Dependent contractors**	Independent contractors
	LOW	Flexihire workers	Mediated services

FIG. 6.2. Dependent contractors: knowledge level, firm specificity, and supplier dependency

forms are emerging, these three provide representative examples of dependent contracting and tend to illustrate how it differs from independent contracting and other forms of work arrangement.

Contracting-In/Leasing

Contracting-in arrangements involving leasing are becoming increasingly popular. The main principles of such arrangements typically include an agreement between a firm and a self-employed individual, or other small business, in which the firm leases or rents assets such as plant, equipment, or accommodation to the contractor and provides other services such as advertising and promotion. The contractor has rights to use of the assets and enjoys the benefit of the services to generate income, from which the leasing fees and other fees are paid to the firm.

An analysis of relationships between taxicab organizations and taxicab drivers by Peter Sherer provides a useful example of how contracting-in and leasing arrangements differ in the context of other types of work arrangement.[9] As Sherer points out, contracting in through leasing has been used in the taxicab industry since the seventeenth century. At that time the owners of horse-drawn hackney carriages contracted with 'hacks' (drivers), leasing them the vehicles for fees. To this day, the modern taxicab firm, the successor to the old hackney cab firm, operates along similar lines. Using agency theory, Sherer shows that whilst all taxi drivers drive cabs, three distinctly different forms of work arrangement may typically occur involving the cab driver and the taxicab organization.

- The first (and least common) form is direct employment, in which the driver is employed directly by the taxicab organization on an hourly wage, or a fixed wage plus commission. This represents a standard principal–agent agreement, in which the principal, the taxicab organization, has direct control over the activities of the agent (the taxicab driver). The taxicab organization owns all the property assets involved, controls all the decision rights, receives all the income, and pays the cab driver a wage or salary.
- The second form involves a 'contracting in via leasing' arrangement. In this relationship, the driver is not employed directly by the taxicab organization. His or her income derives solely from passenger fees, less a taxicab rental or leasing fee paid to the taxicab organization. Whilst the taxicab organization continues to own the taxicab, its rental or lease to the driver implies a transfer of usage rights. The driver also has the right to decide how best to operate the cab for business purposes within certain limits, implying a transfer of some decision rights. Finally the cab driver has the rights to any residual amount from hire fees which is left over after deduction of leasing fees. The cab driver in this case is both self-employed but also dependent on the taxicab organization for the use of the cab, for

radio leads, and for the promotional activity that the organization provides. This arrangement can be described as a 'quasi-agency'.

- A third common type of arrangement is one in which the driver owns the
  taxicab and simply pays a membership fee to the taxicab organization for
  a service which typically includes radio leads and advertising (of the
  organization). In this situation, the driver receives the residual from passenger fees, less membership fees paid to the taxicab organization. Both
  taxicab organization and cab driver are owners of their respective businesses. This type of work arrangement can be described as a 'mutual
  agency' since both the taxicab organization's owners and the owner of the
  taxicab are assumed to be both owners and operators, i.e. principals and
  agents.

Of the three arrangements described above, the first represents a classical
employment relationship and the second an example of dependent contracting. In the third case, despite the fact that both driver and taxicab organization
are owners of their own businesses and the driver owns the taxicab, there is
still a degree of dependence (albeit fairly weak) by the driver on the organization for radio leads and promotional services. These examples illustrate the
spectrum of dependency that can exist in dependent contracting. As supplier
dependency on firm-specific knowledge weakens, the relationship moves in
the direction of *independence* (see Chapter 7).

'Stores within stores' are another example of how dependent relationships
involving dependent contractors and larger businesses may be structured.
Traditionally large department stores have tended to be tightly integrated,
perceiving their strategic advantage as deriving from control of the value
chain from supplier to customer. Nowadays, with increasing competition, rising fixed overhead costs, and a buying public intent on obtaining 'the best
deal', the cost of such control has to be measured against the returns. In some
cases this has prompted department store owners to create shops within
stores, where floor-space is leased or rented out to self-employed individuals
or small businesses. The store management normally provide infrastructure
services, such as building maintenance and security and other value-added
services, such as marketing and promotion. Stores within shopping malls tend
to operate in a similar way.

From the lessor's perspective, such arrangements provide the opportunity
to obtain greater asset utilization, reduce costs, and achieve growth unhin-
dered by growing bureaucracy and management overheads. From the
contractor's perspective, such arrangements offer an opportunity for a fran-
chise-like arrangement without the up-front capital investment and personal
time commitment inherent in standard franchise arrangements. Such work
arrangements naturally have their limitations. On the demand side, where
high conformance to firm-specific standards is required, the flexibility advantages may be offset by disadvantages stemming from loss of control. On the
supply side, typical problems can include the costs of operation, inadequate

support by way of information or marketing assistance, or being placed in an unattractive location in the store or mall.

Apart from illustrating the nature of dependency, the above examples illustrate the benefits of knowledge interchange and uniting cash with knowledge. In the case of the taxicab organization, its major asset is its knowledge of how to organize and control a network of semi-autonomous cab drivers, plus specific knowledge of where and when cabs are required for hire. All cab drivers benefit from this firm-specific knowledge, but also contribute their own, highly specific and tacit knowledge of routes and how to get from (*a*) to (*b*) in the shortest time. The amount of financial capital each driver is prepared to invest then determines his or her level of financial independence. In the case of stores within stores, the centre management's major asset is its knowledge of how to create the right mix of retail operations, and to promote and manage the centre so as to attract the right clientele. All the individual store owners benefit from this knowledge as well as contributing their own specific knowledge of how best to operate their own speciality stores. The financial contribution of each store owner covers the infrastructure and other costs associated with centre management. In both these examples, it can be seen that the key to success is the knowledge contributed by each side, rather than merely the finance, since without such knowledge the financial contributions would be of little value. It can also be seen that dependency in the relationships is determined by which side holds the balance of power in terms of knowledge capital, not just physical or financial capital.

The Franchise Concept

The word franchise comes from Old French *franche* (f.) meaning free. To enfranchise later became associated with the granting of rights, such as the right to vote. The concept of a grant of rights is embodied in commercial franchise arrangements to this day. A franchisor owns the unique idea, name, specific processes, and specialist equipment and/or business system associated with a particular business, plus any goodwill associated with its prior marketing. These assets represent the intellectual property of the franchisor. A franchise is a licence granted by the franchisor to a franchisee, providing rights to use some or all of this intellectual property, usually in a designated territory. In return, the franchisee usually pays an initial licence fee to the franchisor, plus ongoing payments for goods and services received after the granting of the licence. The franchisee is responsible for any losses incurred in the operation of the franchise. A franchise arrangement may be similar in practice as noted earlier to a contracting-in arrangement, the differences typically relating to the requirement of most franchisors for payment of a franchise fee and for the franchisee to follow much more rigidly prescribed operational procedures.

Three broad types of franchise have evolved. Product franchises are those in which the franchisee is granted rights to exploit the franchisor's tradename and/or sell the franchisor's products. Many automobile dealerships, hardware stores, gas stations, and grocery chains operate in this way. The Body Shop, Granny May, Bumpa T Bumpa, and Shell Service Stations are international examples of product franchise operations. The second type of franchise involves the granting of rights to use a unique process or method developed by the franchisor. Examples include many industrial processes involving components and subassemblies. Coca-Cola and KFC are two global brands that are based on process franchises. The third and most common type of franchise is business format franchising, according to which the franchisor licenses the franchisee to conduct a business based on a defined set of principles, specifications, and procedures. Examples of business format franchises based on services range from personal services, such as hairdressing, maid services, lawn maintenance, and cleaning, through to a wide variety of specialist business services ranging from funeral parlours to real estate agencies. All three types of franchise share common principles and particular franchise agreements often incorporate features of more than one type.

The fact that all franchising must be based on some unique and usually secret knowledge that somehow must be transferred to the franchisee has clearly not prevented its growth. As noted earlier, tacit knowledge, once incorporated in a product, process, or system, can be transferred and used without the user needing to understand it fully. Thus procedures for operating a management consultancy practice, bottling a soft drink, selling perfume, or cooking a chicken do not need to include a *full* explanation of the thinking behind the procedures, or the *complete* formula for the ingredients involved. In this way, the core knowledge of the franchisor can be protected—just enough knowledge is transferred and no more.

Growth of Franchising

Franchising is 'big business'. Some commentators believe it could become the single largest form of organized business in the twenty-first century. In 1991 there were over 500,000 franchise outlets in the USA, generating over $US750 billion in annual retail sales. This represented one third of all US retail sales activity. By 1994, franchising employed over 8 million workers in the USA and was forecast to secure 50 per cent of all retail sales by the year 2000.[10] According to *Franchising* magazine, in 1996 worldwide sales averaged $US18.3 billion per country, a total of $US17.5 trillion. In the USA on each working day nine new franchises open on average every sixteen minutes.

Franchising has spread into manufacturing, as well as into services of practically every type. It is not restricted to any particular area of skill or knowledge. Lawnmowing franchises flourish, as do franchises to operate motor accessory stores and funeral parlours. What they all share is their dependency upon the specific knowledge of the franchisor, whether embodied in a business format, a process, or a product.

Scope of Franchising

Apart from external competition from other types of enterprise, constraints on the use of franchising are likely to be determined by at least three major internal characteristics. The first major requirement of a franchise is that it must involve processes that are replicable. Conducting orchestras, writing books, and playing tennis are types of activity which require knowledge which is not precisely replicable—each performance is different from the last and performance rules are not easily defined.

The second major requirement is that *sufficient* knowledge about the product, process, or business format is capable of being defined, transferred to, and properly absorbed (i.e. understood) by another party who may lack any specific knowledge related to the subject matter. These requirements indicate that appropriate applications would be those which are simple rather than complex, which can be conveyed in explicit terms, and for which there is a market which has the necessary 'absorptive' capacity—usually implying relevant past experience. Most adults for example would have had some experience of lawnmowing whereas fewer would be familiar with, or perhaps have the inclination to operate, a funeral parlour. This does not mean that franchising funeral parlour operations is infeasible, but that the market is naturally limited.

The third prerequisite for a viable franchise is that it must involve processes, procedures, or products which have been proven to be commercially successful in a similar commercial setting. This is perhaps the most important requirement for a franchisor seeking to gain market acceptance. Most business processes are replicable, most are capable of being defined and communicated to some audience however small, but far fewer are demonstrably proven commercial successes before they begin. Of course the 'catch-22' with this requirement is that a franchise by definition does not exist before it is launched and thus cannot have a track record as such. Nevertheless the fact remains that unless a closely similar business operation has been shown to operate successfully any franchise concept will (probably justifiably) be regarded with some suspicion.

Franchising is commonly used nowadays as a strategy for growth. Traditionally firms grew by acquiring more assets and employing more people. Apart from the implicit funding requirements, these policies implied the need for greater monitoring and control—hence more managers. Managerial capacity being a scarce resource it frequently became a significant factor inhibiting growth. A longitudinal study by Scott Shane based on 138 firms that first began to franchise in the USA in 1983 analysed the impact of franchising on firm growth and survival over a ten-year period.[11] The firms were derived from forty-nine 3IC codes (Standard Industrial Classifications) across five broad industry categories.

This study showed that the average mortality rate of new franchises was approximately the same as for any new business, i.e. survival in year one, followed by growth decline and then a tail-off. Approximately 75 per cent survived after three years, 43 per cent after five years, and 25 per cent survived at the end of ten years. Franchising however was shown to be a significantly faster method of growth than development of company-owned outlets. Significantly, the age of the firm starting the new franchise seemed to have little effect on its success, implying that prior business experience as such was not especially beneficial to operating a franchise business. This is consistent with the Knowledge Supply Model™ which suggests that, given the franchisor has a proven 'knowledge formula' and can transfer it, there is no reason why the relationship should not be fruitful. Franchise systems which sold the outlets to the franchisees also performed best, indicating the more the franchisee has at stake, the greater the probability of success.

Motivational Issues

Various analyses of franchisor motivation have been conducted. Motivational reasons given by firms who decide to become franchisors rather than to grow by more conventional means have included:

- ready access to financial capital (via up-front fees from the franchisee);
- ready access to human capital (franchisees);
- economies of production, coordination, and promotion;
- reduced chance of adverse selection (due to misrepresentation by franchise candidate) since the candidate is unlikely to benefit from such action;
- reduced chance of moral hazard (shirking by franchisee) since the franchisee is unlikely to penalize him- or herself by such action.

More fundamentally, it can be seen that franchising reflects the overriding importance of the knowledge contained in the product, process, or business format being franchised. Franchising enables the franchisor to concentrate on the core knowledge assets and activities of the firm and to devolve other functions outside the firm while maintaining requisite control. The relationship between the franchisee and the franchisor similarly typifies the use of proven and tacit knowledge, which the franchisee can deploy without needing fully to comprehend or control it. Franchising will become increasingly popular as more businesses begin to recognize that replication/reusability of knowledge is the key to profits, and learn how to communicate that knowledge without losing it.

Preferred Suppliers

In addition to contracting in via leasing and franchising, a third example of dependent self-employment is the use by firms of particular dependent contractors as preferred suppliers. Firms' experience of working with various contractors will inevitably lead to preferred supplier status being awarded to some over others. Other demand side reasons may include a desire to reduce apparent 'headcount' or to avoid the financial and other constraints of direct employment by dismissing, then rehiring ex-employees. Much media comment has been directed at this form of dependent contracting.

Recent studies in the UK book-publishing industry provide evidence of dependency among some self-employed workers, revealing that large numbers of editors and proof-readers, formerly employed in-house, had become self-employed 'freelancers' often working for their previous employers. These freelancers typically relied for over half their work on one client and for over 80 per cent on two main clients.[12] A subsequent case study by the same researchers, involving an analysis of the labour use strategies of fourteen UK book publishers, confirmed that the trend towards externalization was strongly influenced by employers' preferences. Among the older, more established publishing firms, these preferences appeared to be opportunistic rather than the result of conscious strategy. In contrast, the publishing firms in the study that had recently been formed indicated that they had been almost totally reliant on freelance labour from the outset, as part of a conscious policy not to employ people directly.

While the desires of firms to reduce costs and improve workforce flexibility are clearly factors driving firms to contract with preferred suppliers, it is by no means clear how significant such motivations are. The fact that editing and proof-reading, although important activities in book publishing, require knowledge which does not need to be retained in the publishing firms could be argued to have been the major influence underlying many decisions to use such suppliers. The fact that book publishers themselves may not have articulated this as the reason could equally be argued to have stemmed from the traditional 'lenses' through which they view their own industry.

Other factors associated with the use of preferred supplier arrangements can be the time-related benefits of 'early sourcing', a practice traditionally associated with Japanese manufacturing firms and now widely adopted by manufacturing organizations in the USA and other countries.[13] Typically, early sourcing entails firms exchanging information with suppliers at an early stage in the production cycle in order to design products which align better with the supplier's own core expertise and production capabilities. The main goals of such arrangements are to lower eventual product costs and improve product quality.

Early sourcing illustrates the value of dependent contracting as a way for firms to benefit from the specific knowledge of their suppliers, as well as vice versa.

SUMMARY

Far from the classical model of the business entrepreneur, today's self-employed individual is just as likely to be a corporate cast-off, a retiree with more years ahead of him or her than money in the bank, or a home-based worker. The rate of self-employment growth in the 1990s seems to have been more strongly affected by the forces of externalization than before, as shown by the growth in self-employment across *most* industry sectors. Much self-employment has clearly been the product of 'being pushed' rather than 'having jumped'. It is unsurprising therefore to find a new breed of self-employed individual emerging, one who is more cautious, more risk averse, willing to sacrifice autonomy for a better guarantee of return. In addition to the growing pool of 'reluctant' entrepreneurs there is also a growing pool of specialist and niche consultants who, for one reason or another, believe their best interests lie in combining their knowledge with that of other businesses rather than 'going it alone'.

In the short term, dependent contracting appears likely to grow most rapidly in industries with large physical branch networks, particularly those involved in retailing both goods and services, from banking to food and fashion. Some of the largest declines in occupational employment are also likely to occur in these areas as firms switch from physical to electronic mediation. Not all types of retail transaction are however as amenable to being conducted electronically as retail banking and, quite apart from technical feasibility, electronic commerce has some way to go before becoming accepted by the majority of consumers. The net result appears likely to be a period of several years during which the retail sector struggles with increasing internal labour costs, intensifying external competition, and an uncertain rate of technological adoption by the consumer. Three main options appear open to the firms involved: greater use of flexihire with its attendant problems of control; greater use of outsourcing and employee leasing arrangements; and schemes such as those described here, based on the organized use of dependent contractors.

Of the three major groups of externalized work arrangements, dependent contracting would appear to offer the average retailer of goods and services the greatest range of benefits. These include not only opportunities to improve liquidity and flexibility by externalizing physical and non-core human resources, but, importantly, the ability to concentrate on leveraging the value of the knowledge which represents the kernel of any retail operation. Of the three generic types of dependent self-employed discussed here, leasing out of retail facilities and franchising would appear the two most appropriate options.

For some other industries faced with the need to expand, the development of dependent networks of preferred subcontractors may also represent an attractive option. For organizations involved in the provision of services such

as building security, cleaning, and other routine administrative and maintenance functions, their own growth is more likely to be based upon use of
dependent contractors, rather than directly employed or agency-supplied
workers. Franchising would also represent an attractive option to those firms
that had developed a 'recipe for success'.

For manufacturers, the benefits of using dependent suppliers will typically
include streamlining design processes, improving production quality, and
reducing production costs. Such arrangements will also enable such firms to
avoid investing in vertical integration, since the benefits of knowledge access
can be gained without the costs and risks of investing in non-core knowledge
assets.

For the contractors involved, the loss of independence may be more than
outweighed by the benefits of preferred status. For both sides, the ultimate
benefits can be seen to consist in complementary exchanges involving firm-
specific, supplier-specific, and generic knowledge. The balance of power in
such cases however will tend to be maintained by the knowledge buyer rather
than the supplier.

For the dependent contractor, the attractions of a dependent relationship can
be expected to vary according to the characteristics of the contractor, the relationship with the particular firm involved, and the passage of time. Positive factors will include greater levels of guaranteed income, particularly in the short
term, reduced risk through reliance on the knowledge of the principal, and possibly greater scope to evaluate business risks and returns in advance of a major
personal commitment. Negative factors will include greater start-up capital
requirements (leasing or franchise fees), opportunistic behaviour by the principal, reduced independence, and restricted future earning power.

It can be inferred from the incidence of management layoffs that a significant percentage of mature-aged contractors nowadays are likely to have previous people and business management experience. These ex-management
employees are likely to be attracted to working as contractors for firms that
can make use of their particular skills and vice versa. As a result it can be
expected that more dependent contractors will start traditional small businesses, which grow through the acquisition of physical and human capital,
than is likely to be the case with independent contractors.

IMPLICATIONS

The evolution of dependent contracting can be traced to the need for firms to
externalize functions while maintaining a degree of control unachievable via
more conventional arm's-length contracting. In effect, dependent contracting
enables firms to leverage their specific knowledge and to access and integrate
knowledge outside their own boundaries. It also offers many of the benefits of
internalization but without the attendant costs and risks. Little wonder there-

fore that it is a rapidly growing phenomenon and that its future impact can only be guessed.

Management

The central issue for firms' management will involve determining how best to take advantage of dependent relationships with external self-employed individuals and small businesses. In order to determine this, firms will have to improve their internal systems to be able to define and model their knowledge resources. This will involve getting a clearer and more detailed view, not only of what the firm does, but of the knowledge it uses to do it, and the characteristics of that knowledge.

Knowledge modelling will be particularly relevant to firms' growth strategies. As physical assets decline in importance relative to knowledge assets, firms' opportunities for growth will change. Instead of opening physical branches and retail outlets, firms will need to grow by 'virtual replication', i.e. packaging and licensing their know-how to third parties who can absorb and complement it with their own knowledge. As earlier examples have shown, the opportunities for growth through franchising and similar schemes are significant, but fundamentally depend upon having replicable and transferable models of proven business formulas or products.

Having developed a replicable model, the firm will then need to decide how best to market it. The greater the degree of control required over the interface with the final consumer, the more the firm will need to extend its hierarchical influence through contractual relationships with its distributors. For example, a gardening franchise may provide a call centre service, plus advertising and procedural guidelines, to its franchisees, but leave the finer aspects of garden maintenance to them. Conversely, every detail of service in a McDonald's outlet is required to conform to a prespecified standard.

Workers

For workers, key issues include deciding whether they have the necessary resources (i.e. ability, experience, and/or cash), choosing between competing options, and managing the resultant business relationships. A risk many individuals are likely to run is dependency by default, i.e. being forced by circumstances to select a particular contractual arrangement without having an opportunity to analyse other options. As with all forms of externalization, a pre-emptive strategy is advisable, i.e. it is usually better to jump than to be pushed! To this end the development of a career plan, as outlined earlier, should provide the individual with a framework within which to analyse his or her skills and motivations and to research the range of external options available, including various contracting possibilities.

Lack of industry-specific knowledge and experience, particularly in relation to franchising, should not necessarily be a deterrent. Franchisors often tend to prefer experience gained outside their specific industry, since 'insiders' may have preconceived ideas and standards that clash with those of the franchisor. Knowledge of general business management principles and experience gained in some previous self-employed role are however desirable attributes, particularly where a personal financial investment is going to be required.

Once a business relationship is formed, whether involving contracting, franchising, or some similar arrangement, issues will typically resolve around communication and control. For the less fortunate, problems may start before the relationship is off the ground, due to misunderstandings or misrepresentations. As the relationship progresses, the contractor or franchisee may begin to suffer from inefficiencies caused by the other party over which he or she has no control. Success is also likely to be limited by the constraints implied in any dependent relationship. These are risks that can usually be identified in advance and ways around them may be found. For successful franchisees, the answer is often to purchase more franchise outlets. Reportedly the most successful franchise operation in the world today is Subway, providing sandwiches and salads through over 12,000 outlets. Approximately 140 new Subway franchise outlets open somewhere each month—significantly over 50 per cent of all new Subway franchises are awarded to *existing* franchisees.[14]

Government

Issues for governments will entail reducing their support for direct employment, switching the emphasis to self-employment, and incentivizing firms to grow through licensing and franchising arrangements. In particular, organizations in slow-growing industries should be incentivized to devolve control of their non-core operations and to use dependent contracting (among other strategies) as a way to achieve this.

R&D and export incentives need to be joined with other incentives for firms who can demonstrate both innovation and the ability to prove and replicate knowledge models of successful business operations. Arguably more work opportunities and more wealth are likely to be created in future by global licensing and franchising than by firms owning and operating location-specific physical assets.

CONCLUSIONS

Dependent contracting is an interesting phenomenon in several respects. First, it illustrates that there are degrees of freedom and personal autonomy in all externalized work arrangements. Dependent contractors might be described as 'quasi free-agents', who have traded a portion of their autonomy for the higher certainty of economic returns from the firms on which they depend.

Second, dependent contracting reduces firms' costs and risks in investing in their supply/distribution chains, while preserving a degree of hierarchical control. While such strategies could be described as meeting firms' flexibility objectives, they might be more accurately described as using firm knowledge in conjunction with financial and other assets to extend their influence beyond their boundaries. The key words here are knowledge and influence, rather than flexibility.

Third, the development of mutual trust and cooperation implicit in many dependent contracting arrangements suggests that despite the essentially transactional character of such arrangements, they may also take on some of the relational characteristics of employment in the firm.

The stigma attached to dependent contracting therefore needs to be removed. The perception that the firm's role is to employ people has led to the assumption that moves by firms to adopt dependent contracting arrangements are an abdication of responsibility. To level such criticism is to miss the point, such moves are neither good nor bad, but simply an inevitable response to market conditions. Firms would continue to employ workers on open-ended relational contracts if such practices were economically viable. The fact is that they are increasingly non-viable. The media, unions, and other influencers of public opinion will need to reflect these realities to the rest of society.

In the short to medium term, dependent self-employment appears set for rapid growth for the reasons outlined above. Looking further ahead, however, does it have a long-term future? The answer appears to be yes for some people and no for others. Undoubtedly just as part-time employment has suited many women with homes and families, so something less than total independence appears likely to suit many individuals who see their long-term interests best served by combining their knowledge with that of others. Equally there will be those who seek to pursue a more independent workstyle, as we will see in the next chapter.

NOTES

1. R. Wilson (1996), 'UK Labour Market Prospects', in *Review of the Economy and Employment 1996/7: Labour Market Assessment*, Warwick: Institute for Employment Research, University of Warwick: 1–23.

2. L. N. Edwards and E. Field-Hendrey (1996), 'Home-Based Workers: Data from the 1990 Census of Population'. *Monthly Labor Review*, Washington: Bureau of Labor Statistics (Nov.): 26–34.

3. M. Carnoy, M. Castells, and C. Benner (1997), 'Labour Markets and Employment Practices in the Age of Flexibility: A Case Study of Silicon Valley', *International Labor Review*, 136/1 (spring): 27–50.

4. L. Lawrence and R. T. Hamilton (1997), 'Unemployment and New Business Formation', *International Small Business Journal*, 15/3: 78–82.
5. J. E. Bregger (1996), 'Measuring Self-Employment in the United States', *Monthly Labor Review*, Washington: Bureau of Labor Statistics (Jan.–Feb.): 3–9.
6. C. Stanworth and J. Stanworth (1997), 'Managing an Externalised Workforce: Freelance Labour—Use in the U.K. Book Publishing Industry', *Industrial Relations Journal*, 28/1: 43–55.
7. D. W. Naffziger, J. S. Hornsby, and D. F. Kuratko (1994), 'Proposed Research Model of Entrepreneurial Motivation', *Entrepreneurship Theory and Practice* (spring): 29–42.
8. A. E. Polivka (1996), 'Into Contingent and Alternative Employment: By Choice?', *Monthly Labor Review*, Washington: Bureau of Labor Statistics (Oct.): 55–74.
9. P. D. Sherer (1996), 'Toward an Understanding of the Variety in Work Arrangements: The Organization and Labor Relationships Framework', in C. L. Cooper and D. M. Rousseau (eds.), *Trends in Organizational Behaviour*, iii, New York: John Wiley & Sons Ltd.: 99–120.
10. R. P. Dant (1995), 'Motivations for Franchising: Rhetoric versus Reality', *International Small Business Journal*, 14/1 (Oct.–Dec.): 10–32.
11. S. A. Shane (1996), 'Hybrid Organizational Arrangements and their Implications for Firm Growth and Survival: A Study of New Franchisors', *Academy of Management Journal*, 39/1: 216–34.
12. Stanworth and Stanworth, 'Managing an Externalised Workforce: Freelance Labour—Use in the U.K. Book Publishing Industry'.
13. G. Walker and L. Poppo (1994), 'Profit Centres, Single-Source Suppliers, and Transaction Costs', in T. J. Allen and M. S. Scott Morton (eds.), *Information Technology and the Corporation of the 1990's*, New York: Oxford University Press: 298–319.
14. A. Mayfield (1997), *A Guide to Franchising in Australia*, Sydney: HarperCollins.

7

Independent Entrepreneurs and Business Networks

As noted in the last chapter, the dynamics of externalization are changing traditional patterns of self-employment, leading to a spectrum of styles. At one end of the spectrum are self-employed individuals who have dependent relationships with one or a few firms and at the other, those who are inclined to chart a more independent career path. This chapter profiles the latter group: independent contractors (see Fig. 7.1).

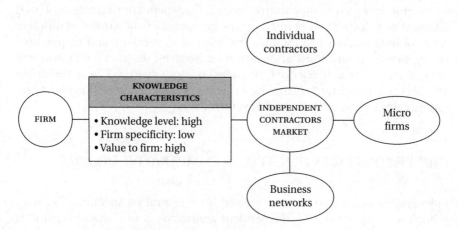

FIG. 7.1. The independent contractors' market

As shown in Fig. 7.1 the basic knowledge characteristics of independent contractors differ from those of dependent contractors in that they generally possess lower levels of firm-specific knowledge. For example, the average doctor, lawyer, engineer, accountant, or IT professional does not depend upon knowledge of specific clients in order to practise his or her profession. Such knowledge is of course necessary to address client-specific problems—a doctor cannot help a patient without patient-specific data, but the doctor is not reliant on any particular patient to operate a successful medical practice. This

Supplier dependency on firm-specific knowledge

		HIGH	LOW
Level of supplier knowledge	HIGH	Dependent contractors	Independent contractors
	LOW	Flexihire workers	Mediated services

FIG. 7.2. Independent contractors: knowledge level, firm specificity, and supplier dependency

example illustrates the fact that independence in contracting derives essentially from the knowledge self-sufficiency of the contractor (see Fig. 7.2).

The aim of this chapter is to describe the independent contractors' market and to discuss the evolution of different organizational structures. The chapter commences with a comparative profile of independent contractors. This is followed by a description of trends in the composition and growth of different styles of independent contracting. The value of networking and its potential emergence as a third form of organization between the traditional firm and the market is then discussed. The chapter concludes with a look at the future of independent contracting and the issues and opportunities it is likely to present to firms, contractors, and other stakeholders.

INDEPENDENT CONTRACTING: A COMPARATIVE PROFILE

Independent contracting can be viewed from several perspectives. From an economic perspective, the independent contractor is one whose income is ordinarily derived from multiple sources and is not normally dependent upon the maintenance of a relationship with one or a few specific clients. This does not imply that independent contractors do not at some time, typically at the start of their career, have to rely on some specific clients. It is rather a reflection of the style of their business operations when viewed over time.

From a contractual perspective, the independent contractor is typically involved in contracts with firms that are 'arm's length', explicit, transaction oriented, and measured by outputs or results, rather than inputs. This contrasts most strongly with direct employment contracts which tend to be relational, open ended, containing implicit promises on both sides, and measured largely by inputs. It also contrasts with the type of contracts entered into by dependent self-employed individuals and firms, which, whilst generally more explicit, transaction oriented, and output based than direct employment, tend to include a degree of control by the firm or reliance on the firm by the self-employed individual. Franchisees and sales agents for example may deal directly with the product market, but they are doing so wholly or partially on behalf of the principals they represent. In contrast, the independent self-employed builder, provider of garden maintenance services, or computer consultant is not restricted as to choice of market, geographic territory, method of operation, or standard of service, by reference to some prior agreement with another party.

From a knowledge-based perspective, an increasing proportion of work externalized by firms will involve knowledge and skills of a high order, but which are not related to the firms' day-to-day operations. Such work will typically include strategic advisory services such as legal, financial, and technical advice, specialist project services, and other niche speciality services which are infrequently required. Independent specialist contractors and small businesses are likely to be better qualified to provide such skills than the general market and to compete effectively with larger outsourced specialists, particularly where the independents' lower overhead structures provide a cost advantage.

Over three-quarters of those in self-employment in the West have no direct employees and, as noted earlier, self-employment without employees is growing much faster than small business growth generally. Within the self-employed category in general, therefore, the majority of work must, by definition, be based on personal exertion, since there are unlikely to be employees to undertake it (other than the owner operators themselves). The profile of dependent contracting as described in Chapter 6, however, suggests that although many dependent contractors will be involved in work based largely on personal exertion, others such as franchisees are much more likely to hire labour to assist them. As a result such enterprises are more likely to be incorporated and to develop into classical small businesses. In contrast, the profile of the typical independent contractor (incorporated or not) tends much more towards that of a consultant or freelance worker, trading mainly with personal exertion and personal intellectual capital, using few physical assets and employing few if any staff. This does not necessarily imply that such individuals will not eventually expand their business operations, but rather that business expansion will take different forms from those chosen by individuals who have a dependent relationship with one or a few firms and/or who employ others.

Like dependent contracting, much independent contracting in future is likely to be the result of individuals deciding to 'go it alone' after having left their previous employment involuntarily. 'Firm push' is therefore likely to play a role in causing such individuals to consider first independent self-employment. Thereafter, however, the direction they take will be less influenced by their past employer and more self-directed. This is because their level of reliance on any particular firm's body of knowledge will be low, and their own general level of knowledge will tend to be generally higher than that of other externalized groups. These and other characteristics typical of dependent and independent styles of contracting are shown in Table 7.1.

Table 7.1. *Characteristics of dependent and independent contractors*

Factor	Typical characteristics	
	Dependent contractors	Independent contractors
Knowledge characteristics	Knowledge level: medium/high Firm specificity: high Value to firm: high	Knowledge level: high Firm specificity: low Value to firm: high
Business structure	Owner operator Dependent contractor Franchisee or similar	Owner operator Independent contractor Small independent business
Relationship to other firms	Agent Quasi-agency	Principal Mutual agency
Relationship with product market	Constrained by relationships with major suppliers	Unconstrained
Business network structure	One to many	Many to many
Network relationships	Subordinate	Peer to peer
Bargaining power	Asymmetrical	Symmetrical
Current demographics	Predominantly older male Above average education	Predominantly male Tertiary education
Psychographics	Independent Self-sufficient High interpersonal skills Risk averse	Highly independent Highly self-sufficient Average interpersonal skills Risk tolerant
Growth potential	Relationship limited	Self-limited

STYLES OF INDEPENDENT CONTRACTING

Three distinct, although often complementary and overlapping, styles of independent contracting include individual contracting (i.e. by self-employed individuals), small and micro business operation, and small business networking. As with dependent contracting, various other examples could be given: however, these three styles illustrate broadly how independent contracting is evolving and how it differs from dependent contracting and other knowledge supply arrangements. The evidence presented here in relation to independent contracting once again strongly supports the validity of the Knowledge Supply Model™. It also provides some useful insights on market trends which we will discuss in the course of the chapter.

Individual Independent Contractors

The 1995 survey of contingent and alternative work arrangements by the US Bureau of Labor Statistics classified workers in alternative employment according to one of four employment arrangements: independent contractors, temporary help agency workers, contract company workers, and on-call workers.[1] The definition of independent contractors used by the BLS included independent consultants, independent contractors, and freelance workers but excluded business operators such as shop owners and restaurateurs.

According to this survey, the typical individual independent contractor was white, male, and middle aged or older. Less than a third of independent contractors were women. Just over 76 per cent of all independent contractors were aged 35 and over, compared to approximately 58 per cent of those in traditional work arrangements. Over 34 per cent had a college degree, approximately 5 per cent higher than the average for those in direct employment and 13–14 per cent higher respectively than those in temporary work or on-call work arrangements (flexihire). The majority of independent contractors were in skilled occupations, the most popular fields for men being managerial, skilled craft, and sales positions and for women services (mainly cleaners, child-care providers, and hairdressers), sales, and professional speciality occupations.

Over 40 per cent of independent contractors were engaged in services and a further 9.6 per cent in finance, insurance, or real estate, compared to 34.4 per cent and 6.4 per cent for the average of those in direct employment. Construction, an industry traditionally associated with independent contracting, accounted for a further 21.2 per cent of contractors. Wholesaling and retailing accounted for only 13.2 per cent compared to 21.4 per cent of the total of all those in direct employment. Very few independent contractors were involved in manufacturing, reflecting the higher capital investment and labour-intensive profile of most manufacturing operations. Over 75 per cent of all independent contractors were single owner operators without employees. Fewer than 6 per cent employed more than five employees.

Consistent with the earlier argument (see Chapter 4) that alternatives to direct employment are not necessarily 'bad', over 83 per cent of independent contractors said they preferred their workstyle to direct employment. Even more significantly, 96 per cent saw themselves continuing in employment through independent contracting.

Small Businesses

As might be expected, no standard definition of small business exists. Small and medium-sized enterprises (SMEs) is the term most commonly used nowadays to describe both small and medium-sized businesses. The basis of measurement is normally the number of employees, the usual demarcation between medium and large business being 500 employees. Across the OECD, using 499 employees as the cut-off point, SMEs represented 99 per cent of all firms in 1995.[2]

Among the G7 nations, significant variations exist in the definition of SMEs with cut-off points ranging from under 500 employees in Germany to under 200 in Italy. Japan uses a combination of capitalization and numbers of employees as criteria. The USA grades small business into very small (sub-20 employees), small (20–99 employees), and medium-sized (100–499). France defines SMEs as enterprises with 10–499 employees. The UK and Canada have no fixed definitions.

The European Observatory for SMEs divides enterprises into micro (0–9 employees), small (10–99), medium (100–499), and large (500-plus employees).[3] Based on this analysis, micro enterprises accounted for 32 per cent of the total employment in the twelve nations of the EU in 1990. Small enterprises accounted for a further 25 per cent, medium enterprises for 15 per cent, the balance of 28 per cent being accounted for by large enterprises employing over 500 workers. The micro enterprise sector, which by this defin-ition would have included the self-employed, accounted for 44 per cent of the total of employment in construction industries, 58 per cent of retail distribu-tion, and 49 per cent of personal services. All industry sectors recorded over 20 per cent of their total employment in the micro sector with the exceptions of extraction (7 per cent), manufacturing (15 per cent), and transport and com-munications (19 per cent).[4]

Net job creation (i.e. gross job creation less gross job losses) appears to be increasing slowly among micro and small firms, and stagnant or declining in firms with over 100 employees. In the USA, for example, based on the size of the firm at the beginning of the period, firms employing 30–99 employees achieved net job creation of 0.5 per cent between 1987 and 1992, whereas all firms with over 100 employees in 1987 recorded net job losses over the five years. The losses progressively increased with firm size, with firms employing over 1,500 workers recording the biggest fall over the five-year period, amounting to 2.8 per cent of those employed at the start of the period.

Over recent years, SMEs in general and micro and small businesses in par-ticular have accounted for both greater job volatility (job losses and job gains) and higher overall net job gains. Less than 50 per cent of SMEs survive for five years. Only about 5 per cent of SMEs are high-growth firms in terms of general business expansion and these high-growth firms account for most net job cre-ation. There is some suggestive evidence that the 'turbulence' caused by the rapid birth and death rates among very small firms is a positive factor in job creation—a case perhaps of the survival of the fittest benefiting the species.[5]

Anecdotal evidence suggests that more knowledge-intensive firms are less likely to grow by conventional means, including direct employment. Support for this notion is revealed in a recent survey of technical entrepreneurs in the UK. This survey involved thirty-eight small independently owned companies which had won awards under a government scheme for technological innovation. Only 37 per cent stated their intention was to grow by conventional means, with 47 per cent stating a reluctance to grow and the balance planning either to grow by strategic alliance or to sell the firm, or not having a strategy. Those that were planning to grow tended to be larger in size already and mainly led by entrepreneurs with a less technical and more market-oriented background.[6]

The fact that self-employment has for some time been growing much faster than any form of small business employment in the West tends to reinforce the view that the trend is firmly towards ever smaller enterprises. Evidence for this continues to grow.[7] Meantime, as the average size of firms reduces, country GDP continues to increase, a further indication of the declining relationship between size (when measured by employment) and productivity. Other related evidence includes the increases recorded in firms' use of intermediate inputs, with firms having 51–500 employees (the main contributors to GDP) tending to rely more heavily on external services than either smaller or larger firms. Since the services sector is dominated by SMEs, as noted earlier, this implies that much of the growth in the micro and small business area is likely to be due to growth in the provision of services contracted out by medium-sized enterprises. Again these trends are supportive of the argument that firms are becoming less reliant on employing labour and increasingly reliant on the services (thus knowledge) of external suppliers.

Business Networks

Somewhat paradoxically the very independence of the independent self-employed individual or small business is likely to be enhanced to the extent they can exploit the benefits of business 'networking'. Support from family and friends, communications involving peer groups in the same industry or profession, plus access to information and other necessary business resources through electronic and other channels, are all positive influences in sustaining and growing a small independent enterprise. The term 'networking' aptly typifies such communications and relationships.

Such business networks tend to exclude those based on the dominance of a particular organization, as is often the case in the *star* or *hub and spoke* models, characteristic of networks involving a single large corporation and its suppliers or distributors. The balance of power in these networks is usually asymmetrical and favours the corporation which controls the network. In contrast to this type of network, the nature of the relationship between the parties involved in small business networking can be characterized as *peer to peer*, i.e. broadly symmetrical in terms of power. Such networks tend to be organized on a communal basis, rather than controlled by one participant, as in the star or hub and spoke model. They are also typically designed to facilitate *many to many* transactions, i.e. so that all parties can communicate with each other.

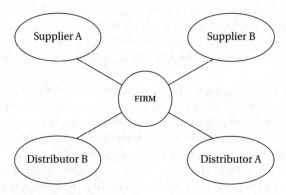

FIG. 7.3. Star, or hub and spoke

Critical success factors involved in business networking have been shown to include trust, informality, redundancy, commitment, and interdependency. Trust between non-associated individuals does not usually come naturally. It is significant that countries with high levels of small business networking are often also those with strong traditions of both family support (including the extended family) and community loyalty, such as in Spain, Italy, and many

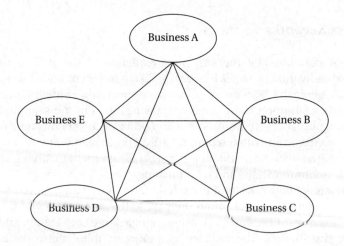

FIG. 7.4. Many to many

Asian countries. Across South-East Asia, reportedly around 6,000 Chinese 'clan networks' provide social and commercial support to their members.[8]

Informality has been shown to facilitate collaboration, much useful collaboration between businesses occurring at a personal, semi-social level, not at a formal level.[9] The use of electronic forums and chat sessions on networks, including the Internet, where individuals who have never communicated with each other before offer ideas, advice, and comment to each other, is a typical example of the value of informal networking. Anyone who has listened in to CB radio involving truck drivers or similar discussions between cab drivers will be familiar with the tendency of the networking medium to induce this type of casual cooperative behaviour.

Dense networks of relationships involving overlapping knowledge domains characterize successful business networks. Too much knowledge exchange appears better than too little. Since business networks tend to be organized along democratic lines rather than controlled by a single firm as in the hub and spoke model, an equal spread of commitment from the members is important. Lack of such commitment tends to be the main reason small business networks sometimes fail.

Firms also frequently collaborate in order to increase their collective market power. Small firms in particular tend to lack the market presence and leverage possessed by larger firms and the development of collaborative networks is often aimed at compensating for this deficiency.

Networking in the biotech industry provides a relevant example of shared commitment and interdependency.[10] Universities and research institutions have played a formative role in the development of the biotech industry since Crick and Watson first mapped DNA over forty years ago. Since that time, much of the ongoing theoretical research which started in academic laboratories has flowed on to be commercialized by the small biotech firms that blossomed in the early 1980s. Since that time also there has been a constant, mutually beneficial, interchange of knowledge between the academic and commercial inputs to the industry. The third major element, the pharmaceutical firms, faced with a constant need to replace drugs when patents ran out, recognized the biotechs as a fertile source of innovative products. In return they could provide cash, commercial knowledge, and ready markets. Thus academia, the small biotechs, and the large pharmaceutical firms have got together. Interdependency protects the collaborators from opportunism by each party and thereby reduces the need for monitoring and coordination costs. The greater the mutual benefits, the more likely that collaboration will be informal, self-organizing, and self-maintaining in the longer term.

Business networking has traditionally been based around physical concentrations of businesses in similar industries in a particular geographic area. Examples range from Silicon Valley in California to the McLaren Vale winemaking districts in Australia and the Prato region of Italy.

While much small business networking has developed spontaneously and tends to operate informally, the Prato regional network has more of the characteristics of a 'virtual organization'. This network was created by Massimo Menichetti in the early 1970s, after he had inherited a large textile mill. After three years of financial losses he decided to break the business up into eight functionally separate companies. He then sold 30 to 50 per cent of the stock in each company to key employees, allowing them to pay for the stock out of profits. So successful was this arrangement that many other textile mills in the Prato region followed Menichetti's example. As a result, by the late 1980s, there were over 15,000 small independent firms scattered across the Prato region with an average of only five employees each. While these firms competed with each other they also established cooperatives for purchasing, logistics, technological innovation, and other tasks where monopolistic practices or economies of scale offered benefits.

The total network is interconnected by *impannatori*, textile brokers or middlemen who act as the networks' links with customers, putting together orders and matching them to the resources of individual firms in the network. The *impannatori* have no equity in the individual firms and no one reports to them, but the system works. While the textile industry in the rest of Europe is declining, the Prato region has grown threefold.[11]

Cooperative business networking today can be seen to be taking new forms as electronic connections both augment physical linkages and provide new and different opportunities for collaboration and inter-working between participants, based on exchange of knowledge as well as physical goods.

KNOWLEDGE-BASED CHARACTERISTICS OF NETWORKING

Key factors influencing business collaboration, from a knowledge-based perspective, are knowledge integration, product knowledge linkages, uncertainty, and timing.[12] Knowledge protection may also be a critical factor in certain situations.

While such factors apply irrespective of the size of the firm involved, they are particularly relevant to independent contractors and small businesses, since knowledge in such enterprises tends to be more highly specialized and concentrated. As a result, the need for external linkages for both knowledge import and export will often be higher among individual contractors and small firms than among larger firms who can afford to maintain more internal resources. The following factors are therefore seen as particularly important to the creation and development of small business networks; however, their general relevance to other styles of enterprise is worth bearing in mind (see also Chapter 8).

Knowledge Integration

Tacit knowledge, as described earlier, can be best integrated within the firm. Tacit knowledge development, however, demands constant 'raw material input' in the form of access to explicit knowledge sources, many of which may be outside the firm. The establishment of inter-firm collaboration provides a mechanism for repeated explicit knowledge exchanges that avoid the need for multiple formal contracts. The protected nature of the relationship also enables more flexible, rapid, and open exchange of ideas and information and may reduce cash outlay, particularly where knowledge is flowing both ways.

In horizontal cooperative relationships of the type which often characterize small business networks, knowledge exchange is frequently ad hoc, informal, and designed to assist with problem solving. As small business networks develop, however, they must develop more formal channels for knowledge sharing and integration. In the Prato network mentioned earlier, the *impannatori* represent efficient conduits for matching specific know-how and production capabilities of many small firms to market demand. Knowledge is thus integrated outside the boundaries of specific firms to the benefit of the network community as a whole.

Product–Knowledge Congruence

Typically, a firm is unable to maintain perfect harmony between its knowledge base and its products. Its knowledge tends to exceed what is required for some products, but to be less than optimum for others. This imbalance implies simultaneous oversupply and undersupply—hence the need for external knowledge trading or bartering to achieve optimum efficiency. The greater the imbalance and the wider the scope of knowledge involved, the greater the potential need for collaborative relationships with other firms. This is one reason that firms need constantly to review their operations in order to maintain a balance between internalized and externalized functions. The examples of cooperation in the biotechnology industry and the Prato regional network noted earlier both reflect the value of networking as a means of optimizing the balance of knowledge between firms.

Uncertainty

A problem for any firm is 'knowing what it will need to know', i.e. predicting future knowledge requirements. Coupled with this, there usually exists uncertainty over how much to invest in knowledge for any given product or service development. Collaboration with other firms provides a way to mitigate these uncertainties and reduce risk of either over- or underinvestment in areas where payback is uncertain. As firms are required to innovate more frequently, this element of uncertainty by definition increases. Examples of collaboration due to uncertainty will thus occur more often in highly innovative industries, and empirical evidence from industries such as biotechnology and IT tends to confirm this.

Part of the problem of uncertainty in a fast-moving, highly innovative industry such as IT is that the industry as a whole is constantly moving forward into uncharted territory. Collaboration between IT firms is thus frequently shortlived. In the mid-1990s IBM, Apple, and Motorola pooled their expertise and production resources to create the PowerPC. When the product failed as a competitor to Windows 95/NT they joined the resource network dominated by Intel and Microsoft. More recently IBM, Sun, and Oracle formed a network alliance to develop the Network Computer as a future competitor to the Windows Intel platform.[13]

Timing

Timing issues, often associated with uncertainty, relate to the time necessary to acquire knowledge regarding products, pricing, markets, or whatever. Given market unpredictability, it is impossible for a firm to internalize sufficient knowledge to enable all events to be managed in the optimum time-frame. As the pace of competition increases and markets become more turbulent, timing pressures tend to increase in terms of both time to market and time to obtain a return on product investment. Collaboration between firms is frequently used as a means to reduce time to market as well as to reduce the risk and costs of overstocking and similar internal inefficiencies caused by poor timing decisions. Most of the examples mentioned above indicate that timing of knowledge acquisition has played a role in the development of network alliances.

Leaky Property

Knowledge has a habit of 'leaking'. Even patents, by definition designed to protect firm-specific knowledge, are required by law to indicate the nature of the knowledge that they are designed to protect. Thus firms learn from other firms' patents. Where a firm believes that it is unlikely to be able to retain sufficient control over its property rights to knowledge for long enough to earn an acceptable return, then there is a disincentive to invest in its development or protection. The availability of information and communications technologies increases the risk of knowledge being illegally copied and distributed. The likelihood is therefore that the incidence of leaky property will increase. One way to avoid this problem is for firms to collaborate. Collaboration can enable pooling of risk, reduction in investment, and the critical mass necessary to obtain an adequate return on investment before competitors gain access to the same knowledge.

Whereas large firms can surround themselves with legal and technical barriers to competition or expropriation of their intellectual assets, small firms and individuals are generally unable to afford such measures. Collaboration between independent contractors is therefore likely to offer them a measure of internal protection which they otherwise could not afford.

SUMMARY

The evolutionary trajectory of independent contracting suggests that far from the classic model of the small business entrepreneur, future knowledge entrepreneurs are likely to grow their businesses through cooperating with other resource owners rather than by seeking to employ them. Likewise, future small businesses appear likely to employ fewer people: to become *micro* rather than *medium*-sized enterprises. For those in the fast-growing knowledge-intensive industries such as IT and in the professions generally, self-employment is already more prevalent and business growth already occurs through loose groupings of associates or partnerships, rather than vertically organized business structures.

These trends suggest that business networking will increase to 'fill the gaps' in the inventories of knowledge and resources possessed by the individual contractors and micro enterprises of the future. Networks of individuals and small businesses are more likely to achieve economies of scale and scope, to compete with larger firms, and to survive financially through cooperation and collaboration. The term 'virtual organizations' has become popular as a way of describing collaborative networks such as these, where the relationships between the businesses involved provide a fluid organizational structure readily adaptable to the needs of the participants. A network of collaborating firms or individuals implies development of more than a series of bilateral arrangements; the system of interactivity between the firms or individuals may offer an attractive structure in situations where 'market-like' efficiency and flexibility need to be combined with 'firm-like' knowledge integration capabilities. Thus the small business network of the future can be conceived of as a potential third form of organization—somewhere between the market and the firm.

In summary, major factors likely to shape the future growth of independent contracting are viewed as follows:

- externalization of workers (mainly from the associate group) with specialist knowledge which is not required for the firm's day-to-day operations, but which may be required on an occasional basis;
- increasing numbers of workers with specialist knowledge already in temporary or fixed contract arrangements (flexihire), usually with their ex-employers, who subsequently seek to reduce their dependence on the ex-employer as a single source of work;
- increasing demand for the supply of external services involving high levels of specialist knowledge, by both end user firms and suppliers of outsourced services;

- the 'demassification' of business activities mentioned in Chapter 1, reducing the need for individuals to work collectively at the same physical location;
- reduced dependency by knowledge specialists on physical premises, plant, equipment, or employees, which will continue to reduce both start-up costs and the average size of small independent businesses;
- declining costs of electronic access to global markets, in line with current trends in telecommunications, thus opening up more growth opportunities for small-scale knowledge-intensive services;
- reducing demand for low-skilled occupations, forcing workers to acquire new skills and to become better equipped in the process to work in an independent mode;
- the attraction of business networking as a means of preserving contractors' independence, while offering them opportunities to benefit through knowledge protection, informal knowledge transfer, and collaboration.

IMPLICATIONS

The growth of individual independent contractors, small and micro businesses, and networks poses a variety of issues for the various stakeholders.

The Evolution of Business Networking

Independent contractors today need to develop knowledge-centred enterprises without having to accommodate the traditional baggage of physical assets, employees, and debt. One route to achieving this is through the medium of business networking, which, as we have seen, can combine many of the benefits of the firm with the flexibility of the market.

The problem is that business networking is still an evolving organizational form. Traditionally, independent business networks have developed around regional concentrations or clusters of firms, usually in the same or similar industries. Access to such networks is generally limited to businesses in the same geographic area. Other traditional networks based on kinship, shared cultural beliefs, or the old school tie tend to be closed to 'outsiders'.

The Internet offers an obvious medium for developing business networking. To date, however, most of the electronic communities which have emerged have been limited to informal knowledge sharing, rather than knowledge trading and the development of cohesive business communities.

A further problem for independent contractors wishing to develop such business communities is that creating a network tends to be a sunk cost. As a result, the original 'network entrepreneurs' may find themselves disadvantaged while those last to join the network will generally get the best deal.

Governments in future may have to play a greater role in facilitating network start-ups (see comments below).

The disaggregation of large firms into multiple smaller firms, as happened in the case of the Prato regional network, may eventually prove the key to the successful development of independent business networks. Many large firms are adopting decentralized semi-autonomous structures (see Chapter 8). The first stage in the evolution of such structures is likely to involve dependency by the externalized suppliers on the firm. Progressively however (as in the Prato example) the networks themselves may tend to replace the firm as an organizing and coordinating mechanism. In such cases, 'many to one' dependence will be replaced by 'many to many' interdependence.

Developing Niche Knowledge Strategies

Conventional niche business strategies are based on the concept that small businesses can best survive by filling weaknesses or gaps in industry value systems and other firms' value chains. As business success in future will depend increasingly on their knowledge, as distinct from other resources, niche strategies will similarly have to reflect the unique knowledge capability of the individual. In a sense, the playing field will be levelled. The difference between the (large) firms and self-employed individuals will now be more a function of how well the firm can integrate multiple, disparate sources of knowledge, versus how well the individual can use his or her individual skills, either alone or through networking with other independent businesses.

Two advantages the individual is likely to possess over the larger firm are likely to be the ability to deploy tacit knowledge more effectively and the ability to respond more specifically to individual customer needs. An example of the former advantage, as mentioned earlier, is the skills possessed by artists, craft workers, sports people, entertainers, designers, and others with individual creative talent. Such knowledge tends to be 'sticky', i.e. difficult to explain and hard for others to understand and absorb, posing problems when it needs to be shared with co-workers, but a positive advantage when used to compete as an individual supplier in the market. Creative ability however is not the only knowledge advantage which individuals can be expected to possess over groups/firms. The second major potential advantage is their ability to develop unique relationships with customers. The small owner operator who is prepared to visit a client to offer (say) a customized tailoring, cleaning, personal tuition, or other personal service is likely to have an advantage over larger suppliers who cannot offer the same level of individualized attention. A similar advantage is available to the craft worker who can design and build custom artefacts for clients.

Tacit knowledge and individualized service together represent the natural advantages individual owner operators possess over the combined resources of firms. In future, it seems likely that market demand will increase for such capabilities, as consumers become aware that they may be able to obtain better value from dealing direct with individual owner operators.

Shifting the Focus of Government Support

The growth in self-employment, micro business, and business networking poses a variety of challenges for policy makers and regulators.

The notion that small and medium-sized enterprises (particularly the latter) are the engines of economic growth and employment no longer accords with the facts. The source of growth in the economy is moving down the scale, from medium to small/micro and progressively towards the individual. Yet currently, businesses need to have reached a certain size, usually measured by employees, to attract much government support. This needs to change; governments need to refocus their support to the individual and to acknowledge that independent self-employment needs fostering *more* than direct employment of individuals by firms.

More funding needs to be provided for entrepreneurship at the individual level. Unfortunately the sins of major corporations in the 'roaring eighties' led to a tarnished image for entrepreneurs. Nowadays the sons and daughters of former entrepreneurs are, as a result, hoping that their educational qualifications will find them a secure, long-term future in some large 'safe' bureaucracy. The climate for risk takers is not auspicious. A greater premium therefore needs to be placed by governments on creation of a knowledgeable, risk-taking working class. Measures to assist this will need to include changes to educational priorities and incentives to bankers and venture capitalists to back start-ups.

Innovation has traditionally been associated with larger firms, who have the financial and other resources needed to sustain R&D. This accords with innovation theories based on those of Schumpeter (referred to in Chapter 2). As a result, much government R&D funding has found its way into medium to large organizations. In the knowledge economy, however, much good R&D is likely to be performed in the garage as well as in the laboratory. IBM may have created the first commercial personal computer, but it took a myriad of individuals and small firms (including Microsoft) to make it a success. Dell computer, one of today's leading hi-tech stocks, started in a college dormitory!

The examples mentioned earlier of the reluctance of leading hi-tech entrepreneurs and innovators to grow by conventional means should ring alarm bells in the corridors of power. Such organizations need assistance to do what they do well, stay small, and innovate. Instead, they are likely to be ignored, while the non-technical entrepreneurs, typically larger, more labour-intensive firms, will continue to receive the bulk of government endorsement and support. The irony is that without the technical entrepreneur, these downstream commercialization specialists would probably lack local products to sell—and would therefore import them from overseas, thus defeating schemes aimed at improving local innovation.

While the 'turbulence' associated with high mortality rates among small businesses may have a stimulating effect on the economy, it is also clearly wasteful. Assistance needs to be provided for independent owner operators and micro firms to survive, underpinned outside the USA perhaps by a similar system to the American 'Chapter 11', which enables struggling companies to trade out of difficulties rather than be bankrupted and their employees and suppliers abandoned. Mentoring schemes, involving well-qualified and experienced retirees assisting entrepreneurs with business planning and guidance, could also be used to better effect and on a broader scale, given more government support.

Business networking, as noted earlier, requires the development of appropriate infrastructure, which, because it implies a sunk cost, represents a problem for individuals and micro firms. Creating science and technology parks and inviting small firms to join in such regional clusters tends to figure prominently in regional government policies, in part at least because such initiatives are seen to be generators of local jobs. In future, assistance with networking needs to be brought down to the level of individuals, who typically cannot afford the investment necessary to move to such locations. It also needs to recognize the changing nature of the infrastructure required. Business networking in the knowledge economy will need to be global as well as local and to be highly flexible, allowing both more open and more casual alliances to flourish. As a result, many science and technology parks may in future stand empty. Investment in improving the information infrastructures required for virtual business networking will probably produce a better long-term payback. Improving access to the Internet and offering incentives and assistance to individuals to create electronic business communities are obvious priorities. Significantly much of this improvement in infrastructure should serve a dual purpose—learning networks and business networks have a lot in common (see Chapter 10).

Other Stakeholders

Industry bodies, including unions and trade associations, need to recognize the growth of self-employment as the 'writing on the wall', spelling their irrelevance, if they do not support individual as well as collective labour. Unions in particular are a dying breed, because they are still fighting the battles of a bygone *industrial era*, rather than preparing for the *knowledge era*. Instead of seeing their role as slowing down the inevitable process of externalization of work, unions need to switch their energies to improving the future lot of independent workers by counselling, skills enhancement, and, where required, assisting their members' transition to fully independent status.

Big business, despite its interest in creating dependent networks of suppliers and distributors, also has a vested interest in the availability of expert independent contractors. These are the suppliers of niche skills and specialist knowledge, which big business occasionally requires, but does not need to control, because the knowledge involved is not central to its routine operations. Contributing to industry assistance schemes for entrepreneurship, sponsoring R&D and innovation awards, and backing 'intrepreneurs' who wish to become 'entrepreneurs' are among the many ways they can assist the growth of the independent contractors' market. Venture capital to assist knowledge-intensive and hi-tech start-ups also needs to become more readily available outside its traditional home: the USA.

This chapter marks the end of our brief tour through the fast-changing world of externalized knowledge supply. We now switch focus once again, to explore how the forces of change are redefining the institution at the centre of the Knowledge Revolution: the firm.

NOTES

1. S. R. Cohany (1996), 'Workers in Alternative Employment Arrangements', *Monthly Labor Review*, Washington: Bureau of Labor Statistics (Oct.): 31–45.
2. OECD (Organization for Economic Co-operation and Development) (1996), *Technology Productivity and Job Creation*, ii: *Analytical Report*, Paris: OECD: 178.
3. European Observatory for SMEs (1994), *Second Annual Report*, Zoetermeer: EIM Small Business Research and Consultancy.
4. OECD, *Technology Productivity and Job Creation*, 233.
5. Ibid. 208.
6. D. Jones-Evans (1996), 'Technical Entrepreneurship, Strategy and Experience', *International Small Business Journal*, 14/3: 15–39.
7. 'New Research: Small Firms' Job Growth Reviewed' (1997), *Labour Market Trends*, London: Office for National Statistics (Feb.): 31.
8. J. Naisbitt (1996), *Megatrends Asia*, London: Nicholas Brealey Publishing Ltd.
9. S. Schrader (1991), 'Informal Technology Transfer between Firms: Co-operation through Information Trading', *Research Policy*, 20: 153–70.
10. W. W. Powell (1996), 'Inter-organizational Collaboration in the Biotechnology Industry', *Journal of Institutional and Theoretical Economics*, 152: 197–225.
11. H. Voss (1996), 'Virtual Organizations: The Future is Now', *Strategy and Leadership* (July/Aug.): 12–16.
12. R. Grant and C. Baden-Fuller (1995), 'A Knowledge-Based Theory of Inter-firm Collaboration', *Academy of Management Best Papers Proceedings*: 17–21.
13. N. Venkatraman and J. C. Henderson (1998), 'Real Strategies for Virtual Organizing', *Sloan Management Review* (fall): 33–48.

PART III

THE KNOWLEDGE-BASED FIRM

Knowledge itself is power.
  (Francis Bacon (1561–1626), *Religious Meditations*)

8

Redefining the Firm

The same techno-economic forces that are driving the externalization of non-core functions and processes from the firm are responsible for the parallel internalization, i.e. refinement and concentration, of core functions within the firm. Previous chapters have described how externalization is leading to a greater variety of supply arrangements between the firm and providers of external services, ranging from flexihire, to independently mediated services, and to dependent and independent contracting. This chapter looks in the opposite direction, at how the forces of externalization and internalization are redefining the firm, in terms of its size, functions, organization, management, and internal incentives and reward systems.

The chapter opens with an analysis of how the firm is becoming physically smaller, but intellectually larger, as it reorganizes its use of externalized and internalized resources. We then move on to examine how the concept of the firm as an institution for integrating knowledge fits well with recent theories regarding models of thinking (cognition), which view the firm as an organism that exhibits learning and self-organization. The focus then shifts to examine how the changing profile of the firm is likely to shape the future role of management. This is followed by a discussion of the need for an overhaul of traditional corporate incentives and reward systems. A 'Knowledge Growth Model^{TM}' of the firm is then presented. This model defines a number of generic stages that the firm is predicted to pass through as it develops into a more highly knowledge-centred institution. The chapter ends with a summary of the predicted effects of internalization and externalization on the firm and discusses the implications for its major stakeholders.

REDEFINING 'SIZE'

As they say, 'it's the size of the fight in the dog that counts, not the size of the dog in the fight!' The same applies to the firm; as the firm begins to focus on its key knowledge assets, its ability to innovate, produce, market, and deliver will be enhanced. Externalization, the process of shedding excess corporate 'mass', is part of the transformation of the firm into a physically slimmer but mentally smarter institution, better able to compete in the global market place.

As firms reduce in physical size, they naturally need less physical infrastructure, such as office space and equipment. As noted earlier, some 20 million Americans already perform some work from home. In the UK in 1995, 29 per cent of employed men and 24 per cent of employed women worked from home at least sometimes.[1] This was the highest rate of homeworking of any EU country, but the trend towards home-based work and teleworking is also growing throughout the West, particularly in the services sector. Fewer office desks mean smaller offices, fewer facsimile machines and telephones, fewer company cars, and fewer office supervisors. Firms are already making greater use of workers' personal resources, such as home offices, computers, and cars, thus reinforcing the tendency for them to view workers as suppliers rather than their 'employees'. A reduction in the scale of physical resources in the firm also implies a switch from capital to expense investment and from fixed to variable cost structures. Firms as a result should become not only physically smaller, but also financially more 'agile'—better able to change course or take advantage of market opportunities.

The declining importance of firms' physical assets and employee numbers is starkly illustrated by the soaring share prices of Microsoft, Netscape, Yahoo, and Amazon.com—all firms with relatively small numbers of employees, and few fixed assets. Microsoft's $US9 billion in sales and $US10 billion in assets gave it a modest 172nd place on the Fortune 500 list for 1996. Nevertheless, despite the fact that it had only 5 per cent of the sales and assets of the industrial giant General Motors, the market value of Microsoft in early 1997 was $US170 billion against GM's $US50 billion.[2]

Externalization does not only imply reductions in excess physical 'baggage' but also reductions in knowledge and skills which do not fit with the core body of knowledge of the firm. Achieving the optimum balance between what the firm knows and what it needs to know at any one time is the knowledge equivalent of cashflow management. Too much and the knowledge is sitting idle, not earning a return. Too little and the firm has a 'knowledge flow' problem. Knowing which knowledge resources to externalize and which to internalize will be critical. The Knowledge Supply Model™, as discussed earlier, provides a basic framework to assist firms in making such decisions and determining the most appropriate sources of supply, from both outside and within the firm.

Thinking Big—Acting Small

While firms in the knowledge economy will generally become slimmer and smarter, technological erosion of industry and geographic boundaries mentioned earlier (see Chapter 1) implies that some firms will increase in size, both physically and logically. What is the rationale, however, for increasing corporate size in an economy where success appears to depend on doing just the reverse? More generally, what are the limits to growth of the knowledge-based enterprise?

Rationales for Knowledge-based Growth

Knowledge-based growth can basically occur in one of two ways: either through increasing the knowledge retained within the firm, or through increasing the strength of the linkages between the firm and external knowledge sources. Either way, the depth or breadth of knowledge available to the firm will be increased.

Increasing the *depth* of knowledge will often involve firms merging with or acquiring other firms in the same industry (knowledge domain) as itself, to improve geographic coverage or increase market share. Other reasons could include improving the efficiency of the firm's vertical value chain; however, as noted earlier, as the economic rules of the game change, this type of efficiency gain is more likely to occur through market contracting or collaboration rather than acquisition.[3]

Increasing the breadth of knowledge in the firm will typically involve acquisition or collaboration with firms in different industries/knowledge domains. The main reasons for such moves will typically be to gain productive efficiencies or to improve innovative capabilities. Flow-on benefits are likely to include increased market/geographic coverage and greater market power. Expansion into unfamiliar knowledge domains however will also carry significant risks, as we will see later.

Plenty of examples of both knowledge 'deepening' and 'broadening' can be seen from a cursory reading of the daily press. Banks are busily acquiring other banks, legal firms other legal firms, and so on. Similarly, cross-industry convergence has become popular once again in the late 1990s, as firms realize they can gain productive and marketing efficiencies through shared use of technical and marketing infrastructures. Broadcasting, publishing, telecommunications, and computing companies are busily forming joint ventures. Banking, insurance, and financial services are linking with travel firms.[4] Suppliers of gas, water, and electricity are similarly capitalizing on the overlap between their knowledge domains to become utility companies.[5] Meantime shrewd investors are busily acquiring 'options on knowledge'. Corbis, for example, which Bill Gates helped start in 1989, acquires rights to photographs and art collections from archives and galleries worldwide. The images are then scanned into digital form for licensing to professionals and consumers. Over 20 million images are currently included in the Corbis collection.[6]

Increasing depth or breadth of knowledge will replace more traditional rationales for mergers or acquisitions, as firms become better able to spot both the opportunities and risks inherent in increasing the size or intensity of their knowledge bases. While, as a result of mergers or acquisitions, firms will inevitably acquire surplus physical and human resources, they are unlikely to retain them for long.

Limits to Firm Growth

Large firms seeking to grow larger still, while maintaining some of the benefits of small size, are currently trying various approaches to managing growth in the emerging knowledge economy. An approach which has attracted considerable interest in the literature is the 'federated firm'. Decentralization of internal functions or the management of dependent or independent relationships with a large number of external suppliers or distributors are often described as examples of 'federalism'.[7]

Asea Brown-Boveri (ABB) and Benetton are perhaps two of the most frequently discussed examples of federal corporate structures. ABB, an electronic transportation and engineering firm whose lineage extends back over a century, was organized in the later 1980s under its then CEO, Percy Barnevik, into 'a federation of national companies with a global communications center'. By the early 1990s ABB had been subdivided into 1,200 companies with an average of only 200 employees each. These companies were then further subdivided into 4,500 profit centres with an average of 50 employees per profit centre. Managing this federation was a head office of only 100 people. By 1997 the group had grown to 213,000 employees in 1,000 autonomous companies in 140 countries. Similarly Benetton, a major Italian-based group, have developed a global textile and clothing empire with finance, design, R&D, purchasing, planning, and manufacturing centralized, and retailing outsourced or franchised via 7,000 independent stores in 120 countries.

A problem with such structures when they become very large, as commentators have observed, is how to stop them flying apart.[8] The forces causing firms to externalize, for the reasons already outlined, are unlikely to allow them to reverse the process. Two future scenarios therefore appear likely. Under the first scenario, federal autonomy grows to the point where the relationship between the 'Head Office' and the rest of the federation becomes totally arm's length, at which time the federation will either disintegrate or will 'elect' its own central management team. Under the second scenario, the 'Head Office' may continue to control the balance of power, through offering its units progressively greater inducements to stay dependent on it. This strategy implies ever increasing support services, and/or greater product standardization, leading to greater brand name strength, as in the case for example of major franchises like Coca-Cola. One or other of these two scenarios appears the likely long-term outcome for any given example of federalism. The implications of both scenarios is that as knowledge becomes the 'glue' that binds firms to their decentralized divisions, or their external suppliers, control will be held by those with the greatest 'knowledge bargaining power' (see Fig. 8.1).

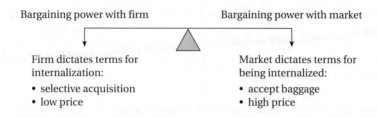

Bargaining power with firm   Bargaining power with market

Firm dictates terms for
internalization:
• selective acquisition
• low price

Market dictates terms for
being internalized:
• accept baggage
• high price

FIG. 8.1. Knowledge bargaining power

Are there, therefore, any inherent limitations to growth of the knowledge-based firm, apart from its capacity to acquire and manage knowledge resources? If there are any limitations they are not obvious—always providing growth delivers the additional knowledge which the firm seeks. The tendency of firm, for example, to buy knowledge with cash has frequently led to small successful firms being acquired by firms with greater financial resources. After the small firms are acquired it is not unusual to see their key knowledge workers set off for greener pastures as soon as they are contractually free to move, leaving the acquiring firm with corporate (knowledge) shells.

In the future knowledge economy, buying knowledge with cash will become increasingly unprofitable unless the key knowledge workers in the acquired firm are motivated to remain post acquisition. This will typically imply offering them a 'smaller piece of a bigger pie' in terms of equity in the merged corporation (see also Chapter 9).

Mergers of course can fail for other reasons. A clash of 'corporate cultures' has spelt the end for many a promising merger. Looked at another way, however, understanding corporate culture essentially implies acquiring *knowledge* of how a firm or its workers behave in certain *contexts*. Most information exchanged before a corporate merger or acquisition unfortunately is decontextualized facts and figures, which provide little or no insight into corporate or personal attitudes and norms of behaviour. A knowledge-based approach, which emphasizes the importance of early exchange of contextual information regarding culture, values, and behaviour, could prevent many a corporate marriage ending up on the rocks.

SMARTER ORGANIZATIONS

Organization and management of the firm needs to reflect its slimmer, smarter profile. From being a producer of physical goods and services, the firm is becoming a knowledge producer, its productive efficiency determined by how well it links and integrates disparate sources of knowledge. Instead of monitoring and controlling labour and physical processes, therefore, the role of management in the firm now must imply managing knowledge. These changes are helping to redefine the firm and its management functions, as we will see.

The Thinking Firm

The organization of the firm in the late nineteenth and early twentieth centuries was often likened to a machine, containing hierarchies of individuals working on defined tasks in a prespecified and sequential manner. This model worked well enough in the days of large, highly specialized labour forces engaged in mass production, but has lost much of its relevance in today's highly service-oriented and knowledge-based economy. Instead, since the modern firm is essentially an integrator of knowledge, the model of how best to organize such an activity is clearly the human brain.[9]

Traditional theories of how the human brain worked envisioned some central processor into which streams of data were fed and subsequently processed. Present theories based on cognitive science suggest that, instead, the human brain may work by configuring many small processors (neural circuits) into large-scale neural networks, with each processor able to communicate to any other. The same concept of massively parallel processing (MPP) is being applied in the development of today's supercomputers.

This peer-to-peer networking concept provides a metaphor for the networked organization, in which functions and workers are loosely distributed, assembling and disassembling as required. The key features of this networked concept of the firm, include the capability of individuals to achieve and if necessary question objectives (learning to learn), to manage themselves (self-organization), and to undertake different tasks (multiskilling). The concept of multiskilling could be seen as in conflict with the notion of specialization or 'sticking to the knitting' but, as we shall see later, these concepts are not necessarily inconsistent.

A significant risk associated with such a loose network structure in the firm, however, is that the neural circuits/knowledge workers become so intermingled and intertwined that they create, in effect, a knowledge 'spaghetti junction'. Fortunately, research in computer science developed the dual notions of coupling and cohesion, to minimize such risks when developing computer programs. Coupling refers to the interaction between teams, and cohesion refers to the team's unity of purpose. Systems designed to maximize cohesion and minimize unwanted coupling have been found to be considerably easier to understand, easier to maintain, and overall more effective.

Underpinning the effectiveness of the network organization is the flow, to all its members, of information that has the requisite richness or variety to enable them to make decisions.[10] Information 'richness' is highest in face-to-face communication and lowest in formal numeric communications. Rich media are useful when dealing with complex issues, but may contribute to information overload when dealing with simple issues. According to cognitive theory, this is why information systems need to be designed with the flexibility to provide different 'views' to different people.

Individuals, however, are boundedly rational[11] (otherwise one of the main reasons for having firms would disappear), so when the complexity of an issue in the firm results in too much informational richness for a single individual to absorb, networks or teams of individuals may be required. While the members of such teams may be homogeneous in various ways, it is important that they bring divergent perspectives to bear on the issue—hence the rationale for using cross-functional teams. Autonomous teams and decentralized organizational control, as proposed in total quality management (TQM) and business process re-engineering (BPR) methodologies, both reflect aspects of the cognitive model of corporate organization.[12]

From People Management to Knowledge Management

Prior to the Industrial Revolution and for a while after it, firms were largely owned and run by their founders, the original business entrepreneurs. 'Managing' a business at that time was inseparable from owning it. The separation of ownership and control, which started with the advent of the joint stock company in the late nineteenth century, gave birth to a new class of worker: the professional manager. Such managers were appointed to control the day-to-day operations of the firm, while the shareholders (now usually including the original entrepreneurs), as the nominal owners of the firm, provided risk capital.

During the industrial era, the firm was essentially an institution geared to mass production, thus massed labour. Productivity was dependent upon narrow, task-based specialization: the division of labour. As workers were divided into groups performing different tasks, they had to be monitored and controlled, i.e. 'managed'. The larger the firm and the greater the diversity of tasks, the more managers were appointed. 'Management', apart from overall management of the firm's affairs, thus became synonymous with management of (relatively low-skilled) people performing particular tasks or functions. In effect 'management' has meant controlling labour.

All that is now changing. Narrow, task-based specialization is reducing, as individual tasks are automated and aggregated. Task management is giving way to process management, which in turn means that fewer managers are required. Computers can now perform many monitoring functions formerly conducted by management, particularly for routine functions normally carried out by members of the peripheral group. The higher the competency of the worker, the less monitoring is required—always providing incentives are properly aligned to achievement of objectives.

Fewer levels of hierarchy, fewer control points, less human monitoring, less need for intermediate layers of management between owners and workers—these are the hallmarks of the modern corporation. Where does this leave the role of the professional manager? Management in the knowledge-based firm will head in two different directions. First, management of people in the old industrial sense of monitoring and controlling low-skilled workers is destined to operate on the periphery of the firm, where such workers will be located. The number of such managers will naturally decline in line with the reduction of peripheral functions, due to automation or externalization. Some managers in this group will carve a new corporate niche for themselves, specializing as interfaces to external knowledge resources. Others, the majority of this group, will join the ranks of former employees outside the firm. Those who accept the challenge of enforced self-employment may find new and highly satisfying careers as dependent or independent agents, distributors, franchisees, and micro firms, as we saw earlier.

Second, management in the strategic sense will move from managing physical resources to managing knowledge.[13] While this will still involve managing people, the emphasis will switch from managing the tasks people perform, to managing their knowledge inputs and outputs. Critical components of knowledge management will include:

- developing more accurate, comprehensive, and up-to-date information systems, reflecting 'hard' information, 'soft' or opinionative information, and contextualized information about the firm's activities and its knowledge resources;
- evaluating and comparing the level of knowledge in the firm with its internal needs, market demand, and the knowledge profile of its competitors;
- protecting and retaining key knowledge, via physical and logical security mechanisms and by appropriate incentives and rewards for people;
- assisting knowledge transfer through directives, routines, and operating procedures;
- developing cross-functional teams to facilitate knowledge exchange, integration, and innovation;
- developing training and research programmes, both in the firm and with external agencies, to enhance the knowledge capital of the firm and to instil a 'knowledge-valuing culture';
- developing measurement and control systems to evaluate the success of knowledge management strategies, both within the firm and as reflected in the firm's market performance.

Emerging Knowledge-based Strategies

As firms start to come to grips with the growing economic importance of knowledge, two broad conceptual approaches to dealing with the phenomenon are beginning to emerge. On the one hand there are those who see measurement and valuation as the logical first step; on the other, there are those who regard knowledge sharing and organizational learning as the first priority.

Dow Chemical provides a relevant example of the first type of approach. In 1993, Dow Chemical appointed one of its global business managers, Gordon Petrash, to lead an initiative aimed at evaluating one of its major intellectual assets, its 29,000-strong patents base. The resultant investigation showed that 30 per cent of the patents were rarely if ever used, leading to Dow cutting its patent tax maintenance bill by $US40 million and reducing its administrative costs by $US10 million over ten years. Based on the success of this first initiative, Petrash and his team moved on to explore new avenues for Dow to capitalize on its patents. This exercise enabled Dow to increase patent licensing income from $US25 million in 1994 to a projected $US125 million by the year 2000. Today Dow Chemical continues to gain from leveraging the value of its patents, having recently signed a number of joint ventures over $US1 billion in value, in which Dow's contribution has been solely via its knowledge base of patents.

According to Petrash, now partner at PriceWaterhouseCoopers in Chicago, successfully managing both codified knowledge such as patents, as well as the broader range of knowledge involved in human organizational and customer capital, implies acceptance of some key principles regarding measurement. These include that 'everything can be measured; that measurements should only be made to the degree of accuracy required, and that appropriateness of measurement is critical'.[14]

Buckman Laboratories are an example of the second approach, which emphasizes knowledge sharing and organizational learning, rather than measurement and valuation. Based in Memphis, Tennessee, Buckman is a speciality chemical company, serving the pulp and paper industry and related industries. The company specializes in solving customer problems through creative chemical treatment technologies and technical service, which implies that there is rarely a standard solution to a customer problem. The company's 1,200 associates, 40 per cent of whom are involved in sales, are spread across 80 countries worldwide. According to Melissie Rumizen, internal Knowledge Management Consultant, some associates may never see anyone from Buckman for up to twelve months.

The company started to address the need to improve internal communications in 1987 with the introduction of a corporate email network. Today Buckman's global knowledge network K'Netix™ and its Bulab Learning Centre provide a platform for communications, distance-based learning, knowledge sharing, and access to case-based and other corporate information to assist associates in the field.

According to Rumizen, Buckman does not focus on measuring its knowledge capital as such, preferring to use other performance indicators such as new product sales and levels of productivity. Following the inception of Buckman's knowledge management programme in the late 1980s, sales of new products more than doubled, with productivity similarly improving.[15]

Dow and Buckman exemplify some pioneering approaches to dealing with knowledge as a key asset and as a means of leveraging business performance.

In Dow's case, its initial business focus was more towards improving how it managed its explicit, codified knowledge. In the case of Buckman the focus has been on knowledge sharing and learning. In both cases, however, the payback has already been significant. The moral of the story is that, as knowledge becomes an increasingly important resource, firms and individuals will have to become as adept at managing it as they are today at managing their physical and financial resources.

The appointment of 'knowledge vice-presidents', 'knowledge officers', and 'knowledge managers' by today's leading corporations signals the birth of a new concept of professional knowledge management. How such roles will evolve over time however is difficult to predict. To a large extent, management of knowledge will become *what all firms do* rather than a distinctively separate function.[16] On the other hand, many firms are currently in a transition from an old industrial mode of operation to the knowledge-centred enterprise model. For these firms knowledge managers will be their change agents, helping them to progress to the next stage of knowledge growth (see Knowledge Growth Model[TM] later in this chapter). Many of these change agents are likely to be drawn from the ranks of the current information systems (IS) and human resources (HR) functions. Rather than managing information or people, both these functions need to reconceptualize their roles as essentially managing knowledge. Merely calling chief information officers 'chief knowledge officers', however, will not produce the required results. Some firms have already moved to appoint a senior executive to oversee the implementation of knowledge-based strategy and to coordinate HR and IS functions in the process.

The Mutual Group, a leading Canadian insurance group, for example has created a Strategic Capabilities function which coordinates knowledge strategy planning via a Knowledge and Technology Leadership Board. The CIO position as such no longer exists, having been integrated with the management of the Board, and the HR function has been reorganized and restructured.

According to Hubert Saint-Onge, Senior Vice-President Strategic Capabilities, the traditional organizational structure which commonly divides functions such as IT, HR, and marketing needs to be re-engineered. Says Saint-Onge: 'for these players to remain in their respective corners, unable to engage by and large in very close collaboration, means that an organization has organized itself to forgo the benefit it could obtain from a coordinated view [of its operations].'[17]

SMARTER INCENTIVES

As firms downsize physically, upsize mentally, and gear their organizations for knowledge-based growth, many are still weighed down with the baggage of outdated incentive and reward structures. In addition to a basic salary, typically determined by the rate for the job, firms have traditionally offered full-time employees a variety of other incentives and rewards, all aimed at maximizing their utility. Such inducements have ranged from attractive working conditions to performance bonuses, promises of promotion, profit-sharing and stock options, and the range of psychological benefits associated with recognition and praise from supervisors and peers.

This complex web of incentives and rewards has been developed within an institutional framework which is now caught up in an accelerating change process. As the firm evolves ever more rapidly towards a knowledge-based institution, so the profile of its internal workforce and the incentive and reward systems necessary to motivate and reward that workforce must undergo a radical overhaul.

The balance of this section describes how and to what extent the two most common forms of incentive, performance-based pay and promotion, have been used to date. This is followed by an assessment of the results of such schemes and the issues that will need to be addressed by firms if they are to survive and prosper in the future knowledge economy.

Use of Performance-Based Incentives

In the 'manufactory' of Adam Smith's day, or on the production line of one of Henry Ford's factories, to pay workers by results would have been both administratively costly and unnecessary. The task specialization that went with the division of labour practically ensured that optimum performance for any given task could be achieved. Providing the worker kept at or near to that optimum, he or she simply received the rate applicable to the job. Failure to achieve the required rate would inevitably lead to dismissal and there were plenty of willing workers waiting to fill any vacant positions.

As the variety and complexity of tasks in the firm continued to grow, they quickly outstripped the capabilities of the, then fairly primitive, internal monitoring systems. Human monitors were required in the form of supervisors and managers. These managers however were not paid by results either. Providing their departments achieved an acceptable level of work, they were generally left in peace, earning the applicable rate for their jobs. A nexus of agreement subsequently developed, typically in large mass production environments, between unions, as the representatives of the workers, and production and human resource management. This rather curious alliance, although marked by regular conflict and disputation, has effectively controlled the monitoring, evaluation, and compensation systems of most western firms.

A hallmark of this alliance has been low levels of *personal* incentives offered to *both* managers and workers to perform above a certain accepted norm. In many cases, over-performance has attracted criticism, with workers who stepped out of line being treated as acting divisively and not in the interests of their peers. Management have been equally reluctant to rock this particular boat, believing that harmonious work relations were worth the loss in overall performance. The traditional reasons given for this apparent anomaly have been that subjective merit pay systems have bred distrust between employers and supervisors and objective merit-based systems have been abused by employees, who learned how to work the system to their own advantage.

Lack of an incentive to differentiate between the performance of individual workers has percolated up through the middle management layers of many firms. According to a survey of salary premia paid for performance involving 7,629 managers in two large, typical manufacturing firms, it was found that both firms ranked over 95 per cent of their management as *good* or *outstanding*. The average salary premium paid by both firms for being *good* was only 3.9 per cent more than for being merely *acceptable* and the difference in premium for being *outstanding* rather than merely *good* was only 2.5 per cent. Additionally in both firms, around 3 per cent of managers were deemed less than *good* and virtually none were deemed *not acceptable*.[18] The almost universally high approval ratings in this study, and the absence of significant incentives, suggests that neither of the firms involved was seeking to differentiate between managers by offering genuinely merit-based pay.

Other studies also confirm that in many organizations claiming to have merit-based pay systems, pay is not very closely related to performance. Research in the UK, for example, involving over 900 respondents to a questionnaire posted to a random sample of fellows and members of the Institute of Management, found strong support for linking rewards to performance but significantly less evidence of it having occurred in practice. For example 63 per cent of the respondents stated it was their organization's policy to support or strongly support merit-based pay. In practice however the majority also reported that their firms had no involvement in individual bonus schemes (57 per cent), executive share schemes (68 per cent), knowledge-based pay (53 per cent), or profit sharing with cash awards (66 per cent). Profit-related pay, profit sharing with shares in the organization, production-based pay, plant-wide bonus schemes, and payment for quality were even less used in practice, with over 70 per cent of firms reportedly not having implemented such arrangements.[19]

Lower levels of personal incentives have not been restricted to the lower ranks. Other research has shown that even when the value of a firm is held constant, for every 10 per cent increase in sales, the salary and bonus of the CEO will on average increase by only 2 to 3 per cent. This elasticity has been shown to be constant both across time and across industries.[20]

Promotion as an Incentive

In any organization, promotion to a higher level in the hierarchy is traditionally viewed as the single most powerful incentive for everyone but the CEO.

Most types of organization from partnerships to corporations and churches to universities use promotion much more heavily than performance- or merit-based pay. Deficiencies with promotion as an incentive are generally only found in slow-growing or physically shrinking organizations where opportunities for promotion are limited or reducing. In such organizations payments based on performance are more likely to provide genuine incentives. In the past, *unlike today*, organizations have tended to expand rather than flatten their hierarchies, so promotion has been the more widely used incentive.

Another deficiency with the way promotion has been used in most firms is that it has implied preference for internal candidates over candidates from outside the firm. The problem with this traditional internal labour market (ILM) approach, as noted earlier, is that it restricts the freedom of the firm and can lead to selection of suboptimal candidates. This problem is exacerbated where there exists no natural promotional path within the firm for a worker with a particular set of skills. This tends to lead to examples of the so-called 'Peter Principle', where workers are rewarded with promotion to positions for which they are not suited.

Among incentive arrangements, the 'up or out' system appears to have been one of the most effective. Since it has most commonly been found in knowledge-intensive, service-oriented industries, the type of industries that seem likely to dominate the future economic landscape, then it would seem worthwhile taking a closer look at how it operates.

The 'up or out' system

The 'up or out' system as traditionally practised by many professional firms, places major emphasis on future promotional opportunities as a means to incentivize workers. Such incentive arrangements typically involve limited rewards for several years to workers considered capable of advancement, whilst the firm trains and evaluates them. After this period and subject to overall performance achievement, those judged to be the best equipped for advancement are, in due course, likely to be offered partnerships which tend to carry the implicit promise of long tenure. Those who fail to match the promotion criteria are fired or 'let go'.

The economic rationale for the up or out system does not appear immediately obvious. Why invest several years in training and preparing a candidate for a position only to fire him or her? From the candidate's perspective, why take the risk of spending several years with a firm when the chances of being fired at the end of the period are obviously significant? Gibson and Mnookin provide answers to these questions using the traditional American law firm as a case example.[21] From the firm's perspective it cannot know in advance which associates will make the grade to partnership and it is faced with the need to evaluate them over several years to find out. The firm therefore needs to feel assured, at the time of hiring, that the associate has an incentive to stay the course. Likewise, when the associate joins the firm, he or she needs to feel assured that the firm will not later act opportunistically and seek to avoid offering a partnership opportunity, by retaining him or her in an associate position on an indefinite basis. By committing itself to fire anyone who does not make the grade to partner, the firm is demonstrating, in the most practical way, that it is eliminating that incentive for itself in advance.

A problem remains for the candidate, however, in that a decision to accept a financially suboptimal package in the short term is no guarantee that promotion will eventuate. The fact that up or out systems continue to be popular, and even preferred to less risky and apparently more remunerative employment options, implies that other factors are involved. The answer appears to lie in the practice of offering outplacement assistance to associates who are not promoted and of ensuring that the training which they receive during their apprenticeship period is sufficiently *generic* to fit them for positions outside the firm. It is important to note, in this context, that the more firm specific the training given the less viable implementing an up or out system can be. The training provided *must* be generic enough to equip the worker to find work at an appropriate level elsewhere—usually in the same industry or profession.

Issues with Current Incentives and Reward Systems

Performance-based pay and promotion have been the two most widely practised methods of incentivizing and rewarding employees for their individual contributions. With the notable exception of the up or out promotional system, both appear to have been only moderately successful from an economic perspective, and considerable anomalies surround their implementation in many firms. These inefficiencies can be traced to the reluctance or inability of firms to reward *outputs* as opposed to *inputs* and the artificial protection to under-performing individuals provided by 'promotion from within'. Why have firms been so reluctant to change their traditional practices? We obviously need to probe a little deeper.

Outputs versus Inputs

The economically poor, or even counter-productive, effects of many merit- and performance-based schemes stem from two primary causes. First, there is an inherent conflict in the notion of rewards for performance where detailed performance goals cannot be specified in advance. This is the norm, however, in standard employment contracts. As discussed earlier (see Chapter 3), employment contracts are designed to be open ended, flexible, and largely unspecific regarding the detailed goals of work performance. They are therefore better suited to performance measurement based on the quality of *input* or *effort* rather than on *output* or *results*. In this respect, employment contracts differ markedly from contracts between the firm and external contractors, which are typically fixed length, rigid, and highly specific about performance requirements. Firms wishing to reward output or results, rather than inputs or effort, will have to look beyond the employment contract.

Second, the repetitive task-based orientation of much work has tended to produce an accepted rate for a particular task or set of tasks. Specialization through the division of labour made 'the rate for the job' a reasonably efficient proposition in the days of labour-intensive mass production. This practice has subsequently spread throughout industry and permeated the firm at every level. From the factory floor to the executive boardroom, comparability or parity, not performance, has become king. What worked on the production line has not however worked as well elsewhere in the firm, and nowadays tends not to work so well on the production line. Standards of compensation based on a rate for the job are generally losing their relevance in the light of global competition. What a worker gets paid in the UK or Australia may now be a function of how well his or her employer can compete with a firm in Thailand or Brazil, where rates of pay for comparable jobs are significantly less. The historical acceptance of these practices stems largely from firms' management being willing to accept a trade-off between maintaining the integrity of the firm's internal labour market (ILM) and achieving maximum economic efficiency. Little wonder that middle management has reacted to the combined pressures of organized labour, and senior management's willingness to compromise, by going along with established practice.

Up or Stay versus Up or Out

Promotion-based incentives have been by far the most popular form of incentive offered by firms to their employees. It is not difficult to see why, since ascent of the corporate hierarchy has offered not only financial reward but increased job security. Promotion as an incentive is also far more consistent with the open-ended, promissory nature of the employment contract since, unlike merit- or performance-based incentives, the conditions under which promotion occurs usually allow the firm a considerable degree of flexibility. Most promotion-based incentive systems, however, have been of the 'up or stay' variety—employees who have not been promoted have generally been retained by firms. The up or out system described above provides an interesting contrast, therefore, in that it has proved generally successful and a strategic advantage to the highly knowledge-based organizations, such as professional partnerships and academic institutions, where it has been traditionally used.

Predicted Changes to Incentives and Rewards

Different combinations of incentives and rewards must evolve for the three major categories of worker retained within the firm in order for the firm to survive in the knowledge economy. For those in the peripheral group, total remuneration can be expected to shift from the rate for the job to payment by results. Computerized information systems can be expected to be used more rigorously in determining how well such workers are performing and to provide more accurate comparisons of the cost benefits of retaining functions in-house or outsourcing. The future of those on the periphery of the firm can therefore be expected to be increasingly precarious, since in addition to being paid by results, their career paths within the firm are likely to be limited to the functions they currently perform. Where the firm decides to outsource the function, personal achievement may count for little either way. Equally, if the function is not regarded as central to the firm's operations, the firm is unlikely to invest in training workers in it—thus unlike the up or out system, workers may find it difficult to find a similar job outside the firm. In effect, 'up or stay' will be replaced by 'stay or go'—with little or no preparation for the next work opportunity.

No easy solutions appear to exist to this dilemma. Exhorting the firm to retain workers where it cannot justify doing so is obviously pointless, as is trying to pressure the firm to invest in training from which it cannot receive an adequate payback. Government imposed training levies have tended to be failures. Equally, the longer such workers remain in the firm without receiving training, the more precarious their position will become. This could be a case of market failure, which can only be fully addressed by external action at an industry or government level. Special awareness and retraining programmes are clearly going to be essential. The sooner workers are made aware of the vital necessity to improve and continuously upgrade their skills, the sooner they can start to help themselves.

For workers in the associate group, performance measurement is likely to be reflected in a combination of input-based criteria, such as attitude, effort, and input quality, and output-based criteria such as productive efficiency, results, team and client satisfaction. Incentives and rewards can be expected to reflect this mix, with an increasing proportion of the total compensation package being derived from quality of output rather than input. Stock options and profit sharing as forms of incentive are likely to be more widely diffused throughout this group of workers. Stock options in particular will replace 'promises' with contractual certainty, another example of the move away from the traditional employment relationship. Up or out systems will tend to become more prevalent and represent options to short-term rewards for performance. Given the benefit of significant generic training, those workers that fail to be promoted and cannot, or do not choose to, join another firm are likely to be well equipped to take on dependent or independent forms of self-employment. The provisions of generic training and the implications for workers are subjects that are discussed more fully later. Finally, for the expanding core group, measurement and incentives will be aligned most fully with the fortunes of the firm—a trend which is discussed in detail in Chapter 9.

A KNOWLEDGE GROWTH MODEL™ OF THE FIRM

How can a firm know how smart it is compared to its competitors? How can governments measure how well industries or indeed national economies are performing on the knowledge scale? Identifying the progress of a firm towards the model of a knowledge-based organization clearly demands some standard measurement criteria. The Knowledge Growth Model™ illustrated below may prove useful for this purpose. From the perspective of organizational learning, such a model can provide a basis for determining potential training and human resource requirements. It can also provide a basis for the development of other models more specifically aimed at modelling human skills in the firm. This in turn can enable better planning of explicit strategies to internalize or externalize particular functions.

Other uses of the Knowledge Growth Model™ may include helping management plan future knowledge investments and assisting analysts and investors to identify corporate strengths and weaknesses. At an aggregate level, such a model could provide the basis for determining future industry policies and strategies, identifying where government assistance might be best directed, and offering 'knowledge best practice' benchmarks against which individual firms could compare their own performance. The stages of growth suggested in the Knowledge Growth Model™ are typical of the progress of any firm towards a 'knowledge enterprise' (see Fig. 8.2).

The following stages are involved.

Stage (1) Knowledge Recognition. The first step is the creation of corporate awareness of the importance of knowledge as a factor of production. Firms will need to conduct 'knowledge audits' to analyse the value of their knowledge assets. During this stage the importance attached to the firm's internal labour market will decline, characterized by external competition for jobs at all levels, individual worker contracts, and output-based performance measurement. Increasing importance will be attached to personal knowledge/competence and less to seniority/experience.

Stage (2) Knowledge Organization. This stage will be characterized by reductions in middle management layers, accompanied by progressive externalization of non-core functions and internalization of core functions. Workers left in residual peripheral functions come under increasing pressure, as automation and externalization reduce the functions they perform. Some may leave the firm voluntarily to take advantage of market opportunities. During this stage, internal systems and processes will need to be re-engineered to take advantage of the firm's updated conception of its knowledge base and to reflect resultant changes to its strategic focus.

Stage (3) Knowledge Networking. Stage 3 will be characterized by diffusion of decision making and increased use of cross-functional teams. Other features of this stage of growth will include increasing homogeneity in worker skills

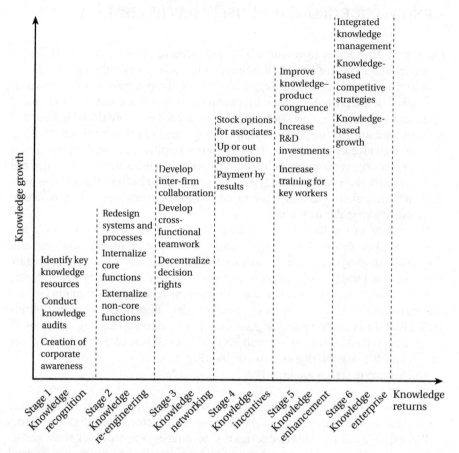

FIG. 8.2. Knowledge Growth Model™ of the firm

and functions performed and greater focus on creativity and innovation. Linkages with external suppliers of intermediary services and with dependent and independent self-employed will increase.

Stage (4) Knowledge Rewards. The firm now needs to realign its incentive and reward systems with its revamped internal structure and knowledge focus. Up or out promotion, team-based performance incentives, and personal stock options will be used to incentivize the associate group. The peripheral group meantime will be offered greater personal productivity incentives.

Stage (5) Knowledge Enhancement. Stage 5 will be marked by increased investment in R&D and in training, and by a refinement in the linkages in the firm between its products and its knowledge base. During this stage, the firm will also improve its external links to providers of training and product development.

Stage (6) Knowledge Enterprise. The firm is now a knowledge-centred enterprise. Knowledge management and business management have fused. Growth and competitive strategies will be knowledge based. During this stage the core group will significantly expand through the addition of workers from the associate group and from outside the firm.

So where are firms today? Using the Knowledge Growth Model™ as a guide, most firms appear to have at least entered Stage 1, and many are well beyond it. Larger, older, more physical and capital-intensive, and more broadly based firms are making slower progress. The majority of leading firms currently appear to be either in Stages 3 or 4 and many in the hi-tech and professional services sector are already into Stages 5 or 6. Most larger firms also appear by now to have gone through Stage 2, involving downsizing, delayering, and externalization of non-core functions. It is notable that business process re-engineering (BPR) became popular in the early 1990s when many leading firms were going through Stage 2. It subsequently received a lot of bad press for not fully living up to some users' expectations. In fact we can now see that the reason for its subsequent fall from grace is because BPR does not take a holistic view of the firm's knowledge growth requirements. In practice, it is focused on the type of changes required in Stage 2, but often not from a knowledge perspective, which is probably why the results have sometimes been disappointing.

BPR of course is not alone in this respect. Many other management strategies, from those aimed at quality improvements to organizational learning and competitive positioning, have been frequently applied piecemeal and without reference to a comprehensive model of firms' knowledge requirements.

Looking at the risk characteristics of each stage in the Knowledge Growth Model™, Stages 1 to 3 typically involve a process of reassessment and restructuring in order to lay the foundations for knowledge-led growth beginning in Stage 4. From Stage 4 onwards, firms begin to accelerate up the growth curve, using their knowledge resources increasingly for innovation and competitive advantage. In the early stages, the main risks for firms are that they will fail to adapt or mismanage the processes of internalizing and externalizing various functions. This will typically result in the type of problems discussed earlier in relation to outsourcing, where firms have not been sufficiently selective in what to insource or outsource. The consequences of failure will include an inability to progress to the later stages and a consequential slowdown in growth.

In Stages 4–6, as firms become more heavily knowledge dependent, the nature of the risks will change. Mistakes made from now on are likely to have a more serious impact on business performance. If team-based decision making leads to 'groupthink' rather than innovation, the firm could begin to stagnate and/or lose out to its competitors. Groupthink refers to a mode of thinking which people engage in when deeply involved in cohesive team decision-making activity. In such circumstances, their striving for unanimity can override their motivation to appraise realistically alternative courses of action.[22] Groupthink has been cited in connection with a variety of bad decisions that have made their way into the press, ranging from the Watergate cover-up to the Bay of Pigs fiasco and the disastrous launch of the space-shuttle Challenger in 1986.[23] Many unpublicized but equally disastrous decisions have been made behind the closed doors of corporate boardrooms.

By Stages 4–6 the firm will need to be in control of the interfaces with the external workforce and other suppliers, since the firm will by this stage have reduced its internal resources to what it considers optimum. Growth and competitive strategy will also need to have changed to reflect a more explicit acknowledgement of knowledge-related factors. The consequences of failure to manage these later stages in the growth process are thus likely to have greater strategic impact on the firm than failures earlier on.

Readers may find it interesting to consider where their firms currently are according to the stages shown on the Knowledge Growth Model™. It is likely that many firms will be between stages or further advanced in some areas than others. Overall, however, the model hopefully provides an indication of some of the critical issues and opportunities that lie ahead for both workers and firm owners.

SUMMARY

Slimmer, smarter, flatter, more flexibly organized, the firm is being redefined by the dynamics of the emerging knowledge economy. As the firm adapts, so must its owners, investors, workers, and other stakeholders who collectively represent the interests of the firm. In summary, the major characteristics of the redefinition process are:

- The firm is shrinking in terms of physical assets, functions performed, and employees, while expanding its internal knowledge base and external linkages to customers, suppliers, and the external workforce.
- Functions requiring knowledge that is not central to the firm's core activities will be externalized, while those which fit within or complement its core body of knowledge will be internalized.
- The composition of the firm's external workforce will change progressively from reliance on dependent flexihire arrangements, to staffing and outsourced services for non critical administrative and maintenance functions. Dependent and independent relationships with self-employed individuals and small businesses will be used for more mission-critical, externalized functions.
- Firms will grow 'strategically' by increasing their depth or breadth of knowledge. Achieving such growth will require that firms become adept at measuring their own knowledge capabilities and at recognizing the issues

and opportunities for synergistic cooperation with other knowledge holders and knowledge domains.

- The model of internal organization best suited to the firm's future role is
  viewed as analogous to a model of human cognition, i.e. loose networks of
  semi-autonomous knowledge workers forming teams as required. Key
  attributes of this organizational form include multiskilling, learning to
  learn, and self-organization.
- For optimum efficiency and effectiveness, team structures in the firm will
  need to exhibit minimum coupling and maximum cohesion.
- The percentage of middle and junior management roles in the firm will
  decline as those in the associate group become more self-directing and
  the functions provided by the peripheral group are progressively externalized. In the short term 'knowledge managers' are likely to be appointed by
  many firms as change agents to help them to make the transition to
  knowledge-centred operation. In the longer term, knowledge management will become integrated with the organization and processes of the
  firm.
- Firms will need to improve how they analyse and model their business
  capabilities and needs, to reflect the value of knowledge to their operations. Models such as the Knowledge Supply Model^{TM} and the Knowledge
  Growth Model^{TM} may prove useful starting points for such purposes.
- Firms' investment in training will focus on staff in the associate and core
  groups. Such training will facilitate the practice of outplacing those who
  fail to progress in the firm.
- Those in the peripheral group will be offered less training and fewer promotional opportunities and their position in the firm will become increasingly precarious. Governments, in consultation with firms, unions, and
  other stakeholders, will have to advise such workers of their vulnerability,
  and make special arrangements to assist them to upskill, retrain, and
  become outplaced. Workers will have to recognize however that it is ultimately their own responsibility, and in their interests, to acquire appropriate skills and manage their own careers independently of the firm.
- Incentives and rewards will change in line with the organizational restructuring of the firm. Key trends will include:
  - greater use of performance- or merit-based rewards for all employ-
    ees;
  - increasing use of personal performance-based incentives for the
    peripheral group;
  - increasing use of personal, team, and corporate incentives for the
    associate and core groups;
  - wider use of the up or out promotional system, particularly to incen-
    tivize workers in the associate group.

SOME INTERESTING ASIDES

An array of challenges faces the modern firm and its stakeholders, as it seeks to reconceptualize its role as a knowledge-based institution.

How to Make Money from Knowledge

A thought that may be intriguing many readers by this point is just how they are going to make money in the knowledge economy. While there are no obvious 'golden rules' there are a few lessons to be learned from previous attempts to link knowledge investments with productivity and profitability.

In the 1980s, economists began to notice that knowledge investments in the form of investments in IT did not seem to improve firms' productivity. They noted that 'IT appears everywhere except in the productivity statistics'. Recent evidence shows that in fact IT has had a substantial positive effect on productivity, but that for many firms increased productivity has not meant increased profitability. The reason for this apparent paradox can be explained by the theory of consumer surplus.[24]

Consumer surplus arises where the cost of a given good or service falls below what a consumer would otherwise be prepared to pay for it. Where technology is used to improve productivity then the resultant benefit may flow either to the producer by way of increased profit, or to the consumer by way of reduced price. Where barriers to competition are weak, there will be a tendency for firms to compete by driving down production costs and then pass a proportion of the resultant benefit to the consumer in order to attract demand. In the ensuing price wars between producers, the consumer is likely to be the winner.

The current use of electronic commerce over the Internet provides an interesting illustration of consumer surplus. Here consumers have rushed to use the world's first truly public global network service, attracted by low access prices, user-friendly access tools, and massive amounts of largely free information. Sensing an opportunity, service providers have rushed in after them. New commercial sites from baby malls to banking services appear by the minute. Yet who is the main beneficiary of the Internet? Apart from a few entrepreneurs, whose stocks have soared, for the most part the main beneficiary has been the consumer. Why? Because in the scramble to offer the consumer a better deal, firms are heavily competing with each other. Internet access costs for example have plummeted from around $US10 an hour to nowadays around $US20 a month. I can now buy my books from the other side of the world at less cost over the Internet than at the lowest-cost book retailer in my home town. That Internet book retailer is growing strongly in popularity and its stock has skyrocketed, but it is by all reports not yet making a profit. Business mortality rates among providers of Internet services are steadily rising, but then so are the numbers of such providers. In the ensuing turbulence there are more business losers than winners, but the big winner is the consumer.

The moral of the story for firms who are seeking to compete on the basis of a knowledge advantage is to ensure they have properly evaluated that advantage. Where it is based on explicit knowledge, such as licensed technologies (thus available to other firms), any advantages gained can only be short run. In such cases, time to market and speed of diffusion will be vital. Where the advantage is based on knowledge which other firms cannot readily emulate (tacit knowledge), the firm with that knowledge may be able to retain most of the benefits from productivity gains.

These aspects of knowledge as a competitive weapon tend to underline the fact that in the long run knowledge which is explicit will only be of value to firms insofar as it acts as raw material for development of tacit knowledge. On the other hand it also underlines the importance of investment in explicit knowledge as a *competitive necessity*. When one bank offers an ATM service, for example, all other banks must follow suit or lose customers. Likewise when electronic shopping really starts climbing up the growth curve, those retailers who do not climb on board quickly will face declining profits.

In the knowledge race, there can be no standing still; keeping up with the pack will be even more vital for survival than it is today. Firms seeking to maintain a market leadership position and increase their profits will therefore have to invest more in the type of basic long-term research which tends to produce major technological breakthroughs and to learn how to package and sell their knowledge products faster. Licensing and franchising the knowledge necessary to produce other goods and services therefore looks set to become the largest and most profitable type of productive activity. Some of the implications have already been discussed in relation to work opportunities (see Chapter 6). Others may include, for example, the development of knowledge franchise systems. Rather than operating a franchise business, knowledge franchisors may specialize in finding existing successful business models and abstract the 'formulas for success' which they then might codify and license through franchise operators. More prosaically, as the success of computer software packages has proven, embedding tacit knowledge in reusable knowledge goods is likely to be more profitable than selling the same knowledge on a 'one off' basis. Thus, consultants who can incorporate their knowledge into software models which can be used by business are likely to be more profitable than those who market the same knowledge as a personal service. One key to making money out of knowledge is therefore clearly reusability, i.e. to be able to replicate and sell the fruits of knowledge without having to part with the original.

A Knowledge-based Approach to Acquisitional Growth

Over the past ten to fifteen years, sticking to the knitting, or the core competencies of the firm, has become the focus of much management attention.[25] The importance of identifying and exploiting what the firm knows best was demonstrated by the failure of many earlier conglomerate diversification strategies, when firms used financial capital from mature businesses to fund new unrelated ventures. The theory was that professional management from the old 'cash cow' businesses would be able to transfer their experience to new industrial settings and help 'rising stars' take off. The results proved it was not that easy. Many business failures that resulted from this strategy can be traced to firms' lack of appreciation of the difficulties associated with managing businesses in unrelated knowledge domains.

In future, firms may again seek to use diversity as a means to improve their global reach, innovative capacity, and productivity. The current rash of cross-industry and global 'mega mergers' is an indication that such a trend is already occurring among large firms. This time, however, it can be expected that firms will have learned from the mistakes of the past and will pay much more attention to the problems involved in operating across multiple knowledge domains. This is likely to lead to more examples of concentric diversification around a core of related knowledge domains.

Future growth strategies will need to take into account, not only issues such as the level of certainty attached to requirements for cooperation and the requirement for first mover advantages, but, importantly, the degree of knowledge transfer required. In situations involving uncertainty regarding the level or term of collaboration, where a need for rapid concerted action is required, and where the degree of knowledge that needs to be transferred is low, then collaboration is likely to be more appropriate. In situations where these factors are different, acquisition or mergers may be more appropriate. Assuming there is a need for a high level of inter-firm knowledge transfer, then firms may adopt a number of different strategies to overcome the problems implied in the transfer process, including:

- adopting systems analysis and corporate modelling techniques which are designed to improve the transfer of knowledge between individuals in different knowledge domains, e.g. by more accurate and unambiguous representations;
- ensuring that not only hard, factual data are transferred but also, where appropriate, soft/opinionative information and case/context-sensitive information;
- hiring contractors with relevant multifunctional skills to act as knowledge brokers between the different areas of specialization in the merging entities, e.g. in the case of multimedia collaboration, a knowledge of video, audio, and text communications.

'Redefining the firm' means not only changing its role, organization, functions, and strategies, but also its ownership. Who will own the future firm? This is the focus of the next chapter.

NOTES

1. 'UK Labour Market Surveyed: Social Trends 27' (1997), *Labour Market Trends*, London: Office for National Statistics (Feb.): 31

2. J. Roos, G. Roos, N. C. Dragonetti, and L. Edvinsson (1997), *Intellectual Capital: Navigating the New Business Landscape*, Basingstoke: Macmillan Press Ltd.

3. B. Klein, R. G. Crawford, and A. A. Alchian (1978), 'Vertical Integration, Appropriable Rents and the Competitive Contracting Process', *Journal of Law and Economics*, 21: 297–326.

4. 'Breathtaking', *The Economist*, Business This Week (4–10 Apr. 1998), *http://www.economist.com*.

5. 'Spliced', *The Economist*, Business This Week (4–10 Apr. 1998), *http://www.economist.com*.

6. Corbis: Putting Online Imagery in Focus, *http://www.microsoft.com/billgates/interests/corbis.htm*.

7. C. Handy (1996), *Beyond Certainty: The Changing Worlds of Organisations*, London: Arrow Books Ltd.: 33–56.

8. J. O'Toole and W. Bennis (1992), 'Our Federalist Future: The Leadership Imperative', *California Management Review* (summer): 73–90.

9. M. Minsky (1989), *The Society of Mind*, New York: Simon & Schuster. D. C. Dennett (1991), *Consciousness Explained*, Boston: Little Brown & Co.

10. R. L. Daft and R. H. Lengel (1984), 'Information Richness: A New Approach to Managerial Behavior and Organizational Design', in L. L. Cummings and B. M. Staw (eds.), *Research in Organizational Behaviour*, vi, Greenwich, Conn.: JAI Press: 191–223.

11. H. A. Simon (1957), *Models of Man*, New York: Wiley.

12. F. A. Wilson (1997), 'The Brain and the Firm: Perspectives of the Networked Organisation and the Cognitive Metaphor', paper presented at PACIS Conference, Brisbane.

13. P. Quintas, P. Lefrere, and G. Jones (1997), 'Knowledge Management: A Strategic Agenda', *Long Range Planning*, 30/3: 385–91.

14. Interview, 10 Dec. 1998. Petrash makes the point that the new business model is how you manage human, organizational, and customer/supplier capital together. Says Petrash, 'To do so implies overcoming traditional forms of organization. For example, functions such as HR and manufacturing may need to get together to solve problems. Organizations who can learn to operate this way in multifunctional contexts can make tremendous efficiency gains.'

15. Interview, 11 Dec. 1998. Rumizen says that while collaboration is now part of the culture at Buckman, the reason for it taking off originally was the strong leadership of CEO Bob Buckman who 'didn't give anyone any option'.

16. B. Kogut and U. Zander (1996), 'What Firms Do? Coordination, Identity and Learning', *Organization Science*, 7/5 (Sept.–Oct.): 502–8.

17. Interview, 26 Nov. 1998. Says Saint-Onge, 'we are now seeing clearly the correlation between the quality of leadership, the quality of services being provided, and the satisfaction of customers, all in one equation, all supported by knowledge'.

18. J. L. Medoff and K. G. Abraham (1980), 'Experience, Performance and Earnings', *Quarterly Journal of Economics*, 95 (Dec.): 703–36.

19. M. Poole and G. Jenkins (1998), 'Human Resource Management and the Theory of Rewards: Evidence from a National Survey', *British Journal of Industrial Relations*, 36/2 (June): 227–47.

20. G. P. Baker, M. C. Jensen, and K. J. Murphy (1988), 'Compensation and Incentives: Practice vs. Theory', *Journal of Finance*, 43/3 (July): 593–615.

21. R. J. Gibson and R. H. Mnookin (1990), 'The Implicit Contract for Corporate Law Firm Associates: *Ex Post* Opportunism and *Ex Ante* Bonding', in M. Aoki, B. Gustafson, and O. E. Williamson (eds.), *The Firm as Nexus of Treaties*, London: Sage Publications Ltd.: 209–36.

22. I. L. Janis (1972), *Victims of Groupthink*, Boston: Houghton Mifflin.

23. G. Moorhead, R. Ference, and C. P. Neck (1991), 'Group Decision Fiascoes Continue: Space Shuttle Challenger and a Revised Groupthink Framework', *Human Relations*, 44/6: 539–50.

24. L. M. Hitt and E. Brynjolfsson (1996), 'Productivity, Business Profitability, and Consumer Surplus: Three *Different* Measures of Information Technology Value', *MIS Quarterly* (June): 121–42.

25. C. Prahalad and G. Hamel (1990), 'The Core Competence of the Corporation', *Harvard Business Review* (May–June): 79–90.

The Rewards for Knowledge

This chapter focuses on one of the most important changes which will occur as a result of the redefinition of the firm: the restructuring of corporate ownership. The tenet of this chapter is that as firms become more knowledge intensive, the structure of ownership must change in unison. The firm's most important knowledge resources in future will be embodied in specific individuals. It is therefore only natural that those individuals' rights to the value their knowledge represents to the firm should be appropriately recognized, and the most appropriate form of recognition is participation in ownership of the firm.

While this central proposition is consistent with the transition to a knowledge economy, why should future schemes involving worker ownership be any more successful than those attempted in the past, which have, on the whole, enjoyed only mixed success? If worker participation in the ownership of firms is to increase, will it affect all firms in the same way? These and associated questions are the focus of this chapter.

EXAMPLES OF WORKER OWNERSHIP

A range of schemes have evolved over the years which have offered workers varying levels of participation in the ownership of the firms in which they were employed.

Employee Stock Ownership Plans (ESOPs)

In the early 1950s, firms started to offer employees stock ownership as a proportion of their annual compensation, thus providing in effect, a deferred compensation plan. In the USA, federal tax subsidies were introduced in 1974, which led to an acceleration of the growth of employee share ownership schemes (ESOPs). By 1988, approximately 1,500 US firms employing collectively over one million workers were majority owned by their employees through such schemes. The motivations for firms to offer such plans appear to have ranged from a desire to protect themselves against hostile takeover, to a desire to obtain greater productivity, to combat growing union power, or to improve their financial flexibility.

Worker participation in ESOPs was essentially limited to earnings. A 1986 US survey found that there were no firms with ESOPs in which the employees had a majority of board directorships and, in general, members of ESOPs had very little voice in the governance of the firm. Even where the ESOP held 100 per cent of the firm's stock, voting rights were not held by the employees but by the ESOP's trustee, who was appointed by a self-perpetuating board. The US General Accounting Office conducted research in the late 1980s which concluded that ESOPs had contributed very little to the firms which had adopted them, in terms of either economic efficiency or decision making.[1]

Worker Cooperatives

Examples of successful worker cooperatives involving workers collectively owning, managing, and controlling enterprises have been relatively sparse in western countries. The Israeli kibbutz system, the plywood cooperatives of the US north-west, and the Spanish cooperative Mondragon stand out as unusually long-lived examples. Many other cooperatives have since come and gone, often the result of worker buyouts of firms, undertaken in adverse economic conditions and usually as a reaction to potential redundancies.

The few successful schemes have all tended to include high levels of worker participation and control in decision making, large workforces, and diverse industrial applications, some of which have been capital intensive and others labour or knowledge intensive. The difficulty has been to replicate such schemes elsewhere. The critical success factors in each case appear to have been either unique or so highly specific to local conditions that they were not easily replicable.

Codetermination

Some firms, notably in Germany, have allowed workers and investors to participate equally in electing board directors, the aim being to improve worker involvement in communication and decision making. The results of these experiments have tended to show that the very different levels of knowledge in the two groups have rendered joint decision making impractical. In effect, they have become communication forums. Their main advantage has been to allow workers to have a greater degree of awareness of corporate issues and directions, but it is doubtful that their involvement has significantly affected firm decision making.

Management Buyouts (MBOs)

MBOs became popular in the 1980s and continue to attract attention, particularly those involving substantial external debt used for leverage. MBOs are however typically restricted, in that only a small number of management tend to be involved. In effect, a management elite become the new investors, the rest of the management and key workers remaining uninvolved. According to research involving fifty MBOs, the average stock holding of those involved in the buyout was already 11.5 per cent before the buyout and subsequently only rose to 16.7 per cent, so even those involved in the MBO did not necessarily increase their ownership of the firm to an appreciable extent.[2] Many MBOs have also been undertaken by management and their financial backers as a short-term strategy designed to gain control before refloating the firm publicly and recouping on their investment.

Services Sector Firms

Here we find a different story. In the services sector, worker-owned firms are quite common. Many firms of accountants and lawyers are almost totally owned by the professional knowledge workers within them. Many management consultants, IT consultants, engineers, scientists, doctors, and bankers also tend to operate in mutually owned practices. Apart from groups such as these, with notably high levels of specialized knowledge, other examples are also to be found of service workers with very different educational backgrounds and skills, such as taxicab drivers, refuse collectors, and milkmen, operating in mutually owned businesses or business networks.

THE DETERMINANTS OF WORKER OWNERSHIP

What lessons can we derive from history? The answer as usual must be to abstract the general from the particular, to note the underlying factors which have proved important to the long-run success (or failure) of worker ownership. From these it should be possible to identify common factors which can be further evaluated in light of the changing profile of the firm.

History shows that employee participation, involving ESOPs, worker cooperatives, codetermination, and MBOs, has delivered mixed results. This is not altogether surprising insofar as the objectives of these schemes have differed markedly. For example, the objectives of those involved in management buyouts or the development of 'defensive' employee share ownership plans can often be traced to personal or corporate strategies which have little to do with worker participation as such.[3] Likewise the kibbutz system and Mondragon appear to have developed as a result of various situation-specific factors which caused worker ownership to have a special appeal at the time of their creation.[4] Many other worker cooperatives can be seen to have emerged as a reaction to firm-specific problems, the alternative in many cases having been mass sackings and plant closures; few of these 'defensive' examples of worker participation however seem to have survived for long.[5]

The services sector on the other hand provides numerous examples of businesses with sustained high levels of worker ownership. Why should this be the case and what is it that doctors, lawyers, taxicab drivers, and refuse collectors have in common, which has led many of them to adopt similar patterns of business ownership and management? One immediately obvious common factor is that they are all service providers, but this in itself is obviously not enough—many other services firms, such as banks and (nowadays) insurers, are not collectively owned or operated.

Key factors which these seemingly disparate groups do appear to have in common however are dependency on human capital (people), low levels of investment in physical assets, and significant levels of specialized knowledge (albeit different types of knowledge). Strongly associated factors include a tendency for individuals within each group to work independently as well as being part of the group, a tendency to be difficult to monitor and control, and broadly similar knowledge levels between the individual workers in each group. Other associated factors are that the firms tend to be small (exceptions include many large professional practices) and narrowly focused, rather than large and diverse in the range of services offered.

While not ignoring examples from other sectors, the prevalence of worker participation in the ownership of service sector firms suggests it may be worthwhile taking a closer look at the characteristics of the firms involved.

Positive Factors

Apart from the tendency to be human rather than physical capital intensive, two factors stand out as being most strongly associated with worker participation in firm ownership: knowledge intensity and homogeneity.[6]

Knowledge Intensity

The knowledge profile of doctors, lawyers, accountants, engineers, and other professional service workers could be typified as follows:

- high levels of explicit codified knowledge including both conceptual and theoretical knowledge as well as high tacit knowledge, usually gained on the job;
- focus on a particular body of knowledge/specialization usually linked to a particular academic discipline;
- continuous knowledge acquisition and updating, while on the job;

- most knowledge acquired through the study of theory.

The typical knowledge profile of taxicab drivers, refuse disposal collectors, milkmen, and many other providers of personal and business services would tend to include:

- low levels of explicit codified knowledge, but high levels of idiosyncratic and (usually) tacit knowledge, such as an individual taxicab driver's knowledge of how to get to the airport in the shortest time, in rush hour traffic;
- specialization on a particular and usually narrowly defined job, trade, or task;
- continuous acquisition of local and situation-specific knowledge, such as knowledge of clients' habits and preferences;
- most knowledge gained on the job.

From this analysis it can be seen that workers such as doctors or lawyers tend to depend upon explicit knowledge derived from previous, largely academic training plus tacit knowledge gained on the job. Other service workers who have not received such training rely almost solely on idiosyncratic and tacit knowledge gained on the job. All service workers tend to update their knowledge bases frequently, i.e. to be engaged in continuous learning. Specialization also appears to be a common factor; it is as unusual to find a doctor who is also an engineer as it is to find a taxi driver who is also a refuse collector.

Aside from its importance in the services sector, knowledge has also played a pivotal role in the creation and ongoing development of worker-owned enterprises in other sectors. The famous Mondragon industrial cooperative in Spain, founded by Don Jose María in the 1950s, was preceded in 1943 by the creation of a school, the Escuela Politécnica, to train boys in industrial skills. In 1955 five of the first students left the school and in 1956 created the first unit in the Mondragon cooperative complex. Subsequently the school has developed significantly, providing engineering training equivalent to third-year level at US colleges.

By the late 1980s the kibbutzim in Israel, which had originated mainly as labour-intensive factories in the 1940s and 1950s, employed only 6 per cent of the total Israeli workforce but significantly used 60 per cent of the country's industrial robots. As a result, no more than 40–50 per cent of the workers in such factories were involved in production, the rest being employed in areas where professional knowledge was needed.[7]

Homogeneity

Workers in worker-owned firms typically enjoy similar educational backgrounds and skill levels, perform similar types of work, and enjoy similar status. This applies particularly to those in the core group of workers who actually own and manage the firm, such as the partners in a law firm. Even in a multi-level hierarchy, however, the skill levels of those in the associate and core groups, such as the associates and partners in a law firm, can be seen to be closely similar. The level of knowledge and other cultural characteristics which tend towards homogeneity among these workers also seems to have some effect on the characteristics of the peripheral group. Legal secretaries, librarians, and receptionists, for example, tend to be better qualified than their counterparts in many other industries.

The relevance of homogeneity to the success of worker-owned firms can be seen to operate in many ways. In the kibbutz system, for example, individuals of widely differing social, ethnic, and educational backgrounds have traditionally worked at the same jobs, thus enhancing the general level of appreciation of the contribution made by each worker, and contributing to cohesion. The greater the similarity in knowledge levels the easier it is for one worker to monitor another effectively, especially if individuals in the firm have highly specialized knowledge. Attitudes to standards of quality and professionalism are less likely to diverge where cultural and educational background is similar. The ability of one worker to deputize for another is easier. Decision making is facilitated where the level of awareness of all involved is broadly similar.

This is not to imply that all the accountants in an accountancy firm, for example, when faced with the need for a group decision on an issue, will automatically agree with one another. It does however imply that they will all tend to have a similar appreciation of the nature of the issue and the implications of the decision. Neither does homogeneity mean that groups of accountants (to use the same example) will necessarily make 'better' decisions than multidisciplinary groups. As noted earlier, one of the benefits of cross-functional teams has been shown to be the diversity of knowledge and thus perspectives which can be brought to bear on a problem.

A problem of homogeneity, particularly noted in the 100 per cent worker-owned cooperatives, but also relevant in partially worker-owned firms, relates to how to compensate workers who may do similar work (and thus might claim similar pay) but whose personal contributions to the firm's success differ. Where taxi drivers are concerned, there is little problem; each earns according to his or her individual effort—an 'eat what you kill' style of remuneration.[8] In a law firm or similar professional practice, however, the problem can become more complex. As a result, either the percentage or the formula system is generally used. Under the percentage arrangement a producer earns a set percentage of his or her billings. Under the formula arrangement, individual contributions in terms of billable hours, introduced business, and other performance measures may be taken into account. Neither approach seems to have been significantly more successful than the other, and each offers proven ways to overcome issues caused by differences in individual performance.[9]

The nature of the work performed by individual workers in firms with high levels of ownership participation tends to be similar. One doctor, taxi driver, or lawyer commonly performs the same generic functions as his or her colleagues in terms of their professional or business activities. The structure of work in an accounting, legal, or taxicab practice resembles a series of nodes in a network, each of which enjoys relative autonomy, performs similar functions, and enjoys a peer relationship with other nodes.

Homogeneity can thus be seen to be an important common factor in most types of enterprise involving high levels of worker ownership. Homogeneity applies not only to skill levels but also to modes of work, monitoring systems, style of remuneration, knowledge of firm systems and procedures, and cultural attitudes. One of the most striking aspects of homogeneity is the facility with which workers in a similar service, profession, or occupation can work either collectively or independently. Doctors, lawyers, or taxicab drivers can operate efficiently, either as independent contractors, within a mutually owned firm, or in a loose business network or confederation. The connection between all involved appears to be most closely related to their shared reference discipline or body of knowledge. It thus seems that knowledge and homogeneity are mutually reinforcing factors, so that when both factors are strongly represented, the chances of ownership by the key knowledge workers in the firm are greater. Conversely, when these factors are not both strongly positive, different ownership structures are more likely to occur (see Fig. 9.1).

| | | Knowledge intensity | |
		HIGH	LOW
Workforce homogeneity	HIGH	Key knowledge workers	Private shareholders
	LOW	One, or a few, knowledge workers	Public ownership

FIG. 9.1. Knowledge intensity, homogeneity, and firm ownership structures

Negative Factors

Four factors, size, capital intensity, diversity, and the tendency for democratically managed enterprises to degenerate into oligarchies, have been found to be negatively associated with worker ownership of firms.

Organization Size

Whilst size, as defined by numbers of employees in the firm, might be expected to limit effective worker ownership, there are significant examples of firms overcoming size-related issues. The big five accounting practices world-wide have many thousands of working partners, and large professional prac-tices of all types run to hundreds of partners. PriceWaterhouseCoopers, currently the largest of the big five, with annual revenues of $US15 billion, has 9,000 partners worldwide. Mondragon, the Spanish cooperative, has over 20,000 owner workers. While size in itself does not appear to be a particularly important factor, when combined with other factors it can however become critical (see below).

Capital Intensity

Both Mondragon and the kibbutzim, in common with many investment banks and some of the larger professional service firms, have shown that increasing financial capital intensity may proceed in parallel with increasing knowledge intensity. Whilst a balance is maintained between the two, worker ownership may continue to flourish. In situations, however, where money is in effect used to buy out knowledge, democratic governance tends to diminish. A typi-cal example of this practice can be observed in the taxicab industry, when local authorities sell taxicab licences. Some cab drivers accumulate licences and start mini-taxi fleets of their own, hiring additional drivers as required, rather than acting privately as owner drivers within a business network. The net effect is the development of privately owned subnetworks involving more subordinate relationships and thus a change to the character of the overall network.[10]

The takeover of Salomon Brothers, the well-known New York investment bank, provides another relevant example. The first generation of partners decided to capitalize on their investment by publicly floating on the New York Stock Exchange. Later, after external investors led by one of America's most highly regarded investors, Warren Buffett, became involved, the most talented income-generating partners departed.[11]

The great majority of successful worker-owned firms are to be found in the services sector, which has a high proportion of firms whose major production inputs are knowledge and human capital rather than physical and financial capital. For a worker-owned firm to raise financial capital can be problematic. Either the owners have to provide the funding themselves, which means each individual taking a personal financial risk, or the firm will have to raise debt finance. This is easier if the firm has significant tangible/physical assets, but is often difficult for firms such as many of those involved in the services sector, where the major assets are people. The penalties imposed on many Lloyd's brokers in recent years are testament to the problems that can occur in firms where individuals have to place considerable personal capital at risk. Even if a worker-owned firm is able to raise the necessary capital to fund projects, it may well be tempted not to do so, unless both the rate of return is higher than would be the case in a normal firm and the risk profile lower. This is because the owners may be staking their personal fortunes on the project's success.

Whilst capital intensity is obviously a significant factor, it does not appear to have prevented organizations such as Lloyd's of London continuing to attract 'names'. Nor has it traditionally inhibited small worker-owned firms and partnerships from operating in capital-intensive industries such as farming and merchant banking, where debt finance can be secured against the tangible assets of the firm. More recently small hi-tech start-ups such as the biotechs have maintained their owner's equity by collaboration with large firms rather than conventional debt or equity funding strategies.[12] As a generalization however it would be fair to say that firms with few tangible assets and significant ongoing needs for external financial funding are less likely to suit worker ownership in the current market.

Diversity

The diversity of activity carried on by the firm has been shown in the past to have a significant bearing on whether or not worker ownership is likely to be viable. Firms which have a common core of knowledge and diversify concentrically around that core tend to attract workers of similar backgrounds and skill groups. Large single-disciplinary professional firms, often with many thousands of workers, tend to have higher levels of worker ownership, for example, than industrial conglomerates.

Since creativity, innovation, and complex decision making are generally associated with cross-functional teamwork involving diversity of knowledge, does this mean that worker ownership is likely to be restricted to organizations characterized by simple decision processes, low levels of innovation, and a single central discipline? Such a profile might well fit many of the service sector firms discussed earlier. If economic success in future however is going to depend on integration of disparate knowledge, then presumably single-disciplinary firms are going to have to become more intellectually diverse. Does this imply less of a future for worker ownership? Conversely, where worker ownership does increase, does this imply less innovation? The central issue here is the nature of diversity as it applies to knowledge.

Unlike integrating dissimilar physical and material resources, integrating knowledge gained in different domains can be achieved efficiently, particularly where the knowledge domains overlap or share some underlying common discipline. Single-disciplinary practices are constantly expanding their knowledge domains and introducing new services. Medical practitioners are for example branching into different areas, many of which demand skills from other disciplines, notably including information systems. 'Multidisciplinary' professional practices are starting to emerge, combining law, finance, accounting, economics, and (again) information systems. The world's largest accountancy practice, PriceWaterhouseCoopers, has recently announced its intention to become the world's largest legal practice.

The profiles of firms with quite dissimilar backgrounds such as EDS and Andersen Consulting for example are as a result starting to look similar. EDS, the brainchild of former IBM salesman Ross Perot, became the leading IS out-sourcing company in the world. Latterly however, with the acquisition of A. T. Kearney, it has moved into management consulting and diversified from its core outsourcing business into business process management, support for e-commerce applications, and a host of related IS solutions and services.[13] Andersen Consulting, on the other hand, an organization originally formed by Arthur Andersen the accounting firm, has shifted aggressively into IS out-sourcing and a broad range of mainly IS services covering many of the same technologies and markets as EDS.[14]

How can multidisciplinary firms grow with such apparent ease? Information systems clearly can help. Instead of operating multiple separate systems to manage their routine functions, merging firms can gain benefits from stan-dardizing their basic routines such as client accounting and billing. Merged practice databases can allow practitioners in different disciplinary areas in the same firm to exploit opportunities for cross-marketing to their respective client bases and for sharing and exchanging ideas. Another factor beginning to facilitate knowledge sharing in professional firms is their habit of recruiting graduates with more broadly based, multidisciplinary qualifications, involving combinations of law, accountancy, IT, economics, banking, and science.

Although size, hierarchical complexity, and cultural barriers still exist, the knowledge bases of many other traditional industries, as noted earlier, are also starting to overlap. Publishing, broadcasting, computing, and telecommuni-cations industries are starting to merge because their underlying production technologies are converging. In future, IT and publishing specialists may as a result know more about each other's disciplines.

In the short term, large single-disciplinary firms are likely to become more intellectually diverse, while smaller firms can be expected to remain less diverse and thus more amenable to worker participation. Over time, even in larger firms, diverse knowledge is likely to be more evenly spread and individ-uals are likely to be more multiskilled; thus barriers to worker participation based on knowledge diversity should progressively reduce.

Oligarchic Tendencies

Anyone who has observed the way the pecking order is established in the farmyard will be familiar with the tendency to oligarchy within groups. In George Orwell's fable *Animal Farm*, for instance, the pigs gradually assumed power over the rest of the animals.[15] Back in 1915, Michels similarly argued that all organizations, even those committed to democratic process and mem-ber control, ultimately degenerate into oligarchies.[16] This classic study has been criticized for its extreme pessimism, but subsequent studies up to the present day continue to point to the tendency of self-interest and opportunism to corrupt democratic structures.

Michels's concept represented an evolutionary view. Over time in any organization, commercial or otherwise, some members will gradually acquire greater influence. Progressively this influence will be formalized. The result is a ruling elite which, through either natural ability or cunning (both reflecting tacit knowledge), or demonstrably greater explicit knowledge, will continue to seek to reinforce its position through various formal or informal mechanisms. Democracy is thus progressively weakened and oligarchy usually triumphs.

According to Michels's theory, age and size of organization are critical factors associated with the development of an elite. Thus it should be expected that the longer a firm has been established and the larger it is, the more likely it will be controlled by a decision-making elite. Apart from size and age, a worker-owned firm may be expected to be more susceptible to the emergence of such an elite than a classical investor-owned firm. In the latter case, the separation of ownership and control provides shareholders with the opportunity to appoint non-executive directors to the board, who can then act as independent monitors of the executive.

A study into the organizational characteristics associated with the decline of democracy in law firms provides some useful insights on the effects of the firm ageing process and also other factors relating to specific categories of decision making in such firms.[17] This study involved two large law firms with offices in twenty metropolitan areas throughout the USA. The findings showed that on average 72 per cent of all partners were involved in appointment of members of the executive committee of a law firm: its ruling body. Promotion decisions involved 62 per cent of all partners but compensation decisions only 28 per cent. These findings correspond to similar research conducted in medical practices, which found that decisions explicitly linked to financial issues were likely to involve fewer participants whilst decisions related to a colleague's competence were more broadly based. The most stable and significant correlate of democratic structure in the case of the law firms was found to be the number of linkages between the firm and business corporations. Law firms closely tied to business corporations were found to be least democratic in their decision making.

Size was consistently negatively associated with democratic or collegial style decision making involving compensation and executive committee appointments, indicating that the larger the firm the more likely it is that oligarchic control will develop over such decisions. Age of the practice however was found to have a significant effect only on the process of selection of executive committee members, and to have little effect on compensation or general promotion decisions. Other indications of a general degeneration of democracy were found in the higher percentage of associates to partner ratios in older firms as well as in firms with higher levels of business linkages.

One of the strongest correlates with continuing democratic governance was found to be the homogeneity of the membership of the firm, which was reflected in lower partner/associate ratios. Firms which had abandoned the commitment to a collegial democratic structure were found to be more frequent employers of non-owner labour, i.e. to have more workers in the peripheral group. A positive relationship was also found to exist between 'membership eliteness' and the partner/associate ratio based on the finding that, where firms selected associates from prestige law schools, the partner/associate ratio, tended to be lower, possibly reflecting both the capabilities and aspirations of the associates.

The findings of this particular study tend to confirm the tendencies noted earlier of worker ownership increasing due to homogeneity, as well as the tendency to oligarchy, particularly in respect to financial decisions and decisions affecting the tenure of the firm's core group. It would seem that an important dynamic associated with the maintenance of more broadly based governance structures is likely to be the up or out system, which constantly infuses new talented workers, who will inevitably seek to have their voices heard in the affairs of the firm.

Analysing the Evidence

Factors considered conducive to worker ownership according to traditional economic theories include situations where metering or monitoring individual worker activity involves high costs. Other traditional reasons include firms' need to protect themselves against the departure of individuals with high levels of firm-specific knowledge. Special measures for example are frequently taken to ensure a small group of managers' interests align with corporate goals, hence the growing practice of offering board members stock options. Such practices suggest why, in the past, employee ownership schemes have been restricted in scope, since they all reflect compensatory or *defensive* rationales, rather than *positive* strategies to capitalize on knowledge resources.

In contrast to such defensive strategies, the analyses of successful examples of worker-owned firms discussed above show that knowledge intensity and homogeneity tend to be strongly positively associated with worker ownership. Some large capital-intensive heterogeneous firms are successfully worker owned. Many highly homogeneous and knowledge-intensive firms are not worker owned. Nevertheless, in broad terms, these two sets of factors stand out as most strongly influencing the success of worker ownership.

Conversely, factors inimical to worker ownership include the need for significant levels of financial capital, firm size where it impedes collective decision making, and diversity where it involves multiple reference disciplines (although these factors are weakening). Oligarchies restrict the *diffusion* of worker ownership, but future oligarchs will tend to be the knowledge workers with the greatest ability rather than the owners of traditional forms of capital.

EMERGING TRENDS

How might we expect the positive and negative factors discussed above to affect the development of worker ownership in future? Taking the positive factors first, firms in general, not just in the service sector, are becoming more knowledge intensive. The educational qualifications demanded of workers alone will produce a more homogeneous, multiskilled workforce. Second, the externalization of non-core functions will generate a more homogeneous work environment within the firm. Both of these factors are conducive to a growth in worker participation and ownership.

Factors that have constrained worker participation in corporate decision making in the past are unlikely to be as significant in future. The hierarchies of large firms are in general already shrinking. Small firms are either growing more slowly than they used to, or reducing in size. Collaborative networking is already replacing direct employment by owner-operated firms. Levels of hierarchy are reducing. Communications and decision support systems are improving. All of these trends point to a diminution in the problems previously implicit in knowledge sharing and collective decision making.

Physical capital requirements similarly are likely to reduce for many firms. Human capital and knowledge, rather than physical plant, equipment, and materials, will be the most highly sought-after forms of capital. For those firms that still require access to significant amounts of financial capital, funding should be easier to obtain. Reasons for this include the progressive opening up of global financial markets, and increased availability of venture capital funding for knowledge-intensive businesses from both private and public sources. Collaboration through knowledge-based alliances provides another route around the problem of capital funding, which will also tend to maintain the independence of the key knowledge holders.

Current trends indicate a growing interest in all forms of worker participation. By the early 1990s, deferred profit sharing in the USA had been adopted by 15 per cent of all firms with over 100 employees. Among other OECD nations, Belgium, Canada, France, and the UK have all experienced rises in profit-sharing schemes over (approximately) the last decade. Anecdotal evidence also suggests the numbers of senior management having stock options or similar entitlements are strongly growing.

High-technology industries are setting the pace in pursuing worker ownership. According to Carl Camden, Executive Vice-President Operations at staffing services provider Kelly Services, equity is now the dominant form of non-wage benefit sought by workers when making a longer-term commitment to a firm.[18] Stan Shih, co-founder of the Acer Group, a leading multinational PC manufacturer, has coined the slogan '21 in 21' to describe his intention of having the Group split into twenty-one separate companies by the twenty-first century. Each company will be owned by its own management, plus home country investors, with (usually) a minority position held by

Acer itself. Shih believes local ownership will unleash the motivation for the new owners to run each company prudently.[19]

Turning to the negative factors, the tendency to oligarchy is not expected to change, inasmuch as human nature is the root cause of this particular phenomenon. Authority relationships are however diminishing across the board as hierarchies flatten. The greater the average levels of knowledge and experience in any organization, the less chance that a ruling elite will emerge. What is likely to occur however is a power struggle between the traditional oligarchs, the owners of financial capital, who at present control much of the corporate sector and the up and coming knowledge capitalists—the 'Bill Gateses' of the future.

Other trends militating against worker ownership include the increasing size of already large firms as global mega mergers continue to proliferate, the increasing diversity of knowledge implied in industrial convergence, and the continuing need for firms to access external sources of funding for growth. Most of these factors tend to apply most strongly at the medium to large end of the corporate scale, which indicates that worker ownership may tend to remain a small firm phenomenon in the short term. On the other hand, although some large firms are becoming even larger, their numbers are few and the average size of large firms is still declining. Many mega mergers, such as those currently occurring in financial services, are already resulting in significant workforce reductions. In the short term, many mega firms themselves will shrink back to an expanded core of knowledge workers. Similarly cross-industry mergers such as those occurring in the media, telecommunications, and computing industries will doubtless be followed by business rationalization, leading to slimmer, smarter organizations, with consequently greater potential for worker participation.

Finally, structural convergence is predicted to occur between business networks representing loose confederations of self-employed workers, and firms representing tighter confederations of worker owners. At present many knowledge workers operate semi-autonomously within formal or informal business groupings while others establish firms. The decision as to which organizational form to adopt will in future be less obvious. Whereas traditionally the firm has offered a clearly superior structure for knowledge integration and ownership protection, knowledge integration via networking is likely to improve through the use of technology. On the other hand, ownership benefits are likely to be diluted through mutual ownership. The result is going to be a reducing differential between the two organizational forms. For many workers, owning their own (single person) micro firms will be the answer.

SUMMARY

- Worker ownership is likely to increase in firms whose workers have high levels of specialized and/or tacit knowledge; and those where worker skills, qualifications, and occupations are homogeneous.
- Other factors positively associated with worker ownership will include the ability of workers to operate both independently and collectively, difficulties associated with independent monitoring, high levels of innovation, and low dependency on external funding.
- Characteristics of firms in which worker ownership is less likely to develop include those with requirements for high levels of external funding, dependency on physical rather than knowledge assets, heterogeneous workforces, highly diverse products, and policies which offer low protection against the emergence of oligarchies/ruling elites. Large size is likely to play a negative role when combined with one or more of the above factors.
- Knowledge oligarchies will progressively replace oligarchies based on control of physical assets in those firms where organizational structure and policies offer low protection against their emergence.
- In the short term, large firms with a profile inconsistent with worker ownership are likely to dominate world stock markets; thus worker ownership of such firms will be limited, whereas worker ownership in smaller privately owned firms will increase more rapidly.
- Membership of networks and ownership of firms are likely to offer increasingly similar benefits for small firms and self-employed individuals, leading to convergence of the two organizational forms.

IMPLICATIONS

A trend towards increasing levels of worker ownership clearly carries with it wide-ranging implications for firms, workers, and investors, many of which will only become apparent over time. A few of the more obvious and immediate implications are discussed here.

Corporate Transition Strategies

It seems likely that as the market leaders in particular industries move beyond decentralized profit-centred management, to progressively greater devolution of power, other firms in the same industry will have to speed up their own internal power-sharing arrangements. The danger for the larger, more diverse, and more capital-intensive firms is that their key knowledge workers will not be content unless they start to receive a share of corporate ownership and play a larger role in corporate decision making. Large industrial conglomerates would appear to be most at risk of key knowledge workers leaving, due to lack of such incentives. The stock market meanwhile will penalize those firms that do not 'bite the bullet' and show they are adapting to the knowledge economy.

The move towards federated structures by industrial firms like ABB, Benetton, and Acer mentioned earlier can be seen as a way of anticipating instead of resisting change, making worker participation a central component of corporate strategy. As a result, such firms have shown their ability to continue to grow and maintain internal cohesion, while at the same time devolving power. Although devolving power clearly implies taking risks, holding on to it will probably entail taking even greater risks.

Democracy or Knowledge Oligarchies?

Counter-arguments to the proposition that increased knowledge intensity implies *more* worker ownership are usually based on the tendency of all groups to degenerate into oligarchies. According to this logic, democratic governance will be no more successful in an economy dominated by people with knowledge than one dominated by people with money. There is obviously some strength in this argument. The organization of the modern networked firm, with its semi-autonomous, informal, team-based structures, might well make it easier for the more ambitious knowledge workers to take control by stealth. Various writers have commented on the danger of 'mafia-like' structures appearing in firms with cronyism and favouritism flourishing in the absence of traditional command and control systems.[20]

Adopting worker ownership as an explicit corporate strategy, however, is likely to reduce the risk of these types of activities occurring. If workers can see their way to achieving a greater say in the affairs of the firm by legitimate (democratic) means they will not have to resort to other means. The danger of collective team decision making becoming suboptimal due to groupthink should also be reduced once team members recognize that their fortunes and those of the firm are more closely related.

The risks mentioned above also need to be viewed in context. The issue is not whether a pecking order will be established, but whether workers on aggregate will have a greater say in the activities of the firm than previously. More egalitarian decision structures, more personal autonomy, and higher average levels of education imply more, not less, democratic governance. Even if the 4 per cent who currently control 40 per cent or so of the economic wealth in leading western nations are joined or replaced by even 10 per cent of the workforce with the highest knowledge levels, this still implies a major redistribution of wealth and power.

Other Stakeholder Implications

The switch from money capitalism to knowledge capitalism is already starting to be reflected in world stock markets. Many hi-tech stocks have been valued very highly, even though the accounting numbers are unable to reflect this value.

During the first half of 1998, the share market value of three leading 'search engines' on the Internet, Yahoo, Excite, and Lycos, all increased by over 500 per cent. Amazon.com Inc., reputed to be the world's largest Internet bookstore, has increased its value by 900 per cent in the last twelve months, even though it has yet to turn a profit. The firm is currently capitalized to the value of America's two biggest book retailers combined.[21]

Valuations of such stocks based on conventional interpretation of their financial results would bear no resemblance to the actual value put on them by the market. They have few physical assets, short track records, and many of them have neither turned a profit nor even appear to have any clear idea of when they will. What does the market know that is not reflected in the accounting numbers? The answer clearly is that the market has decided to place its own value on what cannot currently be measured and recorded in financial reports, i.e. the knowledge represented by these firms. In the absence of any standard criteria for valuing knowledge, the market is doing the best it can. High-knowledge stocks can be expected to continue to perform strongly in overall terms. The lack of standard methods for valuing knowledge however, and thus the lack of surety in the market, is bound to be reflected in continuing market volatility. It is no surprise that the share prices of some of the first Internet stocks to be listed on world stock markets are now on the way down.

In the medium term, markets will clearly have to resolve issues such as how to value knowledge-intensive stocks and human capital in the firm (see Chapter 11). It can be assumed that this will lead to more markets like NASDAQ being developed, which cater specifically for 'high-knowledge' stocks. Other effects seem likely to include the development of 'knowledge auditing' alongside, or as an extension of, financial and information systems auditing and changes to standards of financial reporting to enable better valuation of knowledge assets. Skandia, the Swedish insurance and financial services group, is currently acting as a pathfinder in developing its own internal intellectual capital model and publishing reports based on it alongside the group's financial accounting reports.[22]

The shift towards greater worker ownership seems likely in the short term to boost rather than diminish the importance of stock markets since many more workers will become shareholders in public corporations. What will happen to other schemes such as ESOPs is less obvious. The purpose of such schemes, as discussed earlier, seems to have been less about democratic governance than about workforce stabilization. Given the trend towards externalization of the peripheral workforce, stabilization is not the issue it once was. Workers will have to invest in their own businesses, or alternatively persuade the firms they work for to offer them a share in corporate ownership, based on their individual performance. ESOPs may continue, but the objectives and management of such schemes must change.

The major outstanding issue is: what will happen to the balance of the workforce who are unable to progress to a self-sufficient, business-owning lifestyle? Since nature has been decidedly undemocratic when handing out intelligence, some of us will have to run faster than others to get ahead. Current advances in genetics suggest the parents of the workforce of 2030–50 may well have more say in how smart their offspring are going to be. In the short term, however, the main antidote to the looming disparity in work opportunities and wealth creation is undoubtedly affordable high-quality education for all, coupled with strong incentives for individuals to take advantage of it. The implications of moving from an *employment*-centred to a *learning*-centred world are therefore the focus of the next chapter.

NOTES

1. R. Russell (1991), 'Sharing Ownership in the Services', in R. Russell and V. Rus (eds.), *International Handbook of Participation in Organisations: For the Study of Organisational Democracy, Co-operation, and Self-Management*, ii: *Ownership and Participation*, New York: Oxford University Press: 197–217.
2. H. Hansmann (1990), 'The Viability of Worker Ownership: An Economic Perspective on the Political Structure of the Firm', in M. Aoki, B. Gustafsson, and O. E. Williamson (eds.), *The Firm as a Nexus of Treaties*, London: SAGE Publications Ltd.: 162–84.
3. H. Barkai (1977), *Growth Patterns of the Kibbutz Economy*, Amsterdam: North-Holland.
4. H. Thomas and C. Logan (1982), *Mondragon: An Economic Analysis*, London: George Allen & Unwin (Publishers) Ltd.
5. A. Pendleton, N. Wilson, and M. Wright (1998), 'The Perception and Effects of Share Ownership: Empirical Evidence from Employee Buy-Outs', *British Journal of Industrial Relations*, 36/1 (Mar.): 99–123.
6. Hansmann 'The Viability of Worker Ownership: An Economic Perspective on the Political Structure of the Firm'.
7. M. Rosner (1991), 'Ownership, Participation, and Work Restructuring in the Kibbutz: A Comparative Perspective', in Russell and Rus (eds.), *International Handbook of Participation in Organisations*, ii. 170–96.
8. P. D. Sheier (1996), 'Towards an Understanding of the Variety in Work Arrangements: The Organization and Labor Relationships Framework', in C. L. Cooper and D. M. Rousseau (eds.), *Trends in Organizational Behaviour*, iii, New York: John Wiley & Sons Ltd.: 99–120.
9. Russell, 'Sharing Ownership in the Services'.

10. R. Russell (1985), *Sharing Ownership in the Workplace*, Albany, NY: State University of New York Press.
11. L. C. Thurow (1996), *The Future of Capitalism: How Today's Economic Forces Will Shape Tomorrow's World*, New York: William Morrow & Company Inc.
12. W. W. Powell (1996), 'Inter-organizational Collaboration in the Biotechnology Industry', *Journal of Institutional and Theoretical Economics*, 152: 197–225.
13. EDS Annual Report 1997, *http://www.eds.com/97annual*.
14. Andersen Consulting Annual Report 1997, *http://www.ac.com/overview/annual97*.
15. G. Orwell (1984), *Animal Farm: A Fairy Story*, London: Folio Society.
16. R. Michels (1915), *Political Parties: A Sociological Structure of the Oligarchical Tendencies of Modern Democracy*, Glencoe, Ill.: Free Press.
17. P. S. Tolbert and R. N. Stern (1991), 'Inequality in a Company of Equals: Participation and Control in Large Law Firms', in Russell and Rus (eds.), *International Handbook of Participation in Organisations*, ii. 248–63.
18. Interview, 6 Jan. 1999. Camden says, 'equity-based compensation is the fastest growing form of compensation . . . workers today understand that a lifelong contract is no longer possible, but are increasingly demanding a piece of equity in exchange for a longer-term commitment to companies'.
19. R. E. Miles, C. C. Snow, J. A. Matthews, G. Miles, and H. J. J. Coleman (1997),'Organizing in the Knowledge Age: Anticipating the Cellular Form', *Academy of Management Executive*, 11/4: 7–24.
20. P. Brown and R. Scase (1997), 'Universities and Employers: Rhetoric and Reality', in A. Smith and F. Webster (eds.), *The Postmodern University? Contested Visions of Higher Education in Society*, Buckingham: SHRE and Open University Press: 85–98.
21. P. Kelly (1998), 'American Miracle', *Weekend Australian*, 25–6 July: 17.
22. Skandia Group: Intellectual Capital, *http://www.skandia.se/group/future/intellectual*.

PART IV

*Happy is the man that findeth wisdom and the
man that getteth understanding.
For the merchandising of it is better than
the merchandise of silver and the gain
thereof than fine gold.*

(Proverbs 3: 13–14)

The Learning Imperative

The shift to a knowledge-based economy demands that traditional relationships between education, learning and work are fundamentally reappraised. The long-running debate over whether and to what extent education should be a preparation for work, as well as life, is being overtaken by events, with work and learning becoming increasingly interrelated and interdependent. The need for a new coalition between education and industry is building as the demand by firms for access to more highly qualified and broadly based expertise increases and the demand for low-skilled labour declines.

The current, largely publicly funded infrastructure of schools, universities, and colleges of further education was built to satisfy a model of educational needs derived from an industrial era, in which an educated and wealthy elite employed the less-educated masses. Education for the majority began and usually ended in the school classroom. The economically and intellectually elite (originally men only) went on to tertiary-level institutions, where student–teacher ratios ensured high levels of personal attention. The masses were thus taught, while the future owners and managers of capital acquired the practices and habits of critical thought; of *learning* rather than merely *being instructed.* The negative effects of adherence to this now outdated educational model are starkly evident from current labour market statistics. Systems created in the past to provide and support education are clearly ill suited to cater for the forthcoming explosion in demand for access to learning resources.

According to a recent survey, an average of 21 per cent of men and 50 per cent of women in OECD countries who had received only basic secondary education were non-participants in the workforce, i.e. not among those in work or recorded as seeking work. The participation rate rises as educational levels improve, with only 7 per cent of university-educated men and 10 per cent of university-educated women recorded as non-participants.[1]

In the USA in 1994, the earnings of men with a university-level education were on average over 2.6 times those of men with only a lower secondary education; for women the ratio was almost 2.8 times this.[2] Across the OECD, average earnings of university-educated individuals were typically 50 per cent higher than those that had received upper secondary-level education; these were in turn 10 to 20 per cent higher than those who had received only basic secondary education.[3] The same pattern emerges in relation to unemployment. Unemployment rates for those with an upper secondary-level qualification were two to four times higher than for those with a university education and the unemployment rate was substantially higher again for those with only a basic secondary education.

Current standards of literacy and numeracy are a major cause for concern. The first International Adult Literacy survey showed that the basic literacy and numeracy skills of up to 20 per cent of the total population in seven advanced economies were below that which would generally be required to obtain employment.[4] Problems of literacy and numeracy differ between countries, but the standards in the UK are perhaps illustrative. There, one in five 21-year-olds has problems with basic maths, one in seven has problems with basic reading and writing, and reading standards among 11- and 15-year-olds have not significantly improved since 1945.[5] In the USA, students score below the world average in mathematics, and the top 10 per cent of America's maths students score only as well as the average student in Singapore, the world leader in maths education.[6]

For those leaving the educational system and entering the labour market, the average elapsed time before obtaining work is increasing. An upper secondary education is fast becoming the minimum criterion for entry to the labour market. In 1994 early school leavers, after one year, experienced an unemployment rate of 25 per cent in Australia, ranging up to 62 per cent in France. Unemployment rates after five years for this group were still strikingly high.[7]

Employment of individuals with low levels of education is plunging. By 1994, for those with low educational levels, the rate of employment growth in the majority of major OECD countries was negative, with a low of –8.7 per cent in Canada. According to a recent survey by the Department of Education and Employment in the UK, 74 per cent of employers considered that the skills required of an average employee had increased. Of those surveyed, 20 per cent felt there was a gap between the skills their current employees had and those that were needed to meet their business requirements—a warning signal to those on the periphery of the firm.[8]

The market for 'labour' as such is clearly in terminal decline and is being replaced by a market for *knowledge*. The accelerating shift in demand from unskilled labour to skilled knowledge workers is one of the more obvious and dramatic signs of the move to a knowledge-based economy. Governments that fail to acknowledge the urgency of raising national skill levels will be left with under-performing economies and hostile electorates. Better to prepare such workers for the realities of their situation, while at the same time providing them access to learning resources to improve their situation, than to face the consequences at the ballot box. Individuals and firms will need to focus on maintaining and enhancing their biggest asset: their knowledge capital. The consumer society will become a learning society. Firms that learn faster will beat their rivals. Learning will become a lifelong process, the biggest activity on the planet and the major growth market of the twenty-first century.

As perceptions change regarding the economic necessity to improve basic skill levels and provide access to learning for all on a lifetime basis, technologically assisted methods of teaching and other 'learning technologies' must move centre stage. There are several reasons for this predicted increase in the use of learning technologies. First, such technologies offer the only practical solution to extending access to educational facilities to the total population on a lifetime basis. Second, the technologies involved are capable of generating economies of scale which physical and labour-intensive methods cannot approach. Third, learning technologies offer scope for improving both instructional methods and learning outcomes. The scene appears set, therefore, for a transformation in educational concepts and methods, from a *teacher centric* to a *learner centric* world, with both learners and educators making increasing use of learning technologies.

Transforming the infrastructure of education is not going to be achieved however without the involvement of new suppliers, alongside traditional educational service providers. These organizations, are going to include major players in the communications, computing, and media industries, as well as other specialists. Both competition and collaboration can be expected to result, involving both existing and new providers, as major commercial interests identify learning as the next global growth market, alongside news and entertainment.

Both future work and future learning are likely to be shaped by how these predicted changes to the educational infrastructure, to service delivery, and to the relationship between learning, education, and work all unfold. This chapter explores some of the critical issues and opportunities that are likely to arise, in relation, first, to the use of new technologies, second, to the provision of educational services, and finally, to the roles and relationships involving learners, educators, and firms.

THE POTENTIAL OF LEARNING TECHNOLOGIES

For the past three decades, the use of learning technologies has been increasing at a significantly slower rate than the use of IT for most business applications. This unspectacular growth rate can be partially accounted for by the ingrained culture of face-to-face communications and paper-based systems among both educators and learners. The technologies themselves have been another limiting factor. Early attempts at providing computer-based training (CBT) or computer-assisted learning (CAL) were hampered by the cost of producing and distributing courseware, as well as the cost of the computing power needed to put multimedia applications on the desktop. Nowadays these problems have not totally disappeared, but they have been significantly reduced and are not a long-term issue.

The slow rate of growth can also be explained in part by the lack of availability of low-cost, publicly accessible, global communications networks. Whilst the Internet was adopted by the academic community in the 1970s following its development by the US military, its commercial availability outside the tertiary academic sector only really began in the early 1990s. Prior to that a publicly available global network simply did not exist and even today there is no serious rival to the Internet.

A further and more fundamental reason for the slow innovation and diffusion of learning technologies has been simply the lack of a perceived need to improve education and learning processes. Public perceptions of education, as noted earlier, have been conditioned by traditional ways of thinking about its role, including its relationship to employment and jobs, and socially ingrained acceptance of the traditional roles of educators and learners. Learning technologies are therefore not particularly widely used today, either in the school, in the firm, or in the home. The technologies exist however, even today, to put access to just about any educational or learning resource likely to be required within reach of the majority of the populations of western countries and many inhabitants of third world countries, without users ever having to attend a physical place of learning.

The same technologies are capable of either enhancing or replacing human and other physical resources. It is now technically feasible for a schoolteacher or university lecturer to present his or her lecture, in real time, literally to a worldwide audience, not just a particular class on a single campus. The same lecture, complete with multimedia notes, could be electronically archived and retrieved later by those who could not attend the live performance, from wherever they happen to be, at a time which is most convenient to them. Interaction between student and teacher no longer needs to be synchronized. Queries can be left in voice or data mailboxes and answered when convenient. Test data can be downloaded to students on request and results sent back for processing on completion.

Modelling of real world situations via learning technologies is already capable of replacing much learning on the job with a virtual or actual representation of 'the job' or the work situation. Interactive multimedia technologies are already used for example when teaching pilots how to land passenger jets and medical staff are already beginning to conduct, as well as observe, operations remotely, using a combination of realtime audio and video facilities. The car you drive was designed using powerful 3D CAD software and its performance simulated by computer well before the physical vehicle ever started to be built. These technologies, virtual reality software and a host of associated software, are already technically proven; commercial availability and integration into low-cost educational services and software is a question of economics *not* technology. A volume market is required to drive down costs and that market is set to explode across the globe.

There is nothing new in this situation. The first videotape recorder pro-duced by Ampex in the 1950s was the size of a refrigerator and retailed for $US75,000. Nowadays a VCR is a household item retailing for a few hundred dollars. In the early 1980s mobile phones were retailing for over $US3,000; today they are given away to encourage use of the telephone service. Similar cost–volume relationships have been shown to apply to just about any tech-nological innovation from the computer to the facsimile machine and the television.

The cost of wide-area data network access has already demonstrated the same pattern. Internet access costs have fallen rapidly in most countries over recent years as end user connections have soared, with the current average rate in the USA in the late 1990s at approximately $US20 per month for unlim-ited access. Only a decade previously, major commercial network services would have charged end users the same amount or more per hour of usage—some still do.

The clear message emerging, whatever the technologies used, is that a criti-cal mass of users is required in order to reduce the unit costs per user to an acceptable level. This will also be a necessary precursor to the widespread development and diffusion of more sophisticated learning technologies and services. Meantime even today, television, radio, the personal computer, and the Internet, plus hard copy materials, offer a basic set of infrastructural com-ponents capable of providing low-cost, distance-based, educational services around the world.

EDUCATION AS A BUSINESS

Economic stringency, the need to demonstrate results, and pressure to become more business oriented have already forced many publicly funded educational institutions to reconsider their role in the world. Now they are faced with a potentially massive increase in demand, from existing students staying on, mature-aged workers needing skills upgrading, and firms keen to develop specific research and training programmes.

Some professional educational establishments may be slow to take advan-tage of the opportunities on offer, due either to government regulations, or to an innate desire to provide education for education's sake. Other organiza-tions, particularly in the private sector, will be keen to enter this major new growth market. A small percentage of these newcomers will inevitably be unscrupulous and others only interested in making a quick profit—as in all new markets. This is an area where accreditation and quality assurance stan-dards can assist both prospective learners and employers. The challenge for educators, policy makers, and learners will be to make the decisions that will best help them to make the transition to the knowledge economy. These deci-sions need to reflect the fact that, apart from the education of those up to statutory school-leaving age, education must become a global *business*, as distinct from a locally provided *public service.*

Traditional Suppliers of Educational Services

Changing the tools of the trade from the blackboard to the computer will need to be part of more wide-ranging decisions, about what role traditional suppliers of educational services play in the emerging knowledge economy and global education market. Tertiary institutions, with their stronger traditions of autonomy, can be expected to take the lead in making these decisions, unless constrained by government regulations, in which case the first movers will be those which are privately owned. The initial decision that colleges, universities, and other institutions have to take is how far they go beyond the boundaries of the physical campus and their traditional learner markets. Dependent largely upon the technical resources available to the institution, the next decision will be whether to operate independently as a full distance-learning service provider, or to join a consortium of service providers. Full service providers are those, such as the UK Open University, who are capable of packaging and delivering a total distributed learning service, in which the institution has independent control over its finance, examinations and accreditation, curriculum, and instructional services. In 1997, somewhat surprisingly, only twenty national, autonomous, distance-teaching universities similar to the UK Open University were estimated to be operating worldwide.[9] Traditional universities around the world, however, are moving rapidly to embrace distance-based learning. In China half the 92,000 students who graduate each year with degrees in engineering and technology are taught via distance-based learning provided by traditional universities.

The African Virtual University is aiming to increase university enrolments and improve the quality and relevance of instruction throughout the sub-Saharan region. It has to date installed twenty-seven satellite receiver terminals and to compensate for the lack of scientific journals in African universities it has developed a digital library.[10]

For smaller, less self-sufficient learning institutions, an alternative option is to join a national or international network of similar institutions, plus other private and public interests as necessary, who between them can develop the necessary technology infrastructure and range of services. Such networks are now starting to proliferate.[11]

Other issues involved in extending beyond the campus include the initial disruption that technological adoption may cause, the need to acquire new skills along with new technologies, the unpredictable effect on current staff, and the tendency over time for distributed learning services to overtake on-campus services, thus changing the nature of the institution. All of these however appear to be risks that learning institutions will simply have to take, since the alternatives are even less appealing: progressively less funding, competitors eating into their traditional learner markets, and a tendency for better-qualified staff to join the competition. In any event, over time whether services are delivered on or off campus is likely to become transparent to most learners, since the necessity for physical attendance at a 'place of learning' is bound to diminish. On a more positive note, institutions which do transcend current physical and cultural boundaries are likely to be a lot better off financially, have more ability to influence the future course of education, more resources to dedicate to research, and be better able to maintain educational standards.

Future educational 'brand wars' also promise to have some interesting side effects. Local institutions may be disadvantaged, as students perceive more advantage in the brand value of institutions outside their locality, possibly overseas. The nature of academic tenure may also change as a result of competition between service providers for access to the best academic talent. Some providers will focus on providing educational services to firms and particular industries, whereas others will continue to offer more broadly based education to individuals. Such moves are likely to change the face of education as we know it, but importantly the main beneficiary is likely to be the consumer of educational services, be it the firm or the individual.

New Suppliers

In order for distributed learning to become universally available, new suppliers will need to be involved, including many of the major players in computing, communications, publishing, and software. A variety of niche specialists can also be expected to play a role, from multimedia specialists to suppliers of educational information and brokerage services and providers of supporting services for learners needing special assistance.

New alliances will emerge involving learning institutions with technology providers, plus industry, the unions, and trade associations. In some countries, as is currently happening for example in Singapore, governments are likely to try and take control of infrastructure development, and to develop educational programmes which subordinate distributed learning objectives to other national economic policy goals. In other countries, governments are more likely to take a back seat, trusting that in an appropriately regulated and competitive environment, new educational services will naturally evolve. In the USA under the Clinton administration, for example, the Internet is being massively upgraded (Internet II), partly as a response to the need for improved educational access, but also as a way to improve the national information infrastructure.

The development of learning technologies and the provision of network access for learners is likely to be affected most strongly however by the convergence of the major technology infrastructure providers, leading to new global alliances. These players include the Goliaths of the information age: the providers of content (video audio and print media); the major computer hardware and software providers; and national suppliers of telecommunications services. The combined revenues from these sectors in the OECD alone amounted to $US1.42 trillion in 1994.[12] The diversification of the IT industry into the KT industry looks likely to be a particularly profitable strategic shift, which will be fuelled by the explosion in demand for learning.

To date, content, computing, and telecommunications have been separated, both technically and commercially. Technical separation has been caused by very different production and distribution techniques. Commercial separation has been caused by government regulations which have restricted cross-media ownership and foreign investment, and prescribed state control of telephone and broadcasting networks. The motives for such restrictions have ranged from protection of national interests and maintenance of a 'free press', to a belief in state ownership. The digitization of the underlying structures of all information, as noted earlier, is however rapidly eroding the boundaries between these separate industries. A file transmitted over a telecommunications network may represent a human voice, a film, a book, a musical recording, or any combination thereof. The only real difference is the file size and thus the bandwidth requirements, but with the advent of fibre optic and satellite-based communications, bandwidth is effectively unlimited and competition is becoming global. The technical feasibility and economic benefits of media convergence have been apparent for some years. The growth of the multimedia industry has been inhibited, not by technology, but by artificial restrictions based on outmoded 'industrial era' thinking and misperceptions of what constitutes the public interest.

In a belated response to these realities, across most advanced OECD countries telecommunications are slowly being liberalized. In parallel, restrictions on cross-media ownership are (equally slowly) being relaxed. When the last barriers to open competition are removed, alliances such as those already created between Microsoft, Deutsche Telekom, and Atlantic Vision and many others will be positioned to take advantage of the opportunities. More alliances and mega mergers are then likely to follow as the global multimedia industry takes off. As global competition spreads, services to businesses and consumers can be expected to ramp up quickly and this should include a rapid growth in on-line education services.

Risks and Benefits

As education becomes big business, the influence exerted by providers of content, connectivity, and communications is obviously going to be significant. The new multimedia conglomerates will be in a position to influence the way learning technologies and educational services are provided, since they will be major suppliers of 'connectivity' to learners, via network PCs, set-top boxes, and associated software. They will also include major network service providers, controlling the distribution of distance-based learning services, including availability, access methods, and costs. They will include content specialists, offering access to learning resources from around the world, and will thus be able to determine the availability and cost of such resources.

This impending scenario implies some potential risks as well as benefits to consumers. The user pays principle will inevitably apply, as a result of which recipients of previously subsidized services are likely to feel disadvantaged. There is also a danger that some suppliers will use proprietary standards which lock their customers in and prevent them accessing other educational services. Particular suppliers may dominate certain sections of the value chain, thus allowing them to leverage their own profits at the expense of the consumer. Such risks, however, are not new and are similar in principle to those that apply in relation to many other IT-based products and services and indeed to practically any industry.

On the other hand, governments are in a position to smooth the transition from public to private services in various ways. As the incumbent suppliers of both telecommunications and educational services in most countries, they can to a large extent determine the rules for market entry. Such rules should offer protection to disadvantaged sections of the community from the side effects of open market competition, such as higher prices for delivery of services in remote and rural areas.

Proprietariness is unlikely to be a major issue. Most users of modern technologies (i.e. just about everyone) have become familiar with suppliers' attempts to 'lock them in' and have learned to live with such issues. Proprietariness, where it affects market access to learning resources, is in any event likely to erode, given that sufficient public pressure is applied for adoption of common standards.

Despite its lack of a 'friendly face', the user pays principle is ultimately the only principle that makes economic sense. Prices for electronic services are highly volume dependent and the effect of competition will be to keep driving them down. As a result of existing global competition, production and playback technologies have shown continuous price performance improvements. PC hardware and software, scanning technologies, video camera equipment, and desktop publishing systems are all constantly reducing in price and improving in performance. The much-discussed intelligent TVs and network computers will quickly fall in price to around the cost of conventional television sets and VCRs today, once a volume market is established and competition takes off. The risk of monopolistic practices forcing prices up or quality down is no greater than for any electronically delivered product or service. Anti-monopoly provisions, combined with global competition, should reduce the risk of educational monopolies emerging.

On the positive side, the emerging market for learning-related products and services is massive indeed: at least equal to that for the current news, information, and entertainment industries combined! The same production and distribution technologies that are required for these existing services and future electronic commerce services can also be used for education. The synergistic potential is obviously huge—access to learning resources as a result should become not only universally available, but *cheap*.

A further beneficial side effect of the growth of the global multimedia industry and its involvement in education is likely to be the opportunities for self-employed individuals, micro businesses, and SMEs to become involved as suppliers. A surge in demand has been predicted for multimedia courseware development and other production and distribution functions, which in turn will introduce further diversity and competition at the higher end of the value chain. In Japan it has been estimated that 2.43 million jobs can be created in the multimedia market by 2010. French estimates put the increase in network-service-based employment at 2.5 to 5 times the 1993 level.[13] For those currently facing uncertain futures, the multimedia industry may therefore represent a good career move.

LINKING LEARNERS, EDUCATORS, AND FIRMS

The dynamics of the knowledge economy are changing the characteristics of work and thus demand for knowledge. They are also changing the roles and relationships between learners, educators, and firms. Old demarcation lines between vocational and academic training are becoming irrelevant as the academic and commercial worlds converge. Two key questions emerge from this. First, what should be the future roles of the principal actors in relation to education, training, and learning? Second, how can the pathways between formal education, informal learning, and work be optimized to ensure transition between each state is managed flexibly and efficiently?

Roles and Relationships

Corporate sector investment in vocational education and training is currently growing faster than public sector investment in general education. In the USA in 1995, corporate investment in education and training totalled around $US50 billion, roughly half the total US expenditure on higher education. Firms' investments in training workers have been largely based on the assumption that knowledge acquisition of value to the firm could be most efficiently provided by locating it close to the firm's production processes, i.e. in the firm. Strategies employed by firms to facilitate learning internally have included cross-training by co-workers, job rotation, skill-based pay, quality circles, and rewards for useful ideas suggested by employees. Other associated techniques have included the appointment of particular employees as mentors or tutors for co-workers. In Germany an apprentice is generally supervised by a qualified *Meister*, and the French have created the role of *tuteur*: a person who supervises young trainees in the workplace or who guides regular employees through the requirements for obtaining a vocational qualification.[14]

An increasing number of corporations are turning their in-house training centres from cost centres into profit centres by training non-employees.[15] Motorola for example has set up its own university for staff training and also cooperates with private and public business schools worldwide. Microsoft has set up a campus-style R&D and training function. Two of the leading European business schools, IMEDE and IMI, were originally the company training centres of Nestlé and Alcan respectively. Andersen Consulting, the world's largest management and IT consultancy practice, has its own college at St Charles, Illinois, to ensure a consistent approach and methodology to problem solving. Disney Corporation offers an MBA programme for those interested in learning some of the secrets of its success. In the UK, British Aerospace is reported to be establishing a 'virtual university' complete with vice-chancellor (also called managing director) and faculties of engineering and manufacturing technology and learning, plus an international business school.[16] BT (formerly British Telecom) plans to create a corporate university to provide training for its 125,000 employees and to offer degrees and vocational courses.[17]

The purpose of many corporate training investments is not solely to educate staff in generic or firm-specific processes, but to inculcate firm-specific standards, values, and culture and specific business formulas—as in the case of franchisors such as McDonald's with its famous hamburger universities. Much in-house training nevertheless remains non-firm specific, and the proportion of non-specific training is likely to increase for the reasons described earlier. This throws into question whether, in jumping on the educational bandwagon, some firms may not be simply following a fashion, or seeking to gain a short-run advantage. For those firms who decide to turn their training cost centres into profit centres by extending training to non-employees, the obvious question is, how do such activities fit with their core businesses? The issues at stake here are not whether training staff is a good idea, but the type of training required and to what extent firms are best suited to provide such training. Many elements of training currently provided by firms in-house should be amenable to outsourcing to educational specialists. Such specialists are arguably better suited to satisfy the demand for continuous generic education which is likely to form an increasing proportion of all education and training—even for those in the associate and core groups within the firm.

These arguments suggest the need for a new alliance between business and academia. Greater cooperation between firms and educators should also result in better industry-specific training. Developing industry-related extensions to generic academic courses would help ensure that course content remained relevant and up to date, since learning institutions are usually in a better position to be aware of changes at the leading edge of technologies than commercial firms. From the learner's perspective, qualifications achieved would tend to be valued more highly, since they would more usefully complement qualifications already gained, as well as being more universally recognized in the market place. Such an approach is clearly important, given the increasing trend towards externalization and use of promotional methods such as the 'up or out' system (see Chapter 9).

School-based enterprises have for some time sought to prepare students for the world of work by setting up actual or simulated businesses as part of the school curriculum. A 1992 survey found that 19 per cent of secondary schools in the USA were operating such enterprises. By the late 1980s and early 1990s, 40 per cent of government-supported secondary schools in the UK were reportedly sponsoring mini-enterprises. The Economic Development Board of Singapore and the German Agency for Technical Cooperation have set up the German–Singapore Institute (GSI). GSI, which calls itself a 'teaching factory', carries out development projects for local manufacturers while training technicians and middle managers in various manufacturing-related technologies. The GSI model has been copied in Malaysia, Brazil, and other countries. GSI is organized more like a business than a school, with short vacations, forty-four-hour weeks, and departmental names that represent production functions such as tool and die making, rather than academic disciplines.[18]

Charles Schwab, a leading financial services and investment brokerage company, has undertaken a nationwide school-to-work initiative in the USA called 'School to Careers'. The programme contains three components, school-based learning, work-based learning, and 'connecting activities' that link the experiences students have in school with experiences in the workplace. On average each student spends 150 hours in the programme.[19]

A relevant example of cooperation between American industry, government, and academia is the Michigan Virtual Automotive College (MVAC), the result of collaboration between the state of Michigan, the auto industry, and local universities. MVAC provides a broad range of educational programmes, both face to face and using a variety of learning technologies, to enable existing and prospective workers in the auto industry access to industry training. The cooperative approach taken by MVAC involves major industry competitors such as Ford, GM, and Chrysler sitting on the same executive committee along with members of the industry plus university and union representatives.[20]

The scope for cooperation between universities and industry is not likely to be limited to training its workers. Firm-specific or narrowly applied research is likely to decline and generic or pure research to increase. Major firms in leading edge technologies, such as IBM and Microsoft in the IT industry, have always invested heavily in original R&D, knowing that to stay ahead demands strong generic skills. Microsoft recently invested £80 million in a computer science laboratory at Cambridge University that is run by the university, not Microsoft.[21]

Such examples suggest that schools and universities do not have to prejudice their academic principles when they rub shoulders with corporate interests. Nor do firms have to fear losing their private 'knowledge edge'. The boundaries between academia and work are beginning to fade. For those at the edge of leading edge technologies, such as biotechnology, they never were particularly important. For many other industries, from agriculture to car manufacturing, broadly based cooperative training and generic research programmes are now beginning to appear, which extend beyond highly focused and applied R&D.

In the short term, the advantages of greater cooperation between firms and educators should include improved career prospects for workers, cost savings for firms, and a stronger and more relevant educational system. Learners should benefit from continuity and the transparency associated with universally recognized credentials. Firms should benefit by offloading generic training to educational specialists and accessing their expertise to help improve firm-specific research and training. Educational institutions should benefit from obtaining a better insight into industry requirements, which could be fed back into improving research and extending course design. Firms and educators who fail to take advantage of these synergistic opportunities will have only themselves to blame when they are left by the wayside.

Smoothing the Pathways between Education, Learning, and Work

Many readers will remember the shock of their first encounter with the world of work, when they were fresh out of school or college. Equally, many managers will remember the shock of first having to deal with a batch of new young recruits. Such transitions are never easy. Workers in future however will need to be able to make far more frequent transitions between states of learning and working. Smoothing the pathways between these different states must therefore become a priority for all concerned.[22] The most frequently travelled routes are likely to be between learning and working, between different types of work requiring different skills, and between different educational courses and modes of learning.

Between Learning and Work

The first and most common route, hitherto largely travelled in only one direction, has been between learning and work. For those with tertiary qualifications, this has generally involved moving straight from university to regular full-time employment. For those leaving the secondary educational system, the transition has either been direct or via the bridge of a college of further education, such as provided by the TAFE system in Australia. In future, these routes are likely to be travelled more frequently and in both directions. Most workers will probably need to refresh their skills by returning to a state of learning much more frequently than in the past and vice versa, back from learning to work. Issues likely to surface as a result of this frequent change between learning and work include access rights, access methods, and costs.

Maintenance of access rights by students to reattend colleges or universities after leaving is usually determined by availability of physical 'places' and satisfaction of entry-level criteria. In future, physical access problems should be reduced by greater use of distributed learning. Entry-level criteria would then also diminish in importance, since learning would be self-paced and results or exit criteria would be all that mattered. Open and distance-based learning, using learning technologies as described earlier, largely solves such access issues.

Accessing learning from the workplace poses a different set of issues however. For the self-employed it will simply be a question of personal choice. For core knowledge workers in the firm it can be expected that firms will be prepared to allow them more frequent access from work to learning. For other externalized workers and those on the periphery of the firm, firms will be less predisposed to allow access to learning during working hours and will have progressively less economic motivation to subsidize their learning activities.

It would seem that government intervention will be needed in these instances to incentivize firms through tax credits or other allowances to allow workers to learn while being paid. Imposing training levies on firms designed to force them to undertake employee training have not achieved positive results.[23] It will also be important not to discriminate adversely against self-employed workers and owner-operated businesses, by leaving them to pay in full for their own training while subsidizing firms who happen to be traditional employers.

Measures by governments to improve affordability of education include deferred payment systems like the HECS (Higher Education Contribution Supplement) system in Australia which offers subsidized tertiary training with repayments out of future earnings. Other government policy options include full income tax deductibility of expenditure on training, already claimable by businesses, being offered to private individuals. Exempting educational goods and services from sales taxes and other indirect taxes represents a further policy option.

There is a danger, however, that government intervention could send the wrong signals to the market, resulting in both firms and individuals taking unfair advantage of 'educational handouts'. Both individuals and firms need to see it as in their interests to invest in knowledge. The role of government should be restricted to creating a climate of understanding, both of the issues and of the opportunities, and to creating an appropriate legislative framework to help individuals and businesses to help themselves (see also Chapter 11).

An alternative approach would be for firms to offer workers the option of receiving training which would equip them with the type of generic/industry-specific skills necessary for them to secure future work on leaving the firm. Such services would naturally need to be offered on terms that adequately compensated firms for these expenses. A possible way for firms to recoup these costs would be to deduct a set amount from workers' remuneration on a regular basis, much as firm pensions are currently deducted. For the 'higher fliers' in the firm, transfer fees may be applicable in the same way as they currently are for valuable members of other teams, e.g. basketball teams and soccer teams!

Between Careers

It is likely that more workers in future will be faced with having to change careers, possibly several times during their working lives. These changes are likely to be even more traumatic than the initial shock of moving from the educational system to work.

Many such events however are readily predictable, as for example in the spate of retail bank closures occurring in the late 1990s and due to roll on into the next century. In such cases, most bank branch staff will need to be re-equipped to perform other work. (If there are any bank branch staff reading this who are not already training for a future change of work—they should be.) The same will apply in other highly labour-intensive industries where automation and the consequent need for reskilling and downsizing can be predicted well in advance.

As well as low skill-intensive occupations, many of those involving higher-level skills are also at risk of finding all or part of their knowledge bases redundant. Stockbrokers are a typical case in point, as are many other providers of intermediary services which contain high levels of explicit knowledge. Electronic, direct to the consumer services which will eventually bypass such intermediaries are already beginning to appear, so the need for individuals in such roles to start retraining is already apparent. Both firms and workers will be better able to predict future training and learning needs once knowledge-based models of firms' activities are established.

Where it is possible for firms to predict the need for significant internal retraining, flexible access to necessary learning resources could form a useful adjunct to transition schemes such as work sharing. Work sharing, as discussed in Chapter 4, has proved to be only a partially effective device, spreading work loss more equally among the workforce, but offering little else. Work sharing combined with distributed learning on the other hand could be a much more effective strategy.[24] As part of work-sharing arrangements, firms could offer a retraining package, including access to appropriate distributed learning courses from the workplace or from home. Instead of involuntary leisure, workers would be offered the chance to re-equip themselves to find work in the same industry or elsewhere. This is another instance where cooperation between educational service providers and firms would be helpful, both in designing the appropriate courses and in finding the most efficient and effective ways for workers to participate and benefit from them.

The union movement plus trade and professional associations are potentially well placed to act as intermediaries in such activities. Services which they could offer include development of career counselling services for their members, as part of which future training requirements, both generic and work specific, could be better identified. Such bodies could thus help to inform the dialogue between industry and learning institutions and might ensure that a more holistic approach to their members' learning needs was taken. They would also be in an ideal position to 'sell' the importance of life-long learning to their membership.

Between Work Arrangements

For those in externalized work arrangements, constant transition from one work assignment to another, and one workstyle to another, can be expected to be accompanied by a constant need for incremental learning. This is likely to affect different categories of externalized workers in different ways.

Flexihire Workers. Lacking access to firm-provided training, workers in dependent flexihire arrangements will be forced to develop their own career plans and to become professional flexiworkers, rather than reluctant part-timers. The knowledge and skills to achieve this transition will have to be learned and many individuals will need to seek external counselling in how to replan their careers, what training they will require, and how best to obtain it.

Mediated Services Workers. It may be expected that staffing agencies will progressively take over many of the training activities previously offered by firms through in-company courses, apprenticeships, and other 'on the job' training provision. In turn, the agencies can be expected to form links with the education sector to assist them. For workers joining specialist outsourcing service providers, it can be expected that the contractual relationships will be looser and more distant, placing greater onus on the worker to maintain his or her own skill levels.

Dependent Contractors. For workers who lack the required skills or motivation to operate as either professional temporary workers or fully independent contractors, acquiring knowledge of how to operate a specific type of small business may well be the answer. Considerable potential would seem to exist for cooperation between the corporate and education sectors to improve the availability and quality of training courses based on proven operating business 'formulas'—along the lines of many current franchise systems.

Independent Contractors. The knowledge requirements of the independent self-employed workers are likely to involve an expansion of generic skills in areas such as business, accounting and administration, personal organization and time management, marketing, communications, and business network-ing. Where additional specialist business advice is required, an expanding role can be envisaged for retired professionals to provide mentoring services to small start-ups. Such services are already beginning to flourish as the popula-tion of both retirees and independent micro firms increases. Work experience, often acquired over a lifetime, can thus be reused on a cost-effective and flexi-ble basis to the benefit of all parties.

Maintaining Standards and Equivalence of Qualifications

At present there are a number of gaps in the pathways between learning and work which are caused by lack of appropriate links or interfaces between different educational systems and courses. As far as practicable, the successful acquisition of knowledge, however obtained, should result in the achievement of recognizable and interchangeable 'knowledge credits'. Ideally such 'credits' should be capable of being earned for achievement of micro-skills and small increments in knowledge achievement, as well as more traditional academic achievement.

The New Zealand Qualifications Framework provides one of the most advanced examples of an approach to these issues among OECD countries.[25] Their National Qualifications Framework allows learners to accumulate credits towards achievement of qualifications over time and at their own pace. Learners are assessed against nationally agreed standards, which ensure transparency of objectives and learning requirements and transferability between educational settings. The standards are prepared by expert groups in consultation with relevant stakeholders from different learning areas, industries, and government. Each registered standard carries a defined credit value and fits a specific level in the Framework. Credits can be accumulated from different educational or training centres or in the workplace and contribute to a single qualification. Only accredited organizations are able to assess learners' performance against standards and to award qualifications. Evidence of achievement may include workplace performance measurements as well as more traditional assessment methods. A national database maintains the details of credits achieved. These details can be requested by learners, resulting in the issuance of a Record of Learning, an official document which can be used as a credential when seeking work. By 1997, around 5 per cent of the population of New Zealand had credits on the national database, and some 20 per cent of the credits awarded were based on assessments of workplace performance.

CONCLUSIONS

The requirement for access to learning resources appears likely to accelerate dramatically over the short to medium term, as workers face the necessity for remedial training and skills upgrading, and firms recognize the importance of constantly upgrading their internal skills. The current, largely public-funded educational system clearly cannot cope with either the volume or diversity of future learning needs, nor is it currently equipped to provide low-cost flexible access to learning resources off campus, in the home and at work. To translate lifelong learning into reality implies use of radically different systems and methods of education and the involvement of new types of service provider.

Computers and communications will largely need to replace blackboards and classrooms. Such changes to educational methods are not merely operational, but call for changes to policies and strategies which will represent significant challenges to current educational service providers. Foremost among these challenges will be the need for education to become a business which, like any other business, will sink or swim dependent on its ability to satisfy the requirements of the market—in this case the market for knowledge.

Combining educational specialists with technology specialists should enable the development of a global learning industry that can transcend the limits of classrooms and campuses. Universal access to distributed learning could include many new micro courses which might appeal to a broader audience, and still contribute over time to the qualifications accumulated by individual learners. Learners would arguably be more likely to persevere with such courses if each increment could be seen to add to their qualifications base and thus their market value.

Beyond the initial and largely technical goal of extending access to learning resources, a major requirement exists to improve the links between education, learning, and work. To achieve this goal a more accurate view is required of the type of knowledge which will be required for future work. Far from specific, application-oriented, task-focused training—the model supported by much of industry to date—just the opposite will be required. More emphasis therefore needs to be placed on high-level, generic, and academic training. Theory however needs to be combined much more with practice: 'know what' with 'know how'. Both educational course design and new learning technologies will be needed to provide the equivalent of on the job experience while off the job.[26]

As the bulk of economic activity becomes less firm specific, demand for generic or industry standard training will far exceed demand for firm-specific training. Greater cooperation between industry and academia would seem the best way to achieve this. One reason is that such training usually needs to stay abreast of advances in knowledge related to particular technologies, and to involve research which may be beyond the immediate sphere of interests of the firm. Another reason is that for firms to provide such training efficiently will often demand a critical mass of learners that they simply do not have. By externalizing the provision of such training, firms are likely to improve their 'knowledge–product congruence': the balance between what they know and what they can utilize efficiently. Better asset utilization should in turn improve economic performance.

For the great majority of workers, learning will need to become more of a personal responsibility. Intermediaries will be needed to help part time, temporary, and other externalized workers with career counselling and identification of learning objectives and strategies. Greater cooperation can therefore be expected between staffing specialists and educational specialists. Government assistance is also clearly going to be needed to ease short-term financial pressures on workers who need retraining or upskilling, and in creating an appropriate policy framework which facilitates the growth of knowledge industries including the business of education.

Assuming a happy conjunction of all these factors then lifelong learning may offer lifelong returns to all concerned. This desirable outcome is unlikely to be achieved, however, without a broad community-wide understanding and acceptance of the issues and opportunities involved. The final chapter examines the various methods by which this required level of understanding and acceptance might be achieved. It further examines the implications for all the stakeholders as we cross the threshold of the knowledge economy.

NOTES

1. OECD (Organization for Economic Co-operation and Development) (1997), *Labour Market Policies: New Challenges—Lifelong Learning to Maintain Employability*, Paris: OECD.
2. Ibid.
3. Ibid.
4. OECD (1996), *The OECD Jobs Strategy: Pushing ahead with the Strategy*, Paris: OECD.
5. Commission on Social Justice (1996), 'Investment: Adding Value through Lifelong Learning', in P. Raggatt, R. Edwards, and N. Small (eds.), *The Learning Society: Challenges and Trends*, London: Routledge: 184–206.
6. R. W. Judy and C. D'Amico (1997), *Workforce 2020: Work and Workers in the 21st Century*, Indianapolis: Hudson Institute Inc.
7. OECD *Labour Market Policies*.
8. Richard Walsh (1997), 'Skill Needs in Britain: 1996 Report', *Labour Market Trends*, London: Office for National Statistics (Feb.): 73–6.
9. G. Kickup and A. Jones (1996), 'New Technologies for Open Learning: The Superhighway to the Learning Society?', in Raggatt, Edwards, and Small (eds.), *The Learning Society: Challenges and Trends*, 272–91.
10. Word Bank, 'World Bank Development Report 1998/99: Knowledge for Development', *http://www.worldbank.org/wdr/p148*.
11. Directory of Online Colleges, Internet Universities, and Training Institutes, *http://www.geteducated.com/dlsites.htm*.
12. OECD (1996), *Technology Productivity and Job Creation*, ii: *Analytical Report*, Paris: OECD: 105.
13. Ibid. 109.
14. D. Stern (1997), 'Human Resource Development in the Knowledge-Based Economy: Roles of Firms, Schools and Governments', in *Employment and Growth in the Knowledge-Based Economy*, Paris: OECD: 189–203.
15. G. Stanley (1997), 'Competition and Change in the University Sector', in J. R. Sharpham and G. Harman (eds.), *Australia's Future Universities*, Armidale: University of New England Press: 239–54.
16. 'The Tower of Science' (1998), *The Economist*, 2nd Apr.
17. *The Economist*, Business This Week, *http://www.economist.com*, 22 Jan. 1999.

18. Stern, 'Human Resource Development in the Knowledge-Based Economy.

19. S. Black and R. Tappan (1998), 'Contingent Work: A Bridge to the Workforce of the Future', William Olsten Center for Workforce Strategies, *http://www.olsten.com*.

20. 'About MVAC', Michigan Virtual Automotive College, *http://mvac.org/about.html*.

21. Ibid.

22. OECD, *The OECD Jobs Strategy: Pushing ahead with the Strategy*.

23. OECD, *Labour Market Policies*, 19.

24. M. Carnoy and M. Castells (1997), '*Sustainable Flexibility: A Prospective Study on Work, Family and Society in the Information Age*', Paris: OECD: 31–2.

25. OECD, *Labour Market Policies*.

26. Stern, 'Human Resource Development in the Knowledge-Based Economy.

11

The Transition to Knowledge Capitalism

The decline in the value of traditional capital and the rise of knowledge capital is sending shock-waves through the economy and society. The effects of these shocks can be seen in the widening disparity in earning power between the knowledge 'haves' and 'have nots', in increasing globalized competition, in the disintegration of employment, in the reorganization of the firm, and in falling demand for commodities and low knowledge-intensive products.

Buffeted by the forces of change, many individuals, communities, and businesses perceive themselves to be at risk, yet receive little coherent explanation from governments or the media of what is happening around them or what it means for their future. Cynicism and resentment, bred of ignorance and mistrust, are already apparent among disadvantaged groups throughout the West, notably the rural poor, disaffected youth, and the long-term unemployed, leading to the growth of support for extremist political parties in many countries. Simplistic slogans, a desire to return to traditional values, and victimization of others supposedly associated with the decline in their own living standards are the hallmarks of such groups—as they were in the early years of the Industrial Revolution and more recently during the 1930s and early 1940s in Europe.

Attitudinal surveys of small business and consumer sentiment consistently reflect an undercurrent of uncertainty, apprehension, and insecurity. Even those in apparently secure jobs are reported as feeling at risk. Ignorance and confusion are enhanced by a TV-dominated 'infotainment' culture, which provides a diet of intellectual junk food, occasionally spiced with futuristic visions of technological wonders. Despite the welter of information churned out daily in the media, the notion of a knowledge-based economy is only dimly understood and its fundamental relationship with information and other technologies, globalization, corporate restructuring, and jobs and employment is even less understood. Information is not the problem—understanding is. Society is drowning in information but still left thirsty for knowledge.

Meantime national governments continue to pursue economic and social policies which take little account of the massive paradigm shift in the economic balance of power which is occurring. If governments, along with many of their citizens, are not to be swept away in the 'gales of creative destruction' marking the evolution of the knowledge economy, they will need to fill the vacuum in understanding which currently exists. To do this they will need to develop a vision of what the knowledge economy means and communicate that vision to industry and to society, along with economic and social policies that provide a new sense of direction and purpose. Both governments and industry will need to cooperate in a fundamental reappraisal of priorities, including, most importantly, a radical re-evaluation of the role of knowledge in the economy.

Managing the transition to the new economy and thus to knowledge capitalism is therefore the theme of this final chapter. We discuss the importance of valuing knowledge, issues and opportunities confronting firms and individuals in a globalizing knowledge economy, the role of governments in developing and implementing policies, and finally how knowledge capitalism might be expected to evolve.

VALUING KNOWLEDGE

Government and corporate strategies to facilitate the transition to a knowledge-based economy cannot be developed until the economic value of knowledge is better understood at all levels, in government, by the firm, by workers, and in society. At present, knowledge acquisition (education, learning, skills formation) and knowledge development (research, innovation) are massively undervalued, both economically and socially.

Examples of the mismatch between the actual and the perceived value of knowledge acquisition can be seen in the continuance of institutions, policies, and economic models grounded in the industrial era. Education for the masses is still aimed at producing employees, rather than knowledge entrepreneurs. Between one third and a half of the workforce lack the basic skills which will be needed for access to work in ten years' time. Vocational education is still geared to equipping individuals for narrow industry-specific trades, most of which will cease to exist during the lifetimes of those acquiring the skills.

In relation to knowledge development, application-focused research is valued more highly than basic research, and the 'backroom boys' in the laboratory are valued less than those who commercialize their inventions. The generally low level of public grants, subsidies, and other R&D incentives in many western countries is indicative of governments' inability to appreciate the public value of many private investments in knowledge development.

Innovation is hailed as the key to economic vitality, yet in a financial climate marked by aversion to knowledge-based risk taking many firms find it more prudent to imitate than to innovate. Skilled research workers and knowledge

entrepreneurs are forced to migrate to countries which value them. For traditional manufacturing industry, rather than invest in technological transformation in the West, it often proves more attractive to continue their current
low-tech production in the still industrializing East.

Lack of a sufficiently knowledgeable consumer society is meantime delaying
the diffusion of new knowledge-intensive products and services. Only a
minority of households owns PCs, for example, and even fewer are connected
to the Internet. These problems are not due to failures in specific areas such as
lack of pre-school educational services or lack of basic research in a particular
field. They are endemic, broad scale, and economy wide—the result of a 'sys-
temic failure in knowledge valuation' involving governments, the corporate
sector, and society at large.[1]

Given time, market forces will undoubtedly take care of the situation. Firms
and individuals will eventually recognize the necessity to adapt, or they simply
will not survive. There is evidence however that many workers, firms, and
investors are already coming to grips with the knowledge economy. In the
USA, technology stocks are soaring as investors show their confidence in the
future of knowledge-intensive industries. Throughout the West, and particularly in the USA, the stigma of loss of direct employment is fading, exemplified
in the slogan 'free agent nation'.[2] Demand for adult educational courses, particularly those offering vocational and open distance-based learning, is rapidly
growing, as evidenced by the growth of on-line courses and 'virtual universities' such as Phoenix University, the Open University, and the African Virtual
University (see Chapter 10).

These signs all point to a growing awareness and acceptance of the role and
value of knowledge in the economy. Nevertheless, as the statistics presented
in earlier chapters clearly demonstrate, even in the USA, poorly educated and
inexperienced workers are increasingly disadvantaged when seeking work.
The situation is significantly worse in most other countries.

The risk with leaving everything to the market during the current period of
transition is that while the fittest will undoubtedly survive and thrive, the
already disadvantaged in society and many firms and workers in older physically intensive industries will not. Simply allowing this to happen, as some
laissez-faire economists would recommend, is bound to lead to social and
economic turmoil, to the ultimate disadvantage of the majority of society.

National governments therefore clearly have a pivotal role to play in creating awareness and understanding of the issues, providing an appropriate legislative framework for change and helping those unable to help themselves.
There is a significant risk however that they will go beyond this role and
attempt to introduce well-meaning but ultimately counter-productive measures. To date, most governments' efforts at active labour market programmes
involving job creation strategies, work for the dole schemes, corporate training levies, and the like have been expensive failures. Such failures are indicative of governments' own lack of understanding of the economic value of
knowledge. In a globalizing business environment, the power of individual

national governments to assist the transition process is itself likely to be limited. More initiatives are likely to be needed by regional governments and by supranational organizations (see below).

In short, a degree of government intervention is clearly called for to ease the transition process and help fast-track society from an industrial to a knowledge base. The major force for change, however, remains the free market itself and the capability of firms and individuals to use the liberating power of knowledge to create new wealth and new work opportunities for themselves and others. Before examining how governments might assist the transition process, therefore, it is as well to look at how firms, workers, and other stakeholders might deal with some of the major issues and opportunities confronting them.

MARKET-DRIVEN CHANGE

As we have seen, new markets for knowledge supply are rapidly emerging as a result of firms' demand for different skills and resources. 'Temp' agencies are transforming themselves into staffing services, capable of matching firms' needs for human resources from the mailroom to the boardroom. Outsourcing services are becoming increasingly sophisticated. Firms are finding they can externalize a variety of firm-specific functions and achieve unprecedented growth through networks of dependent contractors via licensing and franchise arrangements. Individuals are finding a wealth of new opportunities to develop and exploit their own knowledge capital.

None of these changes have occurred through state intervention, they have occurred as a spontaneous response to the demands of the market place. The market place itself however is changing, as we saw in Chapter 1. New technologies are appearing, old demarcation lines between industries are eroding, national boundaries are losing their significance, and business is becoming global. The combination of rapid technological change and a borderless business world opens up totally new horizons for firms and individuals in transition to the knowledge economy.

New Technologies

IT, biotechnology, and nanotechnology are three technologies which have the potential to revolutionize how we live and work, and to spawn major new industries in the next few decades. In the IT industry, increasing miniaturization of computing devices is likely to lead to wearable and even human implantable processors, which will be able to back up and extend our physical and mental capabilities. Voice, text graphics, and full motion video will be available seamlessly and via single integrated devices, rather than requiring separate radios, televisions, computers, and telephones. Smart homes, smart factories, and self-piloting, non-polluting automobiles will become a reality. While some old industries will die as a result, major new markets and new industry opportunities will emerge.

Biotechnology, while currently several decades behind IT in terms of commercialization, is likely to catch up quickly as the genomes of human beings and many species of animals and plants are mapped over the next decade. As man gradually takes control of the building blocks of life, new techniques will emerge to feed and improve the health of the inhabitants of the planet, with less impact on its dwindling physical resources. Clearly major risks exist, as with any new technology. Adequate safeguards will need to be implemented on a global basis, including open and transparent dissemination of information about genetically modified products. However, given that these and other safeguards are put in place, less land degradation, lower-cost production, more self-sufficient farming communities, and a better-fed and healthier global population should result. Significant advances are already occurring. Changing the information encoded in a gene in a cotton plant, for example, has led to the production of cotton which repels and resists insects. This has reduced pesticide usage in cotton fields by 60 to 70 per cent in the last two years.[3] At the same time as the world learns to feed itself without destroying its remaining natural resources, improvements in human health should reduce the strain on both governments and families currently coping with problems of birth defects or age-related infirmities.

The infant of this trio of technologies, nanotechnology, has some way to go before its full commercial possibilities are realized, but its effects could be as profound as either IT or biotechnology. In principle, nanotechnology offers the potential to design and manufacture devices by assembling matter an atom at a time. The potential of this technology if realized could result in the production of supercomputers smaller than a cubic micron, vastly miniaturized manufacturing, and devices which could inhabit the human body and be used to fight cancer cells. Futuristic as it may sound, both private and public sector interests are already betting on the future of nanotechnology. The Japanese Ministry of Trade and Industry (MITI) has reportedly already identified nanotechnology as a basic industrial technology for the twenty-first century.[4] Drawing on the same research, Xerox is experimenting with what it calls Smart Matter machines, which use very small sensors etched into silicon or other media. Integrated with computation such machines are able to sense the world around them and respond to it. This type of technology promises to revolutionize the design of systems such as printing and scanning, which today have to conform accurately to tightly defined tolerances, which in turn increase the costs of the devices involved.[5]

All of these technologies imply a replacement of old industries with new and potentially much larger industries. While technological job destruction must occur as a consequence of their introduction, we can as yet only guess at the potential range of new business and job opportunities they will introduce. The challenge for firms and individuals will be to position themselves to take advantage of these opportunities as they occur.

New Business Horizons

The period 1945–60 has been described as one of 'multinational capitalism' characterized by American domination of foreign direct investment, expanded economic imperialism, and the growth of individual multinational enterprises. The period 1960–90 became one of 'globalizing capitalism'. During this period production was shifted around the globe to the countries able to offer the best mix of low-cost labour and facilities and access to new markets. Foreign direct investment was increasingly sourced from European and Japanese as well as American companies. Foreign investment in the European ex-communist bloc countries increased. In the same period inter-firm alliances and joint ventures increased as did offshore sourcing of components.[6]

The current era is best described as an era of 'global knowledge capitalism', in which the need to move physical resources around the world is becoming less important and the need to move knowledge more important. It can be expected that knowledge flows will become as important as financial flows and that the two sources of capital will need to combine more frequently. While knowledge will become more evenly distributed in the developed world, much more knowledge will flow from the developed to the developing world.

Let us take a closer look at some of the implications of these predictions.

'Virtually Global'

As industries become more knowledge intensive, where a particular firm is located will be less important. For example, I happen to be entering these words into a computer in Australia. In a few seconds I can send them by email to reviewers in the USA and Europe for their comments. On receipt of their email replies, I can email my final text to my publisher in the UK. Where I, or my reviewers, or my publisher happen to be located makes virtually no difference. Increasing numbers of businesses in the knowledge economy will similarly become location independent, as both the inputs and the outputs of their production processes become symbolic and thus capable of being transmitted electronically.

Advances in manufacturing brought about by new technologies should enable manufacturing to be conducted equally efficiently in the developing and developed world. Instead of establishing a physical presence offshore, it will become more efficient for many western firms to license their products and technologies offshore. This is likely to result in a proliferation of global networks composed of dependent and independent contractors in a variety of industries. As a result, many more businesses will be able to 'go global while staying local'.

Businesses will increasingly license products and services offshore because they have saturated their home markets, or because of intense local competition. The fast food chain McDonald's, for example, faces major competition in a US market which is expanding at less than 5 per cent annually and in which it already has over 90,000 franchise outlets. The route to increased profitability, which it is now following, is globalization. As a result, two-thirds of its franchise outlets which open each year are outside the USA, and only two-thirds of its total outlets are now inside the USA.[7] While franchising may require the transfer of some physical and financial capital, the major capital transferred is knowledge of how to operate a successful franchise outlet. Increasing numbers of businesses in future can be expected to grow out of their home markets and those who can transfer their knowledge most readily to partners and suppliers overseas are likely to grow fastest.

Combining Financial and Knowledge Capital

Today financial capital roams the world speculatively. In future, knowledge capital is likely to do the same. Rather than adding to the market turbulence caused by massive inflows or outflows of funds, the movement of knowledge is likely to have a dampening or equalizing effect. The reason for this, as we have seen, is that knowledge, unlike money capital, is 'leaky property', difficult to hold on to and (in the case of explicit knowledge) virtually costless to replicate.

High-technology and knowledge-intensive products and services however cannot be sold to those who have neither the education to appreciate them nor the finance to afford them. According to the World Bank, nearly 1.3 billion people, approximately one quarter of the world's current population, live on about $US1.50 per day or less, based on 1997 prices. Nearly 3 billion people, over half the world's population, subsist on just $US3 per day.[8] Transferring knowledge to these populations so that they can develop their own economies and in the process buy western goods and services makes economic sense for all concerned.

Knowledge on its own however is not enough. Third world populations need access to finance to be able to access education and develop new enterprises. Micro credit schemes like that provided by Bangladesh's Grameen Bank have shown that provision of small amounts of finance can be successfully linked to education and the growth of micro enterprises. Since 1986, Grameen's expansion has led to the opening of over 14,000 schools supported by groups of its borrowers. Grameen Phone enables poor women in villages to purchase mobile telephones as economic investments. The women gain an instrument of power and the villages a connection to the markets and business centres of the world.[9]

The success of micro credit schemes shows the potential represented by the third world for knowledge from the West. Modest amounts of financial capital, linked to access to learning resources, can yield significant results. Today over

10 million people borrow from micro finance programmes worldwide but the movement is still in its infancy. Various consortia, including Women's World Banking, the Micro Finance Network, and the Consultative Group to Assist the Poorest, have linked many small and dispersed micro finance institutions into a global network.[10] Rather than view the developing nations of the world as a dumping ground for low technology and a source of cheap labour, western firms may find it more profitable in future to combine knowledge sharing with financial investment in the markets they wish to penetrate.

GOVERNMENT-ASSISTED TRANSITION STRATEGIES

A number of policy recommendations were made in previous chapters to aid knowledge acquisition and development in the economy. Clearly policy prescriptions will differ, depending upon national and local circumstances. Key issues, however, which all governments will have to tackle, include developing a coordinated policy response, assisting industry strategies, supporting essential infrastructure development, and funding policy initiatives. 'Selling the message' of the knowledge economy will have to proceed in parallel and involve not only governments but other stakeholders as well (see below).

Policy Coordination

Government policies affecting labour market programmes, social services, education, science and technology, industry development, and taxation need to reflect a common strategic approach. Labour market programmes, for example, will need to link job creation schemes to education and learning-related programmes. Similarly welfare payments will need to be linked to participation by the recipients in ongoing educational programmes. The objectives of those responsible for collecting tax revenues need to be reconciled with the objectives mentioned earlier, of equalizing the tax treatment of knowledge investments whether by firms or individuals. Certain goods and services will need to be free of indirect taxes to stimulate demand, for example personal computers or Internet access. In principle, tax on knowledge supply and consumption should be minimized.

The integration of policies necessary to address knowledge-related issues might be expected to lead to some reorganization of government functions. Having one ministry focusing on education and another on employment is not conducive to development of policies that link knowledge supply with knowledge demand. Beyond coordination between internal government departments, regional and industry development programmes will need to extend cooperation between government and industry. For example, developing knowledge-based transition strategies for rural economies could well involve public and private education providers, distance-based learning services, and specialist research institutions. Assistance with innovation, commercialization, and business networking could also involve multiple government departments. Managing such projects is likely to demand the creation of high-level quasi-government bodies which can act as knowledge project coordinators, calling in government and industry specialists as required.

Supranational organizations such as the World Bank, International Monetary Fund, World Trade Organization, and the United Nations will need to play an enlarged role in coordination of strategies aimed at global knowledge transfer. Knowledge management, for example, is already a key component of the World Bank's strategy launched in 1996. The Bank's Knowledge Management programme is aimed at both developing a 'corporate memory of best practices' and disseminating knowledge of value from outside organizations to its clients, partners, and stakeholders, particularly in developing countries.[11]

A New Vision of Industry

Government will need to cooperate with industry to help it create a new vision of itself. To achieve this, the first requirement will be new models and new strategies which more accurately reflect how knowledge impacts productivity, profitability and competitive success within the firm. Current measures such as R&D intensity, degree of innovation, and incidence of patents and licensing arrangements will need to be enhanced and extended. There will be a need to evaluate human skill formation in the firm, the degree of specificity or uniqueness associated with firms' knowledge, and how these and other factors combine to achieve improvement in firm performance. In practice, as we saw earlier, this will require a knowledge-based model of the firm.

At an industry level, a similar process will need to be repeated. The first problem will be to remap industry generally, since many of the sectoral definitions and boundary lines are well out of date. Such reclassification may generate some merging of sectors and some new sectors, which are likely to arise from the growth in micro firms and new technologies such as those noted earlier. Banking, insurance, and financial services, for example, are already merging, as are various arms of the media, utility industries such as gas, water, and electricity, and others (see Chapter 8). Distinctions between goods and services, as mentioned earlier, need to take better account of the role of knowledge, which in turn will reduce the significance of these traditional distinctions.

Industry strategies will need to reflect these new industrial models. Investment in developing industry training, for example, as distinct from firm-specific training, should be able to benefit from more accurate models of industrial demand. The value of different occupations in terms of their wealth-creating potential should, as a result, tend to be better understood, enabling better planning by educators, industry, and individuals. Stock market indexes should become more meaningful as stocks are able to be classified by their underlying knowledge characteristics. Analysts and investors should benefit by gaining a deeper understanding of knowledge-based determinants of growth and competitiveness.

Infrastructure Development

Knowledge acquisition and knowledge development are likely to be more efficiently and effectively provided where it is possible to share a common technical infrastructure for production, distribution, and access. The Internet II project in the USA may offer a model which other countries can follow. Each national Internet backbone could be enhanced and used as an infrastructure to access information and learning resources, facilitate collaboration between innovators, and develop business networking and electronic trading. At present, in many countries, there is massive over-investment, particularly by government departments in their individual computing, communications networks, and software. Arguably, this investment would be far better spent improving their national information infrastructures, based on upgrading their local portions of the global Internet.

The creation of a national skills register and accreditation system, similar to the New Zealand model mentioned earlier, is likely to be more efficiently implemented and effectively deployed if planned alongside other similar services. A national backbone service of this type could include informal skill registers, job opportunities, electronic placement services, and links to other information and learning resources.

Funding Issues

Society's willingness to pay for its own education and to invest more in knowledge-intensive business activities and products will be a function of its valuation of knowledge. The 'catch-22' is that it cannot value knowledge until it has been educated to do so. Fear, uncertainty, and doubt about future work opportunities are not likely to motivate workers to invest in acquisition of new skills, particularly those who do not already possess many of the necessary foundation skills.

The escalating gulf between the knowledge 'haves' and 'have nots' will only widen if policies and programmes to improve knowledge acquisition and development carry too high a price tag. The less advantaged members of the community—those typically with the fewest skills and the least ability to pay—will be simply further disadvantaged, while those with greater existing skills and more financial resources will do even better. Thus knowledge inequalities could further widen. Conversely, it will be essential not to waste public funds 'parking' youth in schools rather than on the street. Some existing government schemes, including for example the French government's ambitious programme for achieving near universal tertiary level course attendance, have (rightly or wrongly) been criticized on this count. Equally, many mature-aged workers and the long-term unemployed may be simply unwilling to take advantage of learning opportunities.

Ways around the problems implied by more publicly subsidized education could include deferred payment schemes, whereby individuals learn now and pay later, a pay as you learn (PAYL) system. This would represent, in effect, a public sector version of the private sector approach suggested in Chapter 10. Redundancy payments, work sharing, welfare, and other benefits could also be made conditional upon involvement in approved learning activities.

As noted earlier, the public cost of private knowledge may be significantly reduced through greater involvement by the private sector in provision of appropriate infrastructure services. Providing the potential knowledge market is large enough and all entrants to the market are forced to play by the same rules, experience indicates that market competition should produce a better result than public monopoly. Ultimately, private investments in knowledge acquisition by individuals or research and innovation by firms will have to be paid for by those receiving the investment returns. In the short term, however, there appears no option but to increase public funding to remedy educational deficiencies which prevent some sections of society from being able to help themselves. The emphasis, however, must remain on 'teaching people to fish', rather than 'providing them with fish to eat'.

SELLING THE MESSAGE

Creating a climate of understanding, social acceptance, and willingness to adapt to the demands of the knowledge economy must be the first step along the way to developing a knowledge-valuing society. Governments have a role to play in this, as do all the other stakeholders in society. People have become cynical about political attempts to persuade them of the importance of globalization or open market competition, when all they can see are fewer personal opportunities. Point scoring between political parties, trying to appear more socially concerned, or better economic managers, merely adds to the confusion caused by the lack of a coherent explanation for the strains which are being imposed on society. Explaining the implications of the knowledge economy and helping to develop a knowledge-valuing culture in society is therefore becoming daily more urgent. It is also going to require a significantly greater effort than has been put into 'selling' any other social or economic policy in the recent past. Governments may be able to avoid the issue in the short term, but it will not go away. Worse still, the longer it is avoided, the harder it is going to be to persuade the electorate to support the necessary changes. If this message is not communicated quickly, and across the political spectrum, the transition is going to be harder for all stakeholders—governments included.

The saying 'success breeds success' is a truism, as applicable to countries as it is to firms and individuals. Those who are quickest to face the realities of the situation and capitalize on the opportunities presented will be first to reap the rewards. The same will apply to those governments who have the vision to align short-term economic policies with the demands of the emerging knowledge economy.

In order to achieve understanding, acceptance and a sense of shared purpose—from the boardroom to the factory floor—some broad themes need to be addressed.

Understanding the role of the firm

One of the first requirements is to create a better understanding of the role of the firm. Firms have, sometimes rightly, been accused of only showing concern for their shareholders' profits, particularly during the rash of downsizing and delayering which has occurred throughout the 1980s and 1990s. It is now clear that the forces driving internalization and externalization are beyond the control of the firm. Firms have about as much control over such forces as a farmer has over the weather. It is a question of living with it and adapting to it. The same argument applies to globalization: firms have no option but to compete on a global basis as world tariff barriers come down. If the economic realities of a globalized knowledge economy are ignored, firms will simply go out of business, thus creating more redundancies and layoffs. Society needs to understand that despite the very obvious dissimilarities in wealth, privilege, and ability in the community, in one sense everyone is on the same side against the common enemy—redundancy.

Relationships between firms, workers, and unions will have to change, to reflect the realities of the knowledge economy. The transition will be made easier if these realities are recognized sooner rather than later. Much has been written over recent years about the breakdown in the traditional social contract between firms and workers. This contract represents, in effect, the implicit agreement which forms part of the employment relationship, involving a degree of give and take and fair play on each side. Those who lament its passing point to layoffs, outsourcing, casualization, and other aspects of externalization as failures, predominantly on the part of the firm to honour its implicit promises.

Accurate or otherwise from an historical perspective, these perceptions are now irrelevant. If firms and workers are to make progress new, explicit, knowledge-based work arrangements have to replace old, implicit, employment-centred arrangements. One key to this change will be for firms to offer workers individual contracts which more accurately reflect their likely future relationship. Workers taken on to perform work in peripheral areas, in particular, should be explicitly advised that the work contract is likely to be short lived. Beyond this it will be incumbent on firms to ensure all workers have more accurate expectations in relation to training, promotion, and other career prospects in the firm.

Unions, as the representatives of the workforce, will have to realize that their role must also change. Instead of adopting confrontational tactics, unions will have to accept that they, their members, and the firms they work for have more to gain through cooperation than conflict. Instead of focusing on improvements to workforce pay and working conditions, they will need to focus on assisting their members to become more highly skilled and/or ultimately self-employable. Mass representation will need to give way to individual representation. The union movement will need to specialize in career counselling, outplacement, training, and other services for its members. If it can transform itself quickly enough, the union movement may have a role to play in facilitating the transition of its members to the knowledge economy. If it fails to adapt, it will inevitably lose its 'heartland' and become redundant itself.

Open Discussion

A second theme, which seems essential to creating a climate of understanding and acceptance, is that of more frank and open discussion of economic issues. While government statisticians and researchers may be aware of the meaning of the employment figures, the general public by and large is not. The messages conveyed by much political propaganda to the public are more intended to reassure than to explain. There is no sense conveyed that economic realities are changing as dramatically as they obviously are. The patient may have a life-threatening disease but no one seems willing to tell him or her. Since, on the whole, people tend to respond better when they know the facts, unpalatable or otherwise, open and transparent discussion is likely to pay dividends, both in terms of understanding and of acceptance. Ironically, ignorance will be the major obstacle to progress in managing the transition to the knowledge economy.

Rationality

Debates for or against economic rationalism need to be recognized as sterile. The issue is not whether the arguments put forward are rational but rather whether they are adequate. The problem with many of the neoclassical economic theories reflected in current economic rationalist thinking is their failure properly to value knowledge in the economy. As a result, current economic rationalism may be necessary, but it is certainly not sufficient. Society needs a more comprehensive diagnosis of its economic problems and a more detailed prescription for curing them—plus reassurance as to survival during treatment! The media also need to be more alive to these issues and ensure that they ask politicians harder questions. The debate needs to be taken to those in charge of economic policy, not merely based on what they happen to be doing or wish to discuss.

The Importance of the Individual

A fundamental characteristic of the knowledge economy is the way it will empower and simultaneously isolate the individual. The implications of this 'splendid isolation' need to be taken into account in explaining and promoting ways to handle changing economic conditions. Learning, rather than being educated, for example, will be foreign to many people. Others will find the prospect of an independent workstyle a daunting prospect. For those unaccustomed to operating without supervision, the message has to be one of encouragement and support, both to take control of their own careers and to suggest independent sources of counselling and assistance. For others it will be a case of encouraging and publicly rewarding knowledge entrepreneurship.

For both firms and individuals, redefining work arrangements will involve moving from relational contracts to more market-like arm's-length contracts. Messages previously aimed at encouraging employment will therefore need to encourage independence, self-sufficiency, self-employment, and networking. Above all, individuals should not feel excluded because of real or imagined lack of skills. All types of talent, creative or technical, academic or non-academic, and the willingness of individuals to commit personal effort to pursuing them will need to be welcomed. Personal achievement will need to be publicly recognized as being as important as group or corporate achievement.

Targeted Promotion

Among other themes it is obviously of paramount importance that working is seen to be dependent upon learning, and that the two activities are seen as indissoluble. The notion that learning needs to be a lifelong activity is foreign to most people, hence the value of creating a focus on that aspect in order to start to change preconceptions. The overlap between learning and working can also be encapsulated in national slogans such as 'the clever country' (Australia) or 'thinking for a living' (USA) or 'learning to compete' (UK). Whatever the latest catchwords and slogans used, it is clearly imperative that messages are communicated to those who need to be made aware of them. Youth approaching school-leaving age and adults with only a basic level of education clearly need special targeting.

THE FUTURE OF KNOWLEDGE CAPITALISM

How much government intervention will be required to help society acquire and maintain the skills it needs? Will there be enough work to go round? Will physical assets depreciate in value or just not appreciate as quickly as previously? These are among the many issues that are yet to be resolved as we venture into the new age of Knowledge Capitalism.

Role of the State

State control of the means of production has been one of the big failures of the late twentieth century. With the failure of the communist system, the power of socialism and with it big government- and state-controlled enterprises has been waning. The demise of the public sector is evident everywhere in the West, as privatization has become politically acceptable. The tide of neo-liberal sentiment is sweeping the globe, as the old communist bloc is dismantled. Even China is now espousing capitalist values.

The increasing importance of knowledge in the economy has however caused some commentators to question whether there may not be an argument for a reversal of current trends, leading to an increasing role for the state. The issue, as Thurow succinctly puts it, is 'who represents the interests of the future to the present?'[12] Who in the private sector is going to see it as in their interests to bring the average level of knowledge attainment in society (including the current and future workforce) up to what is evidently required? More specifically why should firms invest in human or any other assets from which they and their shareholders are not likely to get a return? There is no obvious economic reason why firms should. In the USA, the leading capitalist nation of the world, they have not: 10 per cent of its workforce are now less well off than they were twenty-five years ago.

The diminishing association between productivity growth and employment growth has been a widely reported phenomenon. Previous generations, unlike the present one, were able to climb onto an economic 'escalator' which carried them forward, even as they themselves ascended step by step. Now the escalator for many seems to have slowed or even started to go down.[13] Another perspective on the problem is suggested by those who claim that even if, as currently in the UK under the Blair government, resources can be shifted from welfare to education, there simply will not be enough work to employ the better-educated workforce. Improved national skill levels will not be enough, public services will have to be expanded again to offer low-skilled, and probably low-paid, but secure work opportunities.[14]

While symptoms of an underlying economic malaise are appearing everywhere—even in the booming US economy—there is still obviously considerable contention, both about the diagnosis and about ways to effect a cure, or at least sustained relief. Much of the current debate is still focused on how to make short-term adjustments, which will maintain artificially high levels of employment—as in France. National work-sharing schemes such as the current French model however seem doomed to failure, since much of the work saved is likely to require the kind of skills which are already in demand. Sending white-collar workers home will not help blue-collar workers. The emphasis needs to change from saving work to generating new (work-producing) enterprises. Ironically, as the Federal Reserve Bank Chairman Alan Greenspan has indicated, if anything can halt the current US economic boom it will be an acute shortage of skilled workers.

Other problems with pessimistic forecasts of the effects of technological work replacement is that they tend to involve assumptions which simply cannot be tested. All that can be said on the basis of historical evidence is that scientific and technological progress tends to involve 'lumpiness'—discontinuities, caused by both breakthroughs and substitution effects. These discontinuities inevitably produce significant mismatches from time to time between supply and demand for resources, including, most importantly, people. The process of knowledge development, however, has always been, and will continue to be, a voyage of discovery, where each new advance provides a platform for the next. In effect the 'knowledge escalator' is always moving forward—albeit jerkily.

There is every reason, therefore, to be concerned about short–medium-term prospects for work opportunities, but there seems no compelling reason to believe that a knowledge-based economy will not, over time, achieve equilibrium between knowledge supply and knowledge demand. As the comments made earlier indicate, however, time is running out for governments to be able to stand back and leave it to the market to solve the looming gulf between knowledge supply and demand. Sooner rather than later, polarization of earnings and opportunities in the workforce will blow the lid off the pressure cooker and with it whoever happens to be in power. There therefore seems no option but for governments to intervene quickly and appropriately, to avoid having to retreat to old-fashioned Keynesian pump priming economics or, worse still, to revisit the failed strategies of big government and state control.

Assuming appropriate government policies can be introduced quickly and decisively enough, then the level of state intervention can be kept to a minimum. One thing appears certain in the short term, as evidenced by the current policies of the Blair government in the UK, and that is that political ideology of the right or left will have to give way to economic reality. All politics other than the extreme ends of the spectrum are converging—the game after all is the same for all the players: it is called capitalism.

Looking further ahead (always a dangerous pastime) a more knowledgeable, self-sufficient, and self-directing society appears unlikely to require as much governance as in the past. It is also unlikely to be willingly constrained by national borders. The role of the nation state will continue to decline in importance as small and micro businesses and individuals join big business in becoming global players. Supranational rather than national organizations will assume increasing importance.

Owning and Valuing Capital

As knowledge in all its manifestations increases in value, low knowledge-intensive goods and services and basic commodities will decrease in value. This in one sense is the hope of the future. Knowledge will improve productivity and open market competition will force firms to share that increase with the consumer by way of reduced prices. Consumer surplus will thus rise, which in turn will increase demand for more goods and services. So the economic wheel may be turned ever faster.

Conversely, as also discussed earlier, private interests may try to lock up what would otherwise become consumer surplus through market power, thus creating false markets. Diamonds would be a lot cheaper if the world's main supply was not locked up in South African mines. Knowledge however is a most difficult commodity to appropriate and the cost of 'data mining' as compared to physical mining is trivial. Knowledge spill-overs will therefore increase, as firms recognize that to stay in front implies a degree of knowledge sharing.

Side effects of these natural leakage or spill-over effects should be to reduce the importance of government intervention, by way of anti-trust laws and other measures to curb monopolies. If knowledge capitalism works as it should, there will be no way a Microsoft or an IBM will be able to hold on to market leadership indefinitely. It will be a lot easier for de Beers Corporation to keep the price of diamonds high by restricting their production than it will be for any knowledge-intensive firm, even Microsoft, to monopolize the on-ramps to the Super Highway. The faster the growth of knowledge the harder it will be to hold on to any knowledge-based advantage.

In the short term, therefore, while the knowledge economy is still relatively immature, government intervention can be expected to be more frequent in order to protect small players from bigger competitors using their market muscle to stifle competition. Nonetheless, over time the government's role as traffic cop should reduce.

If the value of knowledge assets rises, what does this say for physical assets? Will they actually depreciate in value or just not appreciate as much as before? The answers are not obvious. Knowledge can be applied to reduce production costs or add value to just about any physical process, from diamond mining to cooking hamburgers. Firms that make shrewd investments in technology and improve the skills of their key workers will undoubtedly reap benefits. Those that do not will find their assets depreciating. Farming for example seems certain to be transformed, as genetically designed crops will be able to be grown hydroponically or in factory farms rather than on broad acreage. In the short term this will reduce the value of some agricultural land. Given however that most resources other than knowledge are finite, then a growing population of increasingly knowledgeable and affluent citizens may find other ways to use such real estate.

Logically the less the requirement for physical resources in manufacture or distribution, i.e. the 'purer' the knowledge product and the greater the degree of tacit knowledge embodied in it, everything else being equal, the more valuable it should become. Packaging and licensing knowledge products therefore is likely to become big business. Franchising is currently the world's biggest single industry, built on the principle of licensed use to knowledge embedded in franchise formats. In future it may be expected that the focus of much commercial activity will swing towards licensing knowledge. The gatekeepers of the new society will therefore be the intellectual property lawyers, whose job it will be to protect the packages of knowledge being bought and resold in the future knowledge market.

The voices of doom are heard ever louder nowadays, forecasting a society ravaged by technologically induced unemployment, discontent, and despair. That certainly is a *potential* scenario. The keys to an alternative scenario however are in our own hands, or, to be more precise, in the individual brains of each and every one of us. As the knowledge escalator moves forward, some will still manage to climb the steps faster than others, but everyone should still be better off. The main requirement is for everyone to be on board the escalator!

NOTES

1. OECD (Organization for Economic Co-operation and Development) (1996), *Technology Productivity and Job Creation*, ii: *Analytical Report*, Paris: OECD: 212.
2. http://www.freeagentnation.com (see also http://www.fastcompany.com for articles referring to free agent nation).
3. Speech of Robert Shapiro, CEO Monsanto. Presented at State of the World Forum, Fairmont Hotel, San Francisco, 27 Oct. 1998, *http://www.monsanto.com/Monsanto/Media/Speeches*.
4. *http://nanotech.rutgers.edu/nanotech*.
5. 'Smart Matter', *http://www.parc.xerox.com/theme_sm.html*.
6. M. Waters (1995), *Globalization*, London: Routledge.
7. Ibid.
8. World Bank, 'World Bank Development Report 1998/99: Knowledge for Development', *http://www.worldbank.org/wdr*.
9. Ibid.
10. Ibid.
11. What is Knowledge Management?, *http://www.worldbank.org*.
12. L. C. Thurow (1997), *The Future of Capitalism: How Today's Economic Forces will Shape Tomorrow's World*, New York: William Morrow & Company, Inc.

THE TRANSITION TO KNOWLEDGE CAPITALISM   237

13. M. Miegel (1997), 'Displacing Human Labour: An Epoch Making Phenomenon', in P. James, W. F. Veit, and S. Wright (eds.), *Work of the Future: Global Perspectives*, Sydney: Allen & Unwin: 126–38.

14. C. Crouch (1997), 'Skills-Based Full Employment: The Latest Philosopher's Stone', *British Journal of Industrial Relations*, 35/3 (Sept.): 367–91.

INDEX